PAUL DAVIS
ARSENAL
AND AFTER

PAUL DAVIS

ARSENAL
AND AFTER

FOREWORD BY **MIKEL ARTETA**

Reach Sport

www.reachsport.com

Reach Sport

www.reachsport.com

Written with Tom Watt.

Published in Great Britain and Ireland in 2022 by Reach Sport.

www.reachsport.com
@Reach_Sport

Reach Sport is a part of Reach PLC.

Hardback ISBN: 9781914197352
eBook ISBN: 9781914197369

Photographic acknowledgements:
Paul Davis personal collection, Alamy, Reach Plc.

Editing and production: Adam Oldfield, Richard Williamson.

Every effort has been made to trace copyright.
Any oversight will be rectified in future editions.

Printed and bound by CPI Group (UK) Ltd,
Croydon, CR0 4YY.

CONTENTS

CONTENTS

vi

FOREWORD
BY MIKEL ARTETA

At Arsenal, we aren't inhibited by the club's history. Instead, we're inspired by it. And people like Paul Davis, of course, are a big part of that history. Paul joined Arsenal as a 12-year-old, made his debut – away to Spurs! – at 17, and then went on to win titles and trophies, here and in Europe, during the 1980s and 90s, while playing nearly 500 games for the club. And it didn't end there. He was back at Highbury, coaching young players in the academy, when Arsène Wenger arrived. Paul saw for himself the revolution that led us to so much success and our 'Invincibles' season.

As well as our history, we're proud of our traditions at Arsenal, too. Our home is in Islington, one of the most multi-ethnic and multicultural boroughs in the country, and we've always tried to reflect that identity, on and off the pitch. We're committed to the idea of 'Arsenal For Everyone'. Paul's an important figure in that story, too. When he first started at the club, he was one of only a handful of black players in the English top division. Times may have changed, perhaps, but it's important to take in the experience of a true pioneer, and his views and ideas about diversity within the game.

I first met Paul when he was a coach educator with the Professional Footballers Association, and I was studying for my UEFA 'B' in 2015. He personally and successfully guided me through that coaching qualification. I know he's now a Senior Game Coach Developer with the Football Association and is involved, as well, with the England under-17s team, helping to develop our next generation of young players. He has a unique insight into how the game and the FA work, a vision for how football and coaching can continue to evolve and improve in this country.

So, his experiences as a coach and coach educator, his passion for diversity in football, and 30 memorable years as an Arsenal man. That's a story worth telling. A story worth reading as well. I wish Paul every success with his autobiography *Arsenal and After*.

Mikel Arteta

78

1959: when my mum, Ruby Davis, came to England from Jamaica, she was making the journey to the mother country. The Queen's country. Right or wrong, Great Britain represented values she'd grown up learning to respect, and I know she felt it was kind of a privilege for her to be here. Instinctively, she always deferred to authority figures she encountered: doctors, teachers, the police. She would never question those people. I know she faced real difficulties, like so many others of the Windrush generation, when it came to finding work and somewhere half-decent to live: *No Blacks, No Irish, No Dogs.* Whether she felt resentful or bitter about how she was treated when she first arrived, she never said. Mum always made a conscious effort, I think, not to pass memories of any bad experiences on to me and my younger sister, Sandra.

By the late '70s, I'm sure Mum knew how things were out there in London: stop and search was full on and, out of all proportion, targeting black youth. There were National Front marches all the time, shouting at us to go back to where we'd come from. Kids were attacked in the street and their mums and dads abused if they were in the wrong place at the wrong time. However tense things were, though, Mum said it was up to me to stay away from situations where I might find myself in trouble with the police. That was one of Mum's biggest fears for me. Life was pretty good on our estate, after all. Growing up, I never felt my colour was something anybody was very conscious of. Maybe I was lucky. Our local community was diverse for those times, and everybody around the blocks on Lansdowne Green seemed comfortable with that.

I was perhaps protected a little because I was so involved with football. As a young player, training as a schoolboy at Arsenal, I never had the feeling that being black might hold me back, or that it might put me at any kind of disadvantage. All that mattered to me was being a footballer. I already knew that. And whether I was any good or not seemed to be all that mattered to everyone else. What other boys my age and background were having to deal with on the street didn't directly affect me because of the world I'd stepped into at a big, professional club. I heard stories, read the papers, saw the news, and listened to people talking. Even so, racism didn't seem like something that was going to stop me getting to where I wanted to go.

Once I started training at Arsenal, it took me away from home in Stockwell, away from familiar faces and the places I knew. I was the only young black player at the club. The only black player, full stop. As a youth teamer, I made some good friends, but there'd be moments when I kind of disconnected from the lads around me: tastes in food or music, or humour I didn't share. Jokes which had a racial edge and almost everybody else laughed at, but I didn't find too funny. *Love Thy Neighbour, Till Death Us Do Part:* these were hugely popular weekly TV shows, showing black people in a negative and degrading light, watched, and enjoyed, by audiences of millions. A little later, Chris Whyte and Raphael Meade joined me at Arsenal and, naturally I suppose, I found myself gravitating towards those guys and our common culture as young, black Londoners.

Thing is: you can stay away from trouble all you like, but what do you do when trouble comes and finds you? Everything changes: how you see the world and understand your place in it. I was a first-year apprentice at Arsenal, around '78 or '79, when I was still only 17. We'd had a reserve team game on the Saturday afternoon, and I'd gone to a party with Chris Whyte, down by Hornsey, that evening. Neither of us were driving or earning enough to be paying for taxis. There's no Tube out to that part of North London, either. So, Chrissy and I were walking back: he lived in Blackstock Road, not far from Highbury; I was going to jump on the Victoria Line at Finsbury Park to travel home to Stockwell.

It was late, probably coming up to one or two in the morning. We were walking down Hornsey Road, which leads through from Crouch End to Holloway. Minding our own business. All of a sudden, we were in a scene from an episode of TV show *The Sweeney:* tyres squealing and blue lights flashing all around us. Three, four police cars, maybe. Police piling out of them, running towards us. One of them, shouting: *Stop there, you fucking black bastards!* We're up against a wall: this was how stop and search worked. And they're saying: *We saw you trying to break into that car.* What? *What are you talking about? We were just walking down the road.*

Chris and I were bundled into separate vehicles and driven back to the police station by Seven Sisters Road, where the old swimming baths used to be. They were adamant they'd seen us trying to break into a car. *That fucking car!* Which, obviously, we hadn't been. But they weren't letting it go, and we were locked up in the cells overnight. I'd never had anything like this happen to me before. One minute, I'm walking home, end of a good day: played for Arsenal and then a little house party. Next, I'm sitting on this concrete ledge, behind bars, in a cell smelling like a public toilet which had just been sprayed down with bleach. Not understanding what's going on. Confused and very scared: I know I haven't done anything wrong. But I'm powerless. And the hurt of *You fucking black bastard!* running and re-running in my mind. Me thinking: *Why?* This from an organisation which Mum had brought me up to trust and respect.

It wasn't until the early hours that they let me call home. Mum spoke to Arsenal, and then the club got in touch with Chrissy and me. A solicitor came to get us out the next morning. The police were adamant that we'd been trying to steal a car, but must have decided Chrissy's biggest crime had been being out with me. So, they didn't charge Chris. But they went ahead and charged me. All I could do was say that I hadn't done what I was accused of. It wasn't like there was any evidence either way, though: it was the police's word against the word of a young black kid, wasn't it? They wouldn't drop the charges. And nobody wanted to hear about the name-calling. None of the policemen involved were going to say what had really happened. It dragged on for three or four months, and I ended up being summonsed to appear at Highbury Magistrates Court.

That was the scariest thing: actually, being there in the courtroom. I'd never been in any kind of trouble like this. All the time, until now, I'd been thinking: *This can't go to court. The charges will be dropped. Everyone must see that this is nonsense.* But now I'm standing in the dock, collar and tie half-suffocating me, the prosecution solicitor trying to confuse me. To make me trip up on my words. I'm having to do my best to put into words the details around something that had never actually happened. I'm nervous, sweating, gripping the rail in front of me, fearful I'm not coming across as truthful. All the pressure being pushed on me to prove I'm innocent: that's not how it's supposed to work, is it?

This was my word against theirs. And then I had to listen as these policemen stood up in court and lied about what had happened that evening.

Even at the time, I knew what was at stake. This could have been my career over before it had even begun. If I was found guilty, I would be finished at Arsenal. I told the club the police were mistaken, told them how we'd been treated that night. And they believed me, trusted me. That meant I had a good solicitor speaking for me in front of the magistrates. He stood up and started to unpick the police's story. In no time, the judge threw the case out of court, and I walked out, a relieved young man. Four months worrying, telling my version of what had happened over and over again. And then the whole business was finished in a minute or two. *No case to answer.*

After the court appearance, it started to sink in, how lucky I'd been. I might have looked to the club like a young boy – innocent or otherwise, talented or otherwise – who was more trouble than he was worth. But Arsenal believed in me. Made sure I had a solicitor, support, and good advice. But then I really started thinking. *What if I'd not been a footballer playing for Arsenal? What if I'd just been any other black teenager on my way home from a party that night? What would have happened then?* The fact that I'd done nothing wrong wouldn't have counted for anything. The police would have got their conviction. I'd have ended up with a criminal record which would have hung over me: at school, applying for jobs, finding somewhere to live. Previous would have been pushed in my face the next time I got stopped. And accused for no other reason than that I was a young black man out in London after dark.

The whole experience opened my eyes but maybe it shouldn't have come as such a surprise. Pushed up against a wall, surrounded by uniforms, thrown into a police cell overnight. *You fucking black bastards* ringing in my ears. It's not as if what happened to me that evening was unusual. Stop and search was a part of everyday life for most black teenagers in the UK. It wasn't about if; it was about when. And how often. The hurt and the anger I felt back then, I know many in our communities are still feeling today. After all, stories like mine are still being told, aren't they, 40 years on?

61

Paul Vincent Davis. A friend of mine asked me the other day: *Where does Vincent come from?* I don't ever remember being asked that before. *Well, you could just as well ask: where does Paul come from?* He shook his head. *No, it's always the middle name that stands for something.* I don't know if my friend's right. But the conversation made me realise I had so many questions I should have asked Mum. I know Paul came from Paul in the Bible. But Vincent? I have no idea. Sixty now, I realise there's so much I don't know, that I'll never know. About family, about history, about *why*. Luckily, I have my sister, Sandra, who I can talk about these things with. Vincent, she thinks, might have been my grandad's middle name. He was Samuel Davis. Maybe Samuel Vincent Davis. Sandra met him once. I never did.

My mum's story is, I guess, like a lot of West Indian family stories, which for many are Windrush stories: half-forgotten by the next generation, or the generation after that. When you're thinking about the future all the time – and, for me, that was playing football – the past was of little interest. I was shocked when the Windrush scandal came to light in 2018. But not at all surprised. People born British, or who'd spent their entire working lives in the UK, suddenly being told they weren't welcome anymore. Because they didn't have the correct documents. Documents which, in many cases, had never been given to them, and which nobody had told them they'd need. Worse: passports confiscated, people sent back to the Caribbean, or denied jobs and housing, benefits, and healthcare here.

The Windrush scandal was history being rewritten. A generation being written out, in fact. I wonder what Mum would have made of it. Whether she might even have got swept up in it, what stories she might have shared, if she hadn't passed away in 2016, two years before the scandal became public. Mum's childhood and teenage life in St Andrew Parish and Kingston, before she came to England, weren't things she wanted to talk much about. Not to me, anyway. All I knew when I was a boy: Mum – Rubena Elizabeth Davis – came over from Jamaica, on her own, in 1959. A UK & Colonics citizen. Her older sister, Emily, who we called Auntie Tiny, was already here and helped organise everything for Mum to follow her over: lent her the money for her ticket, a debt her sister never compromised over; a debt Mum was always due to pay back and, eventually, did.

Auntie Tiny had been a midwife in Jamaica and eventually retrained so she could be one here, too. The Windrush generation and the NHS are two stories tied closely together. When Mum first arrived, she was a seamstress and did cleaning jobs to start getting a little money together. For a lot of people from the West Indies, that was the plan: come to England, work, and save for a few years, and then go home with enough to build a better life. While they were here, they would often be doing the jobs that English-born people didn't want to do. The climate was cold, and often they weren't welcomed warmly by everyone. Mum used to send money back to Jamaica: cash, in special blue and white registered envelopes you'd get from the post office.

Mum had left children behind, my two stepbrothers and a step-sister, who were brought up by extended family while she was in London. She sent money so they were always looked after and I'm sure, at the time, she'd have been planning to go back to Jamaica to re-join them before too long. Later on, though, I remember Mum expressing her doubts about returning home. I think she fell out of love with Jamaica because of what she saw and heard from here, it made her think the country had deteriorated. The needless violence and the political divisions made her scared to go back. She was in the UK, trying to get settled and provide for her family.

Mum had me in 1961, in Dulwich, where she was living at the time. Just a single room, no hot water, a shared toilet and bathroom. That kind of place was the first stop for a lot of people coming to London from the Caribbean. I remember getting washed in a tin bath in front of the paraffin fire, long before we moved to Stockwell. Mum never spoke about those times to us. She never spoke about who my father was, either. I didn't ever know him. Mum didn't talk about him, and I don't ever remember him being around. I still don't know anything about him. I started asking questions when I was at school, and I noticed that most of the other children had fathers in their families. But Mum would make it clear she didn't want to have that conversation. Those were questions I didn't need to be asking, right? And I felt that was okay: that, sometime in the future, she would be ready to tell me.

I wondered, though. I was conscious of my dad not being around, especially once I started playing football, nine or 10 years old. Almost everybody else's dad would be on the touchline watching the game and cheering their boys on. I had a couple of good friends at the time who I played with: Robert Bray and Dean Tonkin, who were cousins. I'd spend a lot of my free time round at their family homes, at the weekends after a match and during the school holidays. I always felt welcomed. I liked that their dads were there. I don't think that their mums had to go out to work, but instead looked after the home. They had cars, nice furniture, lovely spongy carpets, and colour TVs, things Mum couldn't afford on her own. We didn't have those luxuries. No dad, no car, no support with my football ambitions. Mum just had to think about how she was going to keep a roof over our heads and put food on our table.

By then, at least, we'd moved away from the single room in Dulwich. First to Bermondsey, and eventually to Stockwell. It took a while before we got a council flat, one that was big enough for the three of us: me, Mum and my baby sister, Sandra, who was born in 1963. We ended up in two bedrooms on the fourth floor of a block called Stafford Court on the Lansdowne Green estate, between Wandsworth Road and South Lambeth Road. Mum had got a steady job, working in police canteens at Marylebone and Bow Street. She was on the catering staff and put in long, long hours, but I think she enjoyed it. She was settled and worked for the Metropolitan Police right through until she retired.

Mum did her very best for us. She worked hard, taking overtime at work to earn a bit of extra money. We were on free school dinners. I hated that. It was supposed to be confidential, but it felt like the whole school knew. I usually couldn't afford to go on any school trips that needed paying for. So, it was quite a small world we lived in: the estate and the school and the shops. You could walk or get the bus everywhere. It was football that started to widen my horizons. I had to think about how I could get to our Sunday League games. Even if Mum was at home, it wasn't as if she had a car. So, I'd get the Tube or a bus. Or a lift with my friends, Rob and Dean. Their dads both had cars. One even had a little van that he would sometimes use if he had to pick a few of us boys up.

Len Bray – Rob's dad – must have been earning good money because he also had a couple of season tickets at Chelsea, the big club closest to where we lived. *Wow!* If Len couldn't go, they would invite me to go with Rob. Those were the first football matches I ever went to. Len would drive us across to the other side of Battersea Bridge and we'd walk up to the ground from there. Early '70s, going to a football match was a scary experience and Chelsea didn't have a great reputation for being friendly, but we'd just be straight there and straight back. We were sitting in seats, too, not standing behind the goal in The Shed.

Mum, Sandra and I would go round to visit Auntie Tiny and her husband, Claude, and their two sons in Brixton sometimes. I still have a scar on my nose I got from playing in the backyard with Cardinal, one of their two sons. My aunt and uncle had done well for themselves. My auntie was at a managerial level in nursing by then, and they lived in an actual house. Which they owned. At Christmas, I remember they'd have a big tree in the front room. They had a car and a lot of the luxuries I'd only ever seen at the Brays' or at the Tonkins' or on television. Everything they had was nice compared to what we could afford; for us, money was always an issue. I had the feeling my auntie looked down her nose at us a bit, living on a council estate, trying to get by. Mum didn't have much time for that attitude. She loved Lansdowne Green: the estate itself and most of our neighbours.

Getting the council flat was when everything started getting a little better for us as a family. Home now was somewhere you had your own front door, even if Mum still had to go to charities to get furniture and clothes for us to wear. She never claimed benefits. The flat was warm, and it was all ours, and we had space to play. As Sandra says: we had the space to be children. For her, that meant the playground downstairs and the bits of green around Stafford Court. For me, it was the cage where I often played football.

Mum's parental principles were good manners and respect for those in authority. We always had to go to Sunday School, down at Stockwell Baptist Church on South Lambeth Road. I so disliked going, but had to. I wanted to be back on the estate playing football with my friends. But Mum insisted we went. She wasn't going to church herself back then, though, so why did she force us to go? It was only when she got older that church became an important part of her life: a social thing as much as it being about her faith. After she retired, Mum started going regularly to the gym, too, and decided to give up smoking, after many years on Senior Service cigarettes, the unfiltered ones with the picture of a sailing ship on the packet. She even learnt to drive and passed her test when she was around 60.

For me and Sandra, as children, we had to learn to look after ourselves. I would iron my clothes and pretty much take care of myself. Sandra soon learned to cook. After school, we'd let ourselves in and warm up our dinner, which Mum had prepared before she left for work in the morning. But, from as early as I can remember, the two of us had our own groups of friends and our own interests. We didn't spend much time together. We went to different secondary schools, too. We had our fights at home, like most brothers and sisters. When you think back to why, you can't believe you fell out over such tiny things: borrowing a pen or a ruler without asking and not giving it back. I used to kick a rolled-up sock around the house when Mum was out and, as soon as Mum got in, Sandra would be trying to get me into some kind of trouble. *Paul's been playing football again, Mum. He nearly broke that vase!* I was no angel towards Sandra, either.

Sandra and I don't have those fights anymore. We grew up and, over time, our relationship has grown to be one of deep respect, I would say. Back then, though, by the time we were 11 or 12, of the two of us, I think I was probably easier for Mum to handle. She always knew where I was and what I was doing: playing football or round at Rob's house or Dean's. I wasn't anywhere I shouldn't have been. But Sandra would be off with her friends, and we didn't know who they were or where they'd been most of the time. When she came back – late-ish! – I remember a lot of rows between Mum and Sandra. I think Sandra would say I was the favourite, and maybe there's some truth in that.

Sandra was better at school than me, academically. But I always knew what I wanted to do, and I don't think she had a clear focus until later in her life. We were different. I had the passion for football and sport, and it helped me keep on the straight and narrow growing up. I got myself a newspaper round when I was 10 and kept it for three or four years. I walked into our local news-agents shop one day and asked if there were any jobs going to deliver the papers. I had to be there at 6.30 every morning. Me and the owner, Ken Green, would pick up the bundles of papers off the pavement and unwrap them inside. He'd write the address on the front of each paper, and I'd deliver them around Lansdowne Green, to the Springfield Estate next door to us, and to the lovely expensive houses which nestled in between the council flats in Lansdowne Gardens.

Doing the paper round taught me so much, but it's left me with a fear of dogs, even now. Through the letterbox, some dogs would bark and growl and snap at your fingers as you tried to push the paper through. Sometimes, there'd be a dog sitting right in the entrance to the block you were trying to deliver to. That was the worst. I'd skip on to another block instead and then come back later, hoping the dog would have gone. But the job was great for me: structure in my life, the discipline of getting up early every morning. It taught me about earning and looking after money. I bought my first pair of football boots from that paper round, which Mum wouldn't have been able to afford. Being independent and self-reliant: those things came more naturally to me when it was time to go off and start a career in football.

Talking to Sandra now, listening to how she remembers times past, has made me much more aware of how much I don't know about my family history. At the time I was out playing football, Sandra was there at Stafford Court, listening to Mum, arguing with her, taking the history in. They went to Jamaica together for the funeral of my grandmother Diana; I never met her or my granddad, Samuel, who was in the army. Sandra made connections with that side of the family on that trip. She met uncles and aunties and cousins. Mum was one of eight children, six girls and two boys. The family had a quarter of an acre of land in St Andrew Parish, the next parish to Kingston. All that family history, all gone, and I'm only learning about some of it now.

Mum used to talk to Sandra a little about growing up in Jamaica: using a fork to straighten her hair because she couldn't afford a hot comb and going off with her friends to dances at the weekend. She had her first child, Queenie, when she was still very young. Then, later, two sons: Tasman and Constant. All with different dads. Mum went to school until she was 15 or 16 and, after she left, worked as a domestic servant and as a seamstress. Once Mum followed her sister, Emily, to England, Samuel and Diana brought up Queenie and Tasman. Constant lived with his father, Hartnell, down in Spanish Town. That was a normal arrangement back then: sons and daughters were a responsibility for the whole family, not just for their mum. Auntie Tiny left two children behind with my grandparents as well.

We remember different things, of course. Sandra remembers more about us living in Bermondsey, after Dulwich and before we moved to Stockwell. I've seen a picture of the block we had a room in, Barnaby Buildings, and I must have forgotten the place on purpose. It looks scary, a run-down tenement, dark with tiny windows, like an old Victorian workhouse. Some of the stuff Sandra remembers makes us smile together now, though: like

Saturday mornings in Stafford Court, when Mum would have the newspaper laid out in front of her, picking horses before going across the road to the bookmakers to put her bets on, and then coming back to spend the Saturday afternoon shouting at the TV, cheering those bets home. That was our mum's fun at the weekend. And Thursday or Friday would be her bingo night down in Clapham.

Other memories come back, too, when Sandra tells me stories. Stories that remind me of the stigma Mum used to have to deal with back then. I'd forgotten how she used to wear a wedding ring all the time, even though she wasn't married, worried what people would think of a woman bringing up her children in London on her own. Sandra never knew any more about her dad than I knew about mine, but she remembers one brief conversation with Mum: she told Sandra that she physically collapsed when the father told her he was going back to Jamaica. But whose father was she talking about? Even Sandra's got no idea. It was a long time ago and Sandra was very young. My sister can go back through it all about Mum and her family. But our dads? It's a full stop. I can't begin to imagine how difficult those times were for Mum, and I know nothing about them.

70

I enjoyed growing up on the estate: bits of green everywhere and a cage area where we could play football. Sunday afternoons, after *The Big Match on ITV*, the blocks would empty into that pen, all of us children trying to do what we'd just been watching on the telly. I would already have played a game for my Sunday morning team, getting back in time to watch the First Division highlights on TV. The night before, too, I'd have stayed up to watch *Match of the Day*. Any time I could, I would go down to that cage and there'd usually be a game going on: one against one, two against two, 20 against 20. All different ages playing together. I used to play on my own a lot, too. There were walkways running underneath the blocks on our estate, with pillars dotted around and walls at the sides. I'd make up games, weaving around obstacles with a ball at my feet. I spent hours and hours practising. Using my imagination and trying things out with the ball and the wall.

And then came the World Cup in 1970 in Mexico, the first World Cup I can remember and, perhaps, the best I've ever seen. That tournament had a major impact on me: the Brazil team were the best of the best, playing football like I'd never seen before.

The scenes we saw on TV throughout the tournament and when they returned to Brazil with the trophy – the joy they gave to their nation – are still clear in my mind. Our TV was probably black and white but, somehow, I think of it all in colour, maybe because I've watched the highlights from 1970 quite a few times since: blue skies and the sun shining every game, enormous crowds, dazzling coloured kits, and the skills. The skills! Plus: lots of these amazing players, like Pelé, were being idolised by everybody. *And they look like me.* So much else in life, when it came to black people, carried a negative reflection. So, it was uplifting for me to see the Brazilians being spoken about on the news and in the papers in such a positive way. I had never experienced that before. Maybe that was when I started believing that professional football could be achievable for me, too.

My love for football came from playing at school and watching *Match of the Day* and *The Big Match.* Clyde Best was the only professional black player I can remember seeing on TV, playing up front for West Ham United. I would look out for him and wanted him to do well. It's a wonder I didn't end up supporting West Ham! After that 1970 World Cup, I looked at Clyde in a new way. *He's doing what I want to do, right?* Clyde became a role model for me, like he did for many players of my generation and those that followed. Pelé was another. He was so far away, but the fact that almost everyone acknowledged he was the best player in the world had another positive effect on me. Yes, black people could achieve: up to that point, I had never seen that idea expressed anywhere.

I had encouragement from closer to home, as well. The PE teacher at Springfield Primary School was Mr Daly. He had seen something in me to make me captain for both our football and cricket teams. I can still see him clearly now: 5ft 7ins, bald, a round face, with spectacles and a moustache. He had a little dent on his forehead, above his left eye, where I think a golf ball had hit him.

He always wore a suit, and collar and tie. When he lost his temper, Mr Daly would go bright red from shouting. He loved what he did and was a bit of a sporting father for me. He gave me support and reassurance, things I needed at the time. I can still remember him saying to me, 11 years old, when I was getting ready to go on to secondary school, that I should consider taking up football seriously. He felt I had what it took to play professionally. He was the first person to say that, to give me the hope that it was possible. I never saw Mr Daly again, but I have never forgotten what he did for me in saying those words.

I suppose I was always slightly different as a footballer: All left foot, always looking to be creative and score goals, but not particularly quick. I was always ready to compete for the ball. Even though I was small, I was always prepared to look after myself if anyone wanted to play that way. One of my biggest assets was my mentality. My first memories of playing are dribbling a little plastic ball up and down the corridor in our flat and, even then, it was: *left, left, left.* For a little while I did try and work on my right foot, to get comfortable using it, but once you're playing games, you go with what feels natural, don't you?

I was playing for the school team, in the pen on the estate against the older boys, and, by the time I left Springfield, I had Sunday football as well: a team called Tamla and then, later, one called Davidson. My friends Rob and Dean played, and a guy I'm still close with today, Gary MacDonald. Back then, Gary played in goal. He was a great person to be around and a good goalkeeper, too, but Macca was always late: we were more often than not waiting for him to turn up. Sunday football started to open up my world. We played at parks all over South London: Brockwell Park, Kennington, Clapham, Wandsworth. Ten years old, but on full-size pitches, 11-a-side. These were great times; I enjoyed my football and being a part of a team.

Len Bray, Rob's dad, was the manager and he put us into a league. I've never enjoyed having coaches who were jumping up and down on the sidelines, shouting at their players all the time. I was lucky: Len – and Dean's dad, Alfie, who was with us later when the club changed its name to Davidson – used to allow us to just play once we got on the pitch. Another coach, Ted Butler, was the same. They wanted to win, but didn't ever let that spoil our enjoyment. Those guys were more than just coaches. They were administrators, managers, secretaries, and bus drivers. Our kits were washed every week, too, by their wives, Jean Bray and June Tonkin. They helped me get to and from games. It's funny: later in my career, when coaches would shout and bawl, I'd keep my head down and do what I had to do. But, inside, I'd be going: *Why don't you shut up? You'd get more out of me if you'd just shut up! Why can't you be more like Len or Alfie or Ted?*

These were some of my best times. Easy: Saturday night making sure my boots were spotless, Sunday morning playing football with Rob and Dean and Gary Mac, and the other friends I got on so well with, off the pitch as well as on it. I've still got a bundle of old red Silvine notebooks, like the ones we used to have for school. Fifty years ago, I wrote as neatly as I could on every page: three or four seasons' worth of match reports. I included all my school and South London district fixtures, too. They used to carry a couple of paragraphs about our games in the *South London Press*. I'd cut them out, stick them in my books, and then carefully write out the score, who'd got the goals, where we were in the table, and anything else that seemed important at the time. Around then, I started to practise doing my autograph. In readiness for that day an Arsenal fan would ask me for it!

The bits of newspaper are going a bit brown now, and some of my spelling isn't the best, but I took a lot of care over those notebooks. Commas, full stops, straight lines, borders around everything. No crossings out: I couldn't afford to make even one mistake. Those notebooks remind me how important football was for me, even then. I didn't go home and have anybody that I'd talk to about my games, obviously. So, in a way, those red Silvine notebooks are me having conversations with myself. What I was really doing was going over the games in my mind, working out whatever it might be that I needed to learn. Like schoolwork, almost. The exercise books are how I was back then. Probably not all that different from the person I still am.

I'm glad I kept them. I'm looking at a page in one of them now: *Saturday 15th of November 1975. Davidson 6, Battersea Boys 0.* I played as a centre-forward back then and I've made a note that I scored two goals that afternoon. But it also says, in my neatest handwriting: *Was sent off for fight on Wandsworth Common.* I don't remember the game and I don't remember getting sent off, but I wrote it down, so it must have happened. There were times our games got rough. These were local rivalries, and we were the team usually getting to finals or finishing top of the league. Even as young boys, we had to learn how to look after ourselves and each other. I was always prepared to do that if I needed to.

Tamla was my big introduction to competition, to winning and losing and to being part of a team. I was following football as well as playing, and it was always Arsenal for me. I've still got the picture in my mind of Charlie George scoring at Wembley in 1971, against Liverpool, when we did the Double, smashing it in and then lying on his back on the pitch in that iconic yellow shirt and blue shorts. The Cup Final was the only live game on TV in those days. I was Arsenal from then on. The next Christmas, the Brays bought me an Arsenal holdall for a present, to carry my football stuff in on Sundays. Even though I went to Stamford Bridge with them, they already knew Arsenal were my team.

The secondary school I went to, Beaufoy, was an all-boys school in

Kennington with 1,500 of us, about a 25-minute walk from where we lived, a stone's throw from the Oval Cricket Ground in one direction and from Big Ben and Westminster in the other. It was a typical inner-city school, more sports-oriented than academic. I had great support from all my PE teachers. There were boys there, older than me, who were already involved at clubs, and I used to follow what was happening to them. In the year above me was Kevin Godfrey, who was with Orient and, three years older than me, Kenny Sansom was at Crystal Palace. Kenny being at Beaufoy was a big deal for me. I remember watching him on TV, playing for England Schoolboys, and wondering what that would be like: Wembley Stadium, a massive crowd, Kenny in his England shirt. Those older boys were important for me. They were local and they went to my school, even though I didn't know them. They made me feel that professional football could be within reach.

While I was at Beaufoy, I started to take an interest in cricket and a whole group of new role models came to my attention. This was the '70s: the West Indies were just starting to dominate with Sobers, Lloyd, Fredericks, all those guys. I felt connected because of my mum, and the joy that team gave to the West Indian community was unbelievable. I fell in love with what they stood for. Whatever negatives might have come with being black in South London were made a little easier to deal with by the West Indies team: best in the world and from where my family was from. Beaufoy was the closest school to The Oval, and sometimes they were asked to send boys over to run the covers on and off during Test matches. I was chosen, and it meant I could see the West Indies play live. It was an incredible time for Test cricket: an amazing atmosphere and the game itself was raw, no helmets or anything. I was right there, within touching distance. I played cricket to county level at school, too, but, when I was 13 and had a decision to make, I chose football. I do still love cricket, though.

After trials, I was selected to play district football for South London, soon after I started at Beaufoy. Always as a striker and usually a year above my own age group. That was quite a big deal: everybody in the area knew who was in the district team, and scouts from professional clubs would go to watch the games. Within a couple of years, almost all the boys playing for South London had been scouted by clubs. Not me, though. I needed to get scouted, needed a scout to see the potential in me. For a long time, I came home disappointed I hadn't been spotted. I'm pretty sure it was because I was so slight at that age and, for a lot of clubs, being big and strong was what the scouts were looking for. I was quite skinny, too. All I could do was try and stand out the next time I played.

That South London team was a good group of players, and we had a lot of success. The English Schools Trophy featured district teams from all over the country at under-15s. A letter would come to the flat on headed notepaper. *Dear Paul. You have been selected to play etc. Meet at Oval tube station, and the rest.* We travelled to games on a coach, played at proper football stadiums. Goals with nets! We won the English Schools Trophy, the first time for South London in 50-odd years. We had games at Hillsborough and at Ashton Gate, but I remember one at Aldershot, the first professional ground I ever played at. Real dressing rooms, with showers, even though they were cold! Stands, and everything so big, especially the pitch. I scored, and we went through to the next round.

Quite often, my weekends were playing football on Saturday mornings for the school or for South London and then again on Sunday mornings for Tamla or Davidson, all on full-size pitches. The English Schools Trophy was all that and more: different cities, miles away from London, playing against boys from very different backgrounds. The first leg of the final, against Islington Boys, was at The Den, which we won 2-0. The second leg was at Highbury and finished 1-1. Chris Whyte and Chris Ramsey were the two Islington players who went on to have professional careers, and I was the only one from South London. Playing a final at Highbury was massive for all of us. There was a crowd of around 10,000, the largest I'd ever played in front of. Mum and Sandra couldn't get there, but plenty of scouts did. We all knew how important it was to perform well. By then, though, I wasn't just a South London schoolboy. I was an Arsenal schoolboy as well.

74

In early 2021, a camp was set up at Loughborough University to watch the England under-17s. The idea was to assess and select 24 boys who'd be the core of the squad we hoped would be going to Israel the following summer to compete at the 2022 European Championships. John McDermott, the FA's Technical Director, had called a meeting to kick us off: all the boys and members of staff. I was at one end of the room with John, Tom Curtis, the new under-17 head coach, and the rest of the technical staff, the medical team, and the welfare staff. The young players, England's best of a new generation, sat expectantly. I was introduced to the players. *This is one of your assistant coaches, Paul Davis.* The boys looked at me. I looked at the boys. There wasn't a sound. But there was a question hanging in the air. *Who's Paul Davis?*

John told them: *When Paul was your age, he was making his first team debut for Arsenal. He was playing top-flight football, senior football, at White Hart Lane, away to Spurs.* That meant something to a few of them. I saw a couple of the boys' heads nodding slowly. Maybe I was imagining it, but it seemed like they were looking at me a little differently now. I'd played at the level they were all dreaming of reaching one day, and had done it while I was still as young as they were now. Part of my role at the camp was to pass on my experiences, to help and support the players' development. Many of them reminded me of myself at that age: quiet, but with a passion and a dream to be a footballer, to have a career in the game.

My district team, South London Boys, played their home games in Dulwich, at Belair Park. That was where I finally got scouted by Arsenal, aged 13. After one game, the South London coach, Mr Richards, came up to me. *There's a scout here from Arsenal who would like to talk to your parents about you going for a trial.* The scout was an older man, bald, wearing a dark-coloured overcoat. That's as much as I remember, meeting him for the first time. We had a brief conversation, with Mr Richards at my side. The scout's name was Mr Ernie Collett. He explained who he was and took contact details so he could come to see my parents. I was a bit self-conscious and thought the fact Mum was on her own might not be in my favour, a reflection of the stigma around single parents in those days.

Mr Collett came to the flat a week or so later: smart, suit and tie, overcoat, very respectable. He was reassuring and explained the process to us. Mum made him a cup of tea, using her best set of china, and he told her that he'd seen me play. Arsenal wanted to have a look at me now. Mum tried to make sense of what was being said. I was just hoping that Mr Collett wasn't going to change his mind. Mum's attitude with me and Sandra had always been straightforward. *Keep out of trouble, be respectful, and do your schoolwork.* She didn't understand the football world, and I had to convince her that was what I wanted to do.

Mum was wondering what a trial involved. I knew what it was, of course: my big opportunity, an opportunity I'd give everything I could to take. Can you imagine? This wasn't the representative of just any football club visiting our home. This was Arsenal, one of the biggest clubs in the country and with a history to match. The club I supported. Before he left, Ernie said we should think about everything he'd said and that, if we had any questions, we were to let him know. The minute he was out the door, I knew it didn't need thinking about at all. *The Arsenal! Look, Mum, I'm doing it. I'm going to go.*

After Ernie Collett came to talk to Mum, everything happened quite quickly. A week later, all the paperwork arrived in the post. I signed there and then. Mum signed her bits. The club needed her permission for me to train with them. She said she was happy for me to go. Back then, clubs didn't have the monopoly on young players that they do now. We weren't playing games for Arsenal because, during term-time, clubs couldn't take you out of school. That meant I was able to play other sports and do any other activities I wanted to: I kept on playing games for Beaufoy or South London most Saturdays, and for Davidson on Sundays. But now I would make my way to Highbury stadium twice a week, every Monday and Thursday, for schoolboy training. I'd get on the Victoria Line at Stockwell, change to the Piccadilly Line at Kings Cross, and then three stops on from there to Arsenal station. Six weeks: that was the trial. I knew I had to do well.

It was the first time I'd ever been to Highbury. I arrived, holding my letter Ernie had written so people would know who I was. *Show this to the staff when you arrive.* I walked up the white steps on Avenell Road, through the black-painted wooden doors and into the marble halls: the big cannon on the floor, a staircase sweeping up on the right, the ticket office and a polished wooden bench on the left. There was a shiny statue on a plinth in front of me: Herbert Chapman, not that I knew who that was at the time. Somebody was there, meeting boys as they came in. I showed him my letter and he pointed me to a door by the foot of the stairs. I pushed through into a narrow corridor and, almost immediately, I was looking into a changing room where all the other lads were getting ready. We were in the away team dressing room. I found a small space and put my bag down on the bench that ran around the room and looked around. This was Arsenal.

There were another 15 or 16 lads already there: I was the only new boy training that evening. The only black boy, as it happened. I don't remember much being said, just somebody showing me where to go. We all got changed, walked back out into the marble halls and then down to the right, through the players' tunnel. Suddenly, I was standing on the cinder track, next to the pitch and between the two dugouts, the stadium looming around me. Away to my right stood the empty North Bank and its terraces; to my right, the Clock End, and the big white clock with its black numbers; and that beautifully manicured green pitch laid out between. I wondered: *What must it be like, playing out there with 60,000 fans cheering you on?*

We walked along the track in front of the East Stand, finding our way through to the back of the old Clock End, where we trained. There was an indoor area with goals marked out on the walls at each end. There were no pitch markings, and the playing surface was Redgra, which burnt your skin off if you went over on it. The session lasted about 90 minutes and it was hard. Plenty of running to start with. Then one or two-touch drills, and a 9 v 9 game at the end. On the walls, they'd painted lots of circles. You had to clip the ball into the circles: a few low down on the wall, and then one or two higher up. The coaches were Roger Thompson, a youth coach, quite jovial, friendly, and talkative, and Ian Crawford, who was the reserve team coach. Ian was tough, more uncompromising, a Scot who demanded maximum effort in everything you did.

We had small-sided games, with the pitch split into two, and those were competitive. We were a couple of year groups mixed.

The lads varied in terms of size, ability, pace and personality. I was one of the smallest and quietest there. There were some players who made a point of testing your character. I remember people being smashed up against the walls, getting cuts and grazes from going over on the Redgra, all of it encouraged by the coaches. It felt like a different level of football: aggressive, intense, talented players all around you. I was nervous walking in that first evening but left wanting more: the ball work, the technical stuff we did; feeling as if every single touch mattered, too. I didn't care about the bumps and bruises. Apart from a few brief sessions with Fulham, these were the most intense coaching sessions I'd ever been part of. I listened carefully to Ian and Roger, trying to deliver whatever they asked of me.

Some sessions took a bit of understanding at first: there were drills where you were only allowed one or two touches, which didn't allow for much creativity. It meant you had to play a particular kind of football. You weren't so free to improvise or express yourself. But I was excited by the opportunity to impress on those Monday and Thursday evenings. In from school, warm up and eat the food Mum had prepared that morning, and then complete my homework. We had to take our own kit. For some reason, I had a West Brom shirt I always trained in, with a proper collar and those thick dark blue stripes. Mum would wash it and I ironed it and my shorts the night before every session, and these went into my Arsenal bag with socks and trainers by the front door, ready to go. I used to leave about 5pm and take the Tube. I'd be there by 6pm, to start at 6.30pm. I was never, ever late.

After the six weeks, they must have seen enough to want to keep me on: my running over distance was good, but my sprinting wasn't so strong. I was physically small – around 10st 6oz – but comfortable with the ball at my feet. We trained during term-time, and then we'd have games against other London clubs during the school holidays. Extra training sessions, too. I always felt I had to be at my very best, on and off the pitch. I'd always show respect to all the staff I met. I felt I was well treated and just wanted to grab this once-in-a-lifetime opportunity. There were regular conversations. Roger Thompson would sit down and talk to me about my game, what I was doing well and what I needed to improve on. From then on, it was pressure all the time, although I didn't find that difficult to deal with. Every stage you moved up to, you were trying to get to the stage after that. To make sure you weren't the next boy released.

I felt like I had to push myself as hard as I could and try to impress. I liked the structure: that was me, twice a week, for the next two years of my life. There was a big turnover of boys, though. You'd see someone come for a six-week trial like I had, but then not see them return. Or a player might be there for five or six months, and then you wouldn't see them at training again. Decisions were being made all the time on players. It was brutal, but I was determined that it wasn't going to happen to me. After a while, I looked around and there were a handful of us who seemed to have been there for some time. My friend from Tamla and Davidson, Dean Tonkin, was one of those; Dean got an apprenticeship, but was released soon after. Also, Michael Pittaway, who I played with for South London. He had a style a bit like Bobby Moore and almost everyone thought he was going to be a cert to play for Arsenal; but Michael got released, too. Chris Whyte joined later and went right through, and we ended up playing first team for Arsenal together. He was ahead of his time, always looking to play football. I remember Don Howe pulling his hair out (and he never had that much anyway) over Chrissy attempting to play out from the back.

I'd get to training quietly excited, always looking forward to the challenge. Once the session was over, the club would always make sure we had our travelling expenses paid to us. I used to make the journey to Highbury on my own, even though there were a couple of other boys from South London. We all had our own routes north. On the walk back to Arsenal station and down the long tunnel to the platform, I'd always replay the session in my head. Another kind of conversation with myself: working out what I'd done well and what hadn't been so good. I was pretty good at being honest with myself. And good at getting over a session if it hadn't been the best. By the time I got home, I'd have replayed the evening over in my mind several times. I learned early on that there wasn't any use in dwelling on bad performances. Or on good ones either. Later on, I came to realise that those self-talk sessions played a large part in my future success.

I had many conversations with myself, but I also received honest advice from others. Even before I started at Arsenal, there were people like Mr Daly, the PE teacher at my primary school, who believed in me, and helped me to believe in myself. At Highbury, there was Alf Fields. Alf was a gentleman, 6ft 3ins tall, with bowed legs. He'd played for Arsenal, but his career had been cut short in the '50s by a knee injury and he'd joined the staff. When I was a schoolboy, Roger Thompson took the team, but Alf was always at every training session and every game. He didn't take sessions, but always had the right words at the right time, ensured we received our travel expenses, and sorted out the kit. Alf seemed to know when I was struggling for confidence or doubting myself, and would always offer me a quiet word of advice. If Alf felt I needed to change something, I thought: *Alf will have done it himself. He'll know.* That gave me confidence. More than anybody else at the club, Alf Fields made me feel that, if I continued driving myself to continually improve, I could have a good career at Arsenal. But I knew nothing was ever for sure in football.

77

I've never been someone who is loud, on or off the pitch. In fact, I would say I'm predominantly introverted as a personality, although at the time I wouldn't have realised that was the name for it. Playing Sunday football and schools football, it never seemed like an issue: playing well and scoring goals was enough. And we were just kids, weren't we? But, when I started training at Arsenal, I felt different from the others: quieter, not as into the banter, not finding the humour all that funny. I was continually working out how much of my true self I was prepared to give up in order to make it in this brutal – but wonderful – world of a professional football club. How I played had to change, too: in midfield instead of up front, for a start. Training in the evenings and playing games in the holidays, this was serious, structured, playing to a system, 1-4-4-2. *How could I fit Arsenal's idea of what a midfield player needed to be?*

Gary Mac, who played with me at Tamla and Davidson, would tell you now: I became a different player to the one I was when I was young. More efficient, more disciplined, more professional. That I played with less freedom. Like every other boy, I needed to find a way to survive, to adapt and fit into an unfamiliar environ-ment. It was a challenge. Every one of us was hoping to get signed as an apprentice at 16. Playing football as a youngster, I was with my friends, competing against other teams. At Arsenal, though, I realised that I was competing against my own team-mates, too. We weren't all going to be kept on, were we? Training, playing matches, building relationships: I had to completely rethink how and why I was doing things. More self-talk, walking to and from the Tube station for every session.

My challenge at Arsenal was to get taken on as an apprentice at 16 years old. I'd seen other boys come and go. I was still there, but that wasn't a guarantee of anything. I remember how scared I was, knowing the club were discussing all our futures in the Spring of 1977. I went to Highbury to find out what would be happening to me. I knew exactly what was at stake. In July, I'd either be starting a full-time football apprenticeship or I'd be needing to look for another club. Or, more likely, I'd be staying on at secondary school.

We were called into the coaches' room at Highbury one by one. Roger Thompson, Ian Crawford, and Ernie Collett were waiting for me when I knocked and entered the room. I found out later that all the staff who'd seen me play had a say on whether to keep me. And it was close: me being offered something came down to one vote. Didn't matter to me at the time, of course. All I heard was Roger saying: *Paul, we'd like you to offer you an apprenticeship at Arsenal. Congratulations.* The mix of joy and relief I felt is difficult to describe. I was on cloud nine on the journey home to Stockwell.

A couple of days later, a letter came through for my mum. Headed Arsenal notepaper, all official, letting her know they were offering me an apprenticeship, reassuring her I'd be well looked after. And confirming that they'd be sending £18 through to her every week to pay for my upkeep. I felt that was the moment Mum realised a career in football was possible; she was so happy for me. I knew if I made it as a professional, I could help relieve her of some of the financial worries she'd always had. I was excited, of course. But there was this overwhelming feeling of relief: I knew that my next target was in two years, and that was to get a professional contract offer by 18. I left school after my CSEs in June. My mind hadn't been on my studies for a while, and I didn't do as well as I would have liked. All I'd been thinking about was whether I was going to be offered an apprenticeship at Arsenal. Everything else seemed insignificant.

I don't remember anything more about that meeting with the coaches. Maybe that was partly because I didn't talk to anyone about it at the time. Mum was pleased for me, of course, but she didn't know how it all worked, or even understand that there was a future for me in football. I'd given up a lot for this moment: no parties, no hanging out late at night, no smoking, no girlfriends. But all I was thinking was: *What's next? What happens now?* I had to do even more for the next two years so that I would be offered a professional contract. It was almost as if I cleared everything from my mind. It was instinct now. *Listen. Take on instruction, work hard, improve, be mentally strong, learn how to get on with other people. But, at the same time, look after yourself.*

The apprenticeship was a completely new world. From Arsenal being a part of my life – a small part, in terms of the hours I spent there – it became my whole life. Instead of travelling up from Stockwell two evenings a week, I now had to get the Tube every morning, meet the minibus at 9am at Highbury to go up to London Colney, the training ground out in Hertfordshire, and be ready to start at 10.30am. Missing that bus meant you missed training, and I couldn't ever let that happen. We'd have sessions on the pitch every morning. Afternoons sometimes, too. If we weren't training, we'd be doing jobs: cleaning boots, tidying dressing rooms, preparing the balls and bibs for the first team, even washing Roger Thompson's car. Some days, we'd go back to Highbury after training to do jobs at the stadium. This was all part of being an apprentice. There was a lot of learning to be done very quickly. Learning how to handle relationships with staff and my team-mates from day to day was as big a challenge for me as the football was in many ways.

I finally stopped wearing my favourite West Brom shirt. All our kit was laid on now. It'd be there, waiting for us, freshly laundered every morning. I was number 26, on my training kit, and on my shirt, sweater and tracksuit, too. Boots were supplied as well. The biggest change, though, was seeing and being so close to the first-team players every day: Pat Jennings, Liam Brady, Willie Young, Malcolm MacDonald, Arsenal's stars. We all trained at Colney, and they were just a few pitches away from us. We changed in the same building: we used the dressing rooms at the bottom end of the corridor, which meant that we'd be walking past the first-team dressing rooms and the manager's office most mornings. And at lunchtimes, they'd already be in the canteen when we came in to eat. We were just out of school, but senior football was within touching distance.

I recognised the senior players' personalities and watched how they behaved. Liam Brady was my favourite player. My hero in many ways. A role model: a midfield player, a little over 5ft 8ins, and all left foot. He could pass, dribble, create and score goals: Liam was a class apart. Kevin De Bruyne is maybe the closest comparison I can see in today's game. If you'd asked Arsenal supporters at the time, they'd all have told you Liam was the best player they'd ever seen. He was the best I ever played with. I'd watch him in games – play alongside him, even – and he was on a different level. I watched and watched and tried to adopt what I could. He was one of the out-standing players of that generation.

There was a lot to learn as an apprentice. And the running: there was a lot of that, too. In fact, running in pre-season was the one thing we all did together: apprentices, young pros, reserve-team players and first team. I was up with the best over longer distances, but sprints weren't such a strength. Full-time football meant I had to learn and adapt, improve physically and mentally. And it was during those first few weeks out at Colney that I got a sense of just how big a club Arsenal was, and how many players there were for me to get past if I was ever going to play for the first team: older apprentices, first- and second-year pros, reserves. All those players were competing against each other. I was competing against all the other midfielders, and there were plenty of those.

Things would be said by the older boys sometimes, testing you, digging away at your confidence. There'd be tackles flying in during sessions. It felt like people would try almost anything to get ahead, and stay ahead, of you. I wasn't at Arsenal to mess around, or to take the mickey or belittle anybody else. But I soon realised I had to look after myself and, if someone was pushing me, I needed to be ready to push back, regardless of who they were. I was serious about having a future in the professional game. I could have a laugh and a joke, but I always felt there was a very fine line between that and taking the piss out of someone. I never wanted to cross that line. I never wanted to be bringing someone else down in order to build myself up, even though I saw that happen many times.

As a young player, you were challenged every single day. I can still remember, when I was first getting involved around the first team, on a Friday we'd finish training with a 20-minute small-sided game. Everyone enjoyed these games – North v South or Young v Old – and afterwards, everybody would get to vote. *Who was your worst player in the game today?* Whoever got the most votes would get presented with the yellow bib. It could be anyone: Pat Rice, Willie Young, Brian Talbot. And sometimes it was me. Fair enough. But I would always, always, get at least one vote every Friday morning, no matter how well I'd trained. It bugged me.

Years later, Alan Sunderland told me he was the one voting for me every week: just having a bit of fun. I promised myself I'd never do anything like that to anyone, least of all a young player.

I realised quickly that I wasn't going to hit it off with every coach or player I worked with. I took what I could from every session, though. The more time I spent training with senior players, the more important it became to find ways to adapt. These guys were established professionals; older than me and living completely different lives, most of them married with kids, a big home out in the suburbs and nice cars. We had nothing in common apart from football. And I knew it was down to me to adjust and adapt to try to fit in. *They aren't going to adjust to me, are they? Why should they?* I had to figure it out. *How much can I bend here but still be true to myself?*

As first-year apprentices, we played in the South East Counties League. It was a brutal 90 minutes of football on Saturday mornings. The league was made up of clubs in and around London, every single game felt like a derby. We were playing big rivals – Spurs, Chelsea, West Ham – every other week. Twenty-two boys trying to prove themselves, tackles flying in: those were the games where I learned just how competitive professional football was going to be. South East Counties was a world away from the academy games 16- and 17-year-olds play now. Our games were fierce, physical, and the results mattered. You learnt how to deal with winning and losing, playing well and playing badly, injuries and the psychological challenge that came with them.

I was driven. I was determined to succeed. Even on our day off, Wednesday, I would travel back to North London because we had to attend college on Holloway Road. I'd get back to Stafford Court, have something to eat, watch TV and then go off to bed: I slept well that first year as an apprentice. My connection to South London, my friendships at Sunday football, at school and on the estate, started to loosen a little. We were all out in the big wide world trying to find our own ways, weren't we? But my world now was in North London. I started thinking about moving, to be nearer to the training ground at Colney, nearer to Highbury. It wasn't until I signed professional forms, though, that I'd have the money to do so.

All my time growing up and as a young player at Arsenal, I only ever had one injury I can remember. But it made me realise how fragile this idea of a career as a professional footballer was. I was 16, a year into my apprenticeship, and we went away to play in an international tournament in Germany. Amazing: first time I'd ever been out of the country. I was excited and looking forward to the new challenges. I was playing well; the team was playing well. But a few games into the tournament, somebody came through the back of me. My knee buckled. I knew straight away that I was out of the tournament.

I limped off and couldn't play in any other games. I couldn't walk, just hobbling around on crutches for the last few days in Germany. I remember watching on, fearing the worst. The real concern was not being able to find out how serious the injury was until we came home, and I could have a scan, and get looked at by the club doctor. As apprentices, we had so little time, really, to convince the club we were good enough. What would happen if I missed weeks – or months, even – out injured? Back in London, the club sent me to see a doctor in Harley Street. They said I didn't need an operation, which was great news, but I had my whole leg put in plaster for weeks: couldn't train, couldn't play. I was out for three or four months, frustration stretching on into the summer.

I spent a lot of time on my own after that injury: resting up at home, Mum and Sandra both out all day. After the plaster came off, I would go into Highbury and do my rehabilitation in the small gym above the home dressing room. I was aware of how much I was missing, which made what happened next even more surprising. Usually, at the end of your two years as an apprentice, you'd find out whether you were going to be offered a professional contract. But even though I was injured, Arsenal made the decision with me early, before that tackle in Germany. After just a year as a youth-team player, the club offered me the opportunity to sign my first professional contract.

I think it was Roger Thompson who took me to one side and told me the club wanted to offer me a contract. Told me I had to go into the office at Highbury and sign the papers. Out of the blue: this was a full year before I'd have expected to find out about my future. I didn't even have time to get nervous or excited. I've still got the letter from the Arsenal manager, Terry Neill: dated June 12th, 1979, confirming what was on offer. *£100 a week, plus £100 per first-team appearance, plus any bonuses.* A couple of sentences is all: but this was telling me I was about to become a professional footballer. I was 17. It's amazing, really: in the same letter, Terry said the club doctor, Dr Sash, was sure my knee would be fine after some rest and rehabilitation work. So, reading back over that letter now, I realise I was out injured when I signed professional forms for Arsenal.

Turning professional after just a year as an apprentice was unusual. I didn't dwell on that, though. I just jumped at the opportunity. A couple other lads turned pro that same summer. Paul Vaessen and I were the same age. We'd known each other from district football in South London. Paul played for the first team when he was still very young, while he was an apprentice. He was a big, strong centre-forward. Incredibly powerful shot, good passer, a very technical player. We all thought he was going to have an important future at Arsenal.

Paul came on as a sub and scored a famous goal in Turin against Juventus that took us into the Cup Winners' Cup Final in 1980.

He played quite a few first-team games that season. But a football career's fragile, isn't it? One bad injury can cost you everything. Paul damaged ligaments in his knee and struggled for a couple of seasons before he had to retire. Operation after operation, but the problem never got fixed. I remember seeing him around the training ground when he was in for treatment, looking so down. It all fell away and the rest of us watched it happen. I don't think he ever got over having to retire so young, at just 21. It cost him his life, really. It's a difficult, painful story: Paul died, from a drug overdose, before he was 40.

In '79/80, while Paul Vaessen was making his mark, I was full-time with the reserves, playing games in the Football Combination. That meant training with senior players – guys who had played for the Arsenal first team – and being up against experienced professionals every weekend. It meant home games at Highbury, with supporters watching. Terry Neill or Don Howe, maybe, up in the Directors Box, too. I knew there were more experienced players ahead of me: Liam Brady, Brian Talbot, David Price, Graham Rix. There were midfielders in the reserves as well, who'd already played first-team football, like Richie Powling and Jim Harvey. I was competing against them. But the Football Combination was a fantastic chance to impress. I had that in my head every time I played. *You never know who's watching you, Paul. Be brave!*

I wasn't big. I wasn't quick. But I could get around the pitch, and my positional sense meant I was where I needed to be. I didn't mind getting stuck into tackles. I wasn't the striker I'd been at school and playing Sundays for Tamla. Instead, I'd worked at becoming the kind of footballer Arsenal were wanting me to be: efficient, effective, competitive, with a mentality to win every game and to play well under pressure. I was determined to get the most out of whatever ability I had. I used to go into the little gym at Highbury and do weights on my own, trying to build up my physical strength. I started thinking and reading about anatomy, diet, lifestyle: anything I could do that would help me improve. When some of my team-mates were talking about going to play snooker in the afternoon, I found myself thinking there had to be more productive ways to spend my time after training. I did my first coaching qualification, the old FA Preliminary, when I was still just 17, getting up early to go down to Clapham for full-day sessions on Sundays.

Late '70s, clubs didn't really work with the idea of squads. There was only one sub allowed in a game. At Arsenal, everybody knew who the first team were, and those players played pretty much every game. It was only if there was an injury, a run of bad results or a suspension that the team would change. There wasn't such a thing as rotation. Teams stuck with a tried and trusted first XI, which made it more difficult to break into the starting line-up. Nevertheless, I started to get the call to leave training with Ian Crawford and, instead, to go over and join the first team with Terry Neill and Don Howe. I might work with the first team in the week, but I always knew that, even if I didn't play for them on Saturday, I'd still have a reserve game to look forward to and learn from every weekend. There wasn't a loan system like today. It must be frustrating for young players now: lots of them train all week – travel to games, even – but end up on the bench or in the stands when, really, they'd be best off learning in competitive games. Instead, some can go weeks without playing.

I can still remember the first few times I trained with the first team. There were a few strong characters. Most of them were established internationals. It was what I'd been working for, though. I was still a way off being a first-team player, but I could feel myself edging closer. The guys used to challenge you: they'd give you a kick in training or give you some banter to see how you reacted.

They were seeing whether you had the mental and physical skills to survive. Even at that age, though, my personality was: *If you're going to give me some, you'd best be prepared to get some back.* It was scary. Holding my own against senior players like Sammy Nelson, Pat Rice, Frank Stapleton or Graham Rix took a bit of doing. You were tested, all the time, by coaching staff and team-mates alike. I quickly learnt you had to have the courage to stand up and give as good as you got.

What shocked me, though, was the players' attitude towards the manager. Don Howe was the assistant and did most of the coaching. The players all recognised how good he was at his job and put the work in for him. Terry Neill was the manager, so he was more the public face of Arsenal. He was always a good talker, always had a story. But during training sessions and in team meetings, a lot of the players didn't show Terry the respect I thought he should have as the manager of the football club. People like Willie Young would just dismiss what he had to say, swear at him, even. *You don't know what you're talking about, Terry.* I'd just be listening, open-mouthed. *Can you really do that? Can you say that? He's the manager!* Willie was a big character and didn't suffer fools, obviously. But I have to say he also stood out as someone who'd look out for you as a young player, on and off the pitch.

Given that he gave me the opportunity to start my career and had the patience to stick with me through challenging times early on, I wouldn't ever say a bad word about Terry. I found it difficult in Don Howe's training sessions, though. Don was a great coach, extremely well respected. Even now, four decades later and after his passing in 2015, Don's name is still highly regarded through-out football. He had passion, drive, and knowledge to match any other coach of his time. He had a great sense of humour as well and would love telling a joke or two at the right time. But I always had a problem with coaches shouting at me while I'm trying to do my job.

And Don shouted a lot! That was just him. It wasn't anger. It was his enthusiasm and passion. For example, if I was closing a player, having someone scream at me to do it quicker didn't ever help. Don always wanted one-touch and two-touch football. But, when the ball's coming towards me, nothing's going to upset my first touch more than someone bawling *instructions to me*. That said, Don did improve my game. He always demanded more, always challenged me to be quicker and stronger. He helped me grow as a player.

80

'79/80 was a unique season for Arsenal. We did okay in the League. For a while, we were pushing for the title. But that team was a cup team, really. We ended up in two finals. By Easter, that meant a lot of games in a very short space of time. We had Norwich away on April 2, Southampton at home on April 5. The big one was Juventus in the first leg of the European Cup Winners' Cup semi-final at Highbury on April 9. In between, though, we were away to Tottenham on the Bank Holiday Monday. Arsenal asked for the game to be moved to give us time to prepare for the Wednesday night, but Spurs refused. Of course they did. Terry Neill made a fuss in the papers about how he'd have to rest players. People thought he was getting his excuses in early, and he got criticised for the fact that he was going to name a weakened team.

That's how I got my chance. At 17 years old. I'd trained with the first team at London Colney, but I hadn't ever played, hadn't ever been named as a sub. I'd never even travelled to a game. I got the call to join up that Monday, though. The team always met at South Herts Golf Club for games in London. I'd just passed my test and had bought myself a car, so I drove up to Totteridge in my light blue Ford Escort. I was around it all for the first time: everybody together, laughing, and joking, some nerves, the pre-match meal. Around midday, we filed through to a meeting room for the team talk, which was when Terry named the starting XI. I was excited: I felt there was a 50/50 chance I could start from all the talk leading into the game, but couldn't be sure.

Terry and Don stood at the front of the room. Terry lifted the paper on his flipchart and began to read out the team. I saw my name on the sheet before he even got to say it out loud. I felt as if my heart was going to pump out of my chest, I was fighting hard to contain my emotions. There were a few lads around the first team getting a game: Paul Barron in goal in place of Pat Jennings, Paul Vaessen up front instead of Frank Stapleton. Five of the regulars were playing, including Liam Brady, Pat Rice and Willie Young. And then Terry said it: *Davis. Paul Davis.* That was me: debut, in midfield with Brian Talbot, away to Spurs. But I couldn't allow the joy of that moment to last too long: I had to listen to the instructions the team was getting from Don now. There wasn't time for celebrating anything. There wasn't time to call Mum or Sandra or any of my friends from home to say I was playing, either, or to arrange for any of them to come to the game.

After the team was announced, we received 15 minutes of instructions from Don. Who was doing what on corners, free-kicks, those sorts of details. Reminders about what we'd been working on in training. Not that there'd been much training because there had been so many games. My key instructions were to play my normal game, but also to stop Glenn Hoddle getting on the ball and running the game for Spurs. Glenn's three or four years older than me and was one of the most naturally gifted players of his generation. I'd still say he's the best I ever played against. I knew without being told: if Glenn was given too much space, he'd either create or score a goal. I had half an hour, then, to relax. *Relax?* Well, to let it all sink in before we got on the team coach that was taking us to the Lane.

There wasn't a cloud in the sky that day. It was almost like Cup Final weather. The senior players were towards the front of the coach, playing cards. I sat by a window, the sun streaming in, so bright it made you squint. It's not a long drive from the golf club to Spurs: Cockfosters, Southgate, Wood Green and across to Tottenham. I started to see supporters making their way to the game: just a few at first, then more and more as we got towards the High Road. The coach had Arsenal written on a board in the front window, so everybody knew who we were: a few of the fans – Arsenal fans – waved and cheered us as we went past. Spurs fans were either ignoring us or verbally abusing us. We were in their territory now.

I was nervous. Excited, too. Wanting to be there and to get on with it. This was all new to me. But I was used to having quiet conversations with myself in my head. I'd learnt how to do that, never having had anyone at home who was interested in talking about football. Now, I was just trying to think about my first game for Arsenal. Think about what I needed to do, putting positive thoughts and feelings into my mind, trying to cut out any negatives that tried to creep in: *play my normal game but also stop Glenn Hoddle.* We turned out of White Hart Lane into the High Road and, even though this was an hour and half before kick-off, it was packed: Spurs supporters chanting, jeering at us, snarling, faces all angry and twisted up. The tension and pressure are always heightened when Arsenal play Spurs. That afternoon was no different.

A couple of hundred yards further along, we turned left into the old ground. The White Hart pub on the corner, and *Tottenham Hotspur Football Club* in big letters on the back of the main stand in front of us. This narrow bit of street was so full of Spurs fans the coach could hardly move. And we were the enemy. We just had to edge forward, inch by inch, while they opened the gate for us. Eventually we pulled up a little way from the players' entrance, and we climbed down off the coach. Now I could hear the shouts and the anger at full volume. Stewards walked alongside us. Protecting us, I suppose, because there were home fans in the car park, too, waiting to get into the ground.

We were shown through to the dressing room. Suddenly, everything was quiet and calm. It was just us: the lads milling about, chatting, asking for cups of tea, arranging to get tickets left for friends and family. It was still early. I looked around and nobody was getting changed yet. So, this was time again to gather my thoughts. All the lads had wished me well for the game. The surroundings, at least, were familiar. I'd been here for Football Combination games. But this was the biggest moment of my life, and the sense of anticipation and excitement was like nothing I'd ever experienced before. I needed to do well. A bad game and that could be my Arsenal career over. In a situation like that, there are so many things that could scare you, distract you from what you are there to do: win. I had the concentration, the discipline, and all the training I'd done, to keep me focussed. I needed to feel excited, not fearful, about the challenge ahead. I'd taught myself how to do that.

We wandered out: turned right out of our changing room into the tunnel, then a short walk, past the referee's office and the home team changing room, up onto the perfectly manicured pitch. It was still early. There were more stewards around than fans, but there were already a few Arsenal supporters, chanting. *Arsenal! Arsenal! Arsenal!* And: *We all agree, Brady is better than Hoddle.* Then, back in the dressing room. Players prepare themselves in different ways. Willie Young and Pat Rice were cracking jokes, to break the tension, I suspect. Others, like Brian Talbot, David O'Leary and John Hollins, got ready in silence. I don't remember anything that was said to me particularly. But I do remember I was made to feel a part of it all. Not the new kid: I was an Arsenal player. Tony Donnelly, the kit man, had been at the ground for a while. Our kit had been laid out, neatly folded, on the benches round the room, our boots on the floor, tucked underneath. I could see where my spot was, where I needed to get changed.

Everybody got on with doing what they needed to do in their own time and went out to warm up in twos and threes for five or ten minutes before Don called us all together for a team warm-up across the pitch. It was now about 45 minutes before kick-off, and the stadium felt like it was already packed, a crowd of more than 40,000. Then back into the changing room: shin pads in, a few of the older lads shouting encouragement and then, just before kick-off, Terry and Don saying their final reminders. I tried my hardest to listen but, by then, all I wanted was to be out there, the game kicking off and me getting a good first touch or tackle in. *Where's Glenn?* It was a feeling of anticipation: all the laughing and joking was over. This was serious, now. Everybody was ready to play, ready to fight to win the game. I felt supported, secure. I knew we were fielding a weakened team and that not many people had us down to win, but I didn't allow those thoughts to stay in my mind for long. The noise of the crowd, the tension and pressure of the occasion: Spurs versus Arsenal isn't for the faint-hearted. I had to be ready. *I won't get another chance.* This was it: *Do or die.*

The afternoon mattered so much to both sets of fans. But the game itself? I don't remember too much. That might seem strange, but I've spoken to many players who've told me they've felt the same. I made a few mistakes early on: a misplaced pass, a missed tackle, losing Glenn and wondering where he'd gone and fearing it was going to cost us. One thing I hadn't appreciated was the speed of the game. It was quick; it took me some time to get to the pace of it. But I'd already learned you forget about mistakes as soon as you've made them, and then find the courage to put yourself back in the line of fire. You have to develop that strong-mindedness to be a professional footballer. *What's just happened doesn't matter anymore. It's gone. It's all about what's happening next.* Finding my feet, I couldn't stand there, thinking: *Well, this is going okay.* It did go okay, though, didn't it? In fact, it couldn't have gone better. Vass and Alan Sunderland scored, and we beat Tottenham 2-1, with half a team of reserves. That felt good.

Afterwards in the dressing room was fantastic. Nobody from outside had expected us to win, which made it even sweeter. Sitting in my place, dripping sweat, and kicking my boots off, my heart was beating out of my chest. I knew our fans would now be able to look forward to going into work over the next couple of days. I thought I'd done okay in the game. Some of the senior players came over. *Well done, son.* Terry and Don, too. It was hard to take in what had just happened. I'd won plenty of games of football before, but all of them had only been building up to this, right? *First game for Arsenal. North London derby. Winning at their place.* The intensity of the physical exhaustion and the emotional high was new to me. When I looked around the dressing room, I loved that I could see my team-mates, experienced players, feeling the same. You can't beat beating Spurs.

What an afternoon. I'll never forget that togetherness, before we went out and in the dressing room after the final whistle: a group of players making something special happen, for the club, the fans and ourselves. That's the best feeling in football. An hour later, we were back on the coach. Some of the players got dropped off at the Cherry Tree in Southgate to celebrate. That was the Arsenal pub back then after games, that, or The Orange Tree in Totteridge. I wasn't a drinker. I was actually still too young to get served in a pub. Nobody said anything to me, and I didn't feel like inviting myself. I was happy, adrenaline still rushing through me and my head in a spin. I stayed on the coach all the way to South Herts, head resting against the cold window. The noise from the Lane was still ringing in my ears. At the golf club, I climbed into my Escort and drove to South London. Back home to Mum's.

Next day, I think what I'd done hit home to Mum, once she read some of the reports in the newspapers. She was proud of what I'd achieved. All through the rest of my career, she would often embarrass me, whatever company we were in. *Did you know that my son, Paul, plays football for the Arsenal?* I'd stand there next to her, feeling like I was about six years old again. *Thanks, Mum!* But it made me feel good that I was able to make her feel so proud. Later in my career, I'd ask friends who knew their way around Highbury to meet her, help her pick up her ticket, and then make sure she got to her seat. Saturday afternoons, huge crowds, me out there playing: I think it was all overwhelming for her at first. But she grew to love coming to watch some of my games.

The morning after we beat Spurs, I wanted to see what was being said about the game and about me. I went out and got a few papers from the shop where I used to do my round. The headlines were all about Arsenal's reserves having beaten Spurs' first team. Nobody was saying it had been a great game, but a few reports mentioned how I'd looked calm and collected in midfield, which was pleasing and a relief. None of them mentioned Glenn Hoddle doing much. I knew that I'd only played because of the situation the club found itself in. The fixture congestion had given me my opportunity. But I wanted some reassurance: that I'd done okay, hadn't let anybody down, and that I was a young player with a future at Arsenal.

A month later, away to Coventry, I got another chance. After an FA Cup semi-final and three replays against Liverpool, one or two needed a rest. I was sub at Highfield Road and came on second half for David Price. We won that game, too. 1-0. Really, though, I wasn't involved much. By the time it came to the big games at the end of the '79/80 season, I was back playing in the Combination. I was at Wembley when we lost in the FA Cup to West Ham, but sat up in the stand along with the other young players and club staff. When we played Valencia in the Cup Winners' Cup Final, at the old Heysel Stadium in Brussels, I didn't travel. But, from then on, I started asking the question. It was scary most of the time, but I started knocking on the manager's door to ask why I wasn't getting more games. I wanted Terry Neill to know how desperate I was to play for Arsenal.

Liam Brady left for Italy that summer, and I thought it might open the door for me to play more. As it turned out, though, I only made a few appearances, scattered through the '80/81 season. Arsenal finished third in the league and I struggled to get games. Brian Talbot and John Hollins played together most of the time in midfield. Another player my age, Brian McDermott, was the only youngster who got the opportunity to make a mark, playing wide on the right. People were always talking about the club signing another midfield player to replace Liam. Thinking back, playing ten games that season at 17, turning 18, wasn't bad. But I wanted more. In the midst of all the talk about Arsenal needing to buy a midfield player, I was thinking: *Believe in me! Show some confidence in me, please!* I never for a minute thought I could replace Liam, but I was sure I could save the club lots of money on a new signing.

81

After making my debut and then beginning to find my way as an Arsenal player, I think I was in people's minds: Arsenal fans, and newspaper journalists, too. I was around the first team. Chris Whyte was coming through, along with Raphael Meade. At the time, there were three players from West Indian backgrounds making a huge impact at West Brom: Brendon Batson, Cyrille Regis and Laurie Cunningham. Brendon had played for Arsenal half a dozen times in the early 1970s. Laurie came from Archway and had been a schoolboy at Arsenal before he was released and went to Orient. Now, together with Cyrille, they were getting called The Three Degrees and were setting the First Division alight. Three black players in the same team? That was something new. Maybe the papers were looking for the same kind of story elsewhere.

I've saved a few cuttings, reports from the match at White Hart Lane and feature articles that I was asked to do during 1980/81 and the season after. I know Mum kept a few more. Those newspaper reporters said some very nice things about me. About Chrissy and Raph, too. I can remember how, at the time, those match reports and articles made me feel good about myself.

They gave me confidence. I'd always carefully cut out everything I could find about Tamla and Beaufoy and South London when I was younger, pasting tiny paragraphs neatly into the exercise books which were my record of a schoolboy hopeful's career. So, it made an impact on me when those little cuttings became pages and half-pages in the national press.

Looking at the cuttings now, of course, I notice what I didn't really see at the time. I don't think there's a single article which doesn't describe me, somewhere, as black. Like that was the most important thing about me. Maybe it was to the people who wrote up those games and did those interviews. White players weren't described by their colour. Black footballers were still some sort of novelty. I don't think the journalists meant any harm. I didn't really see it then. And, even if I did find myself wondering why, I brushed it off. I was comfortable enough with my family background and my culture. I'm more aware now, reading these articles again.

Whenever I'm in South London these days and pass by my old estate, it still looks pretty much the same. Lansdowne Green seems well looked-after, quiet, secure. They were nice flats when we moved in – still are, probably – and you have to remember where we were coming from to live in them. Our estate was somewhere people could have a better life, families getting out of single rooms with no hot water, paraffin heaters to keep warm, and crammed in together with little space to breathe. Lansdowne Green had electric heating, gas cookers, and caretakers who looked after the blocks. It was low-rise and well laid out, so you were always near a bit of grass or next to a flowerbed. We had room to play. A bit of care had gone into designing the estate, and that made a difference.

We were probably about 90 per cent white English and maybe 10 per cent of us from Caribbean backgrounds, but there was never any tension. No name-calling, no bullying, no feeling of separateness. Nothing I noticed, anyway. Mum made good friends with our neighbours, and I made good friends, too, from different backgrounds: English, West Indian and Irish. On the Lansdowne Green estate, we were the Davis family. I felt comfortable and safe. Mum provided for us, even though money was tight. She'd just have to tell me she couldn't afford a lot of everything I asked her for. I'd be disappointed, but came to understand that was how it was. I walked everywhere without thinking about it. It was football, eventually, which took me away from that environment I felt so at home in.

When I went to watch those first games at Chelsea, I was 10 or 11, I'd guess. Back then, crowds were largely male, white and aggressive, and the songs and chants were often threatening. Violence amongst fans was commonplace, inside and outside stadiums. Going to a game in the '70s was a brave thing to do if you were black. I was a little fearful, but that didn't stop me going back for more. Going to a game was something out of the ordinary. There was a group of people who called themselves skinheads, who stood up for the values of the National Front, around Stamford Bridge and football in general back then. The Front was a well-supported political party committed to having all black people repatriated out of the UK. Outside the ground beforehand, and inside during the game, there was racist chanting if a black player was on the pitch. I was aware of it, of course, but I was still just a boy, and I was there with my friend or his dad, who were white. I was never picked out or attacked, but I was scared nonetheless: these people were around us, even in the seats. Maybe they didn't even see me. Maybe it was as if I wasn't really there.

Especially if I was going to Stamford Bridge, Mum always used to tell me I had to stay away from any trouble, and make sure I didn't put myself in the wrong situations. She was more aware than me of how the UK was at the time. She worked for the

Metropolitan Police, in the canteens at Marylebone and at Bow Street police stations. She enjoyed what she did and got on well with the officers she was serving up teas and sandwiches for. But I remember Mum going for a few promotions and not getting those jobs. I felt for her. I knew how hard she worked. But she never went into any of the details of why she'd missed out, and never talked about how she felt. Mum just got on with it. And, for obvious reasons, her big thing was that I mustn't ever get myself in trouble with the police.

Getting arrested when I was an apprentice at Arsenal and everything that followed, having to appear in court and listen to policemen lie, made me stop and think about things – about colour – almost for the first time. It crossed my mind that perhaps those police officers had really believed I'd been trying to steal that car, and that they'd just been doing their jobs. I'll never know their true motivations, but I do know that the racist words which got used said a lot about those officers' mindsets. Before that experience, overt racism hadn't been something I'd come into contact with. I wasn't aware of the ways subliminal racism shows itself: being watched, being followed around in shops, white people crossing the road to avoid me.

Racism wasn't part of the picture Mum had drawn for me, either. *Stay out of trouble's way, Paul.* I don't think I ever heard Mum question anyone in authority, and I guess I picked up some of that from being around her when I was young. It's worth remembering that there was, generally, more of a sense of an accepted hierarchy in those days, too. Looking back now, it seems to me that Mum was subservient in many ways. But I wanted to break out of that. I wanted to be able to challenge or speak on the same level as authority figures when I needed to. What happened in Hornsey Road that night turned everything upside down for me. I started asking questions. Lots of those questions I'm still asking today.

Being a young player at Arsenal, other players were always looking to challenge you, but I don't remember any of that having a racist undercurrent. I felt different from most of the people around me, but I'm pretty sure that was more of a cultural thing, especially when I started being involved with the first team and was mixing with a different generation. I was ten years younger and from South London. I had a short afro hairstyle and always had my afro pick and wet gel products in my bag so I could keep my hair straight, and lotion to keep my skin moist. We lived different lives, those first-teamers and me. Came from different experiences altogether. But, as I remember it, the gap between us wasn't about the colour of my skin. Or theirs.

Even so, without them thinking, there'd be jokes told in and around the dressing room. Jokes that depended on race for their punchlines. And I remember stopping to think. *That's me.* It wasn't directed at me, but it was me on the end of the joke. Even though I was still a teenager and surrounded by senior players, I felt there was something not right about it and, after it happened a few times, I decided I needed to say something: *I don't like that. It's a joke for you, but for me it's an insult. So please don't.* To be fair to those senior players, me speaking up wasn't ever a big problem. Once or twice, I remember guys replying: *Paul, it's only banter. Get that chip off your shoulder.* But that would be as far as it went. I didn't ever feel the need to explain any further.

Back then, I might not have known how to express what it was I felt anyway. This wasn't racism directed at me, specifically. This was mainstream culture: white, British culture in the '70s and '80s. Like most other black people, I felt frustrated. I was made to feel different, which I suppose I was. But was I of less value as a person in the minority rather than the majority? It felt as if it was something I had to live with. That's what our parents for the large part had to do, after all. I didn't know then how to spell it out for people: that those jokes led in a straight line to boys like me getting stopped in the street, arrested for no reason other than being black.

When I first broke through into Arsenal's first team, I was our only black player. That wasn't something to bother me, or that I even thought much about. All I wanted to do was play, and my colour wasn't stopping me from doing that. The fact that I was a little apart from the senior players was more to do with age and lifestyle. My background was different to theirs. In the couple of years after my debut at Tottenham, other black players joined me in the first team: Chris Whyte was my age and started getting games at centre-half; Raphael Meade was a bit younger, but he came in for Alan Sunderland up front. Players like Dave Rocastle and Michael Thomas were schoolboys at the time, and others – like Kevin Campbell and Gus Caesar – would follow. Everyone was aware of them as talents for the future.

And then, in '84, Viv Anderson signed from Forest. That was a big deal for the club: Viv had won everything already in his career, including two European Cups, and was an England international. He arrived and fitted in straight away with the senior players. He already knew a few of them from international duty. Viv was a character, a bit like Ian Wright: loud, extroverted and at the centre of everything. Everybody used to call him 'Busy' because he was always in the middle of things. Compared to someone like me, Viv related to the other senior players in a completely different way. He was in on jokes, giving people stick, and wanting to know everything that was going on. Viv had a great energy about him.

Viv's way of dealing with racial abuse or racist jokes was to laugh them off, to roll with the punches. I wasn't so forgiving. Not that I could do much about it other than saying something whenever I plucked up the courage. Whether Viv's approach was his personality or whether he was having to bury stuff, I don't know. It was great for me, Chrissy, and Raph to have Viv in the dressing room. It was good him being there, almost like having an older brother around. Viv was a pioneer of the same generation as Cyrille Regis and Brendon Batson. He was the first black player to be capped by England. He knew all about what it could be like going to some of those away grounds in the '70s.

I knew what that was like, too: places you went to play football, but where the game itself wasn't the only battle you had to have. Where the tension was like a cloud swirling around the stadium, abuse directed at black players spilling down from the terraces first whistle to last. It was part of every black footballer's working life. At away grounds, there would be thousands booing, making monkey noises, shouting at you every time you were on the ball. Individual fans saying stuff like: *Fuck off, you black bastard.* Spitting at you, or throwing bananas or coins at you. Those things happened to me at a lot of grounds, and a lot of the time.

It's hard to find words to describe the experience. At some games, it was actually scary. You saw supporters' faces, all twisted up, when you were near the touchlines. It felt like, if they could, these people would get on the pitch to try to do you physical harm. I know supporters will do anything to undermine the opposition's players if it means their team will win. I know football can bring out the worst side in human nature. But I never got used to being treated like that, and I had to fight to make sure it didn't ever distract me from playing my game.

As a player, Stamford Bridge was one of the grounds I always dreaded going to. When I went there as a kid, with my friend, Rob or his dad, I heard the chants and the insults. I can only think of one non-white player I saw playing league football there: Paul Reaney of Leeds, an outstanding right-back. Paul was mixed-race, and many people didn't identify him as 'Black'. Around the stadium, there was only ever a handful of young black supporters, so I stuck out like a sore thumb and, of course, felt uncomfortable. Perhaps one of the reasons I was such a quiet teenager was I learned not to attract attention to myself. I was extra polite and courteous, so nobody would single me out or make trouble for me.

Playing at Stamford Bridge was a different experience, though. And one game sticks in my mind more than any other. Mid-'80s, Chelsea were only just back in the First Division. It was a few years after my debut and I was playing central midfield. There was another level of tension around Stamford Bridge that day. It took a while for me to realise what was happening. Midway through the second half, I could hear some racial abuse. I knew it wasn't directed at me because I wasn't on the ball. But I noticed Paul Canoville, Chelsea's young black substitute, warming up alongside the pitch and realised, to my horror, that he was the target for the abuse. From his own team's fans, from Chelsea fans. That really shocked me.

It wasn't until afterwards that it really sank in. I'd never experienced that. It took a while for Arsenal fans to appreciate me, but there was never any element of racial abuse: they just didn't like the way the team or I were playing. How Paul Canoville was treated, though, has stayed with me ever since. *How could that happen? How could people do that?* Paul was a talented player, and we were around the same age. Down the line, the abuse took its toll on him: his career went out of control. He left Chelsea and found life, as well as football, very difficult. I got to know Paul after we both stopped playing. He retired after a bad injury, got involved with drugs and had several battles with cancer. Paul's a brave and dignified guy, and he's come through the worst of it now. A few years ago, Chelsea fans, many of them now in their 50s and 60s, and the club itself officially acknowledged what had happened and finally apologised to Paul. These days, there's a lounge at Stamford Bridge bearing his name.

Back then, Paul was just left to deal with it. That afternoon was a warning for me. I saw the direct impact the abuse had on Paul, as a player and as a person. Paul was on his own with it and I was, too, really. When Arsenal played and I'd get abused and screamed at by opposing fans, my team-mates and the coaching staff must have heard it. But it didn't affect them personally, so it wasn't a problem as far as they were concerned. Early on in my career, I was often the only black player in the team. On the pitch, even. I wonder now what the other lads were thinking: it was never talked about in the dressing room or in team meetings. Racist abuse was accepted by wider society as normal behaviour, which very few people questioned or criticised. I had to get my head down, ignore it, deal with it. But I do believe these experiences have a psychological impact. It doesn't ever just go away. Thinking about it now, it's difficult to believe how alone black players were back then.

Football wasn't going to fight for us on this issue. Football denied there even was an issue. It was up to each individual to handle it in whatever way he could. I do think there was a rising tide of solidarity that started to emerge, though. I began looking out for established black players at other clubs: Brendon and Cyrille and Laurie at West Brom, Garth Crooks and Chris Houghton at Spurs, Remi Moses at Manchester United, Howard Gayle at Liverpool, Vince Hilaire at Crystal Palace, and others. They were my contemporaries, and I followed their careers with interest, watched what happened to them, listened to anything they had to say. Whatever else, I knew for sure they'd be experiencing the same things I was. *How were other guys dealing with it?* But when we met up – I used to see a bit of Garth and Chris because we were all North London – we'd never discuss it.

Racism was that deeply embedded in the culture around us that it just seemed a fixed part of our lives. We buried the experiences, not feeling that we had the support to be able to challenge the situation. I'd be thinking: *This is wrong. Things shouldn't be like this.* But it was a part of the day-to-day away from football, too. I felt powerless and my response was to try to ignore it and get on as best I could. What could I do anyway? Gareth Southgate recently talked about some of the young players in the current England side and how he thought they took the racial abuse they were getting on social media almost as a given. Taking the hatred on as a part of their lives. Which is exactly what we had to do 40 years ago. I recognise that mindset. You can say things are different now, that we've made progress. And we have, but we've still a long way to go.

Racism's impact was insidious, too. I could try to ignore the abuse I'd get on Saturday afternoon, but it was there in everyday life. How I saw the world around me began to change. I became aware of when I was the only black person in a room. *Maybe this isn't a good situation to find myself in.* If I was aware of it, other people must have been. 'Can I help you?' started to mean: 'What are you doing here?' After a while, your intuition becomes super-sensitive. You become aware of people's subtlest behaviours. Maybe the fact that I was black wasn't always the issue, but racism distorted every-thing anyway. Being abused as a player, I'd find myself weighing up situations from that perspective. On the football pitch, people shouted at me because of my colour. It's no surprise that, away from the game, I'd think some people were making negative judgments about me because of it, too. My life has proved to me that, more often than not, whenever I've been brave enough to trust my intuition, it's served me well. Particularly as I've got older, I've noticed more and seen situations repeating themselves.

It can be damaging having that stuff constantly playing on your mind if you're not really conscious of why it's happening. Making it as a professional footballer is hard for anybody. It always has been. I'm very aware that, whatever other pressures black players were dealing with in the 1980s, the issue of race within wider society was another thing again. Whether you believe it existed or just believe we had chips on our shoulders, it affected all of us psychologically. It's not surprising that, for some lads, it became overwhelming. My first few years as an Arsenal player, I didn't feel comfortable at all about Mum and Sandra going to games. I didn't want them to hear the stuff I was hearing week in, week out. And, from their point of view, all football grounds were the same: aggressive and intimidating unless you were white and male. Football grounds weren't places where many black people or women were made to feel welcome. So my mum and my sister didn't come to watch me early in my career.

That whole part of my experience as a young player has stayed with me. How could it not? Even now, I watch and listen. When I see or hear what players still experience today – being booed for taking the knee or being racially abused on social media – it's like a trigger, as if I'm experiencing the raw emotions all over again. I can't help but react instinctively. What's happening to them is what happened to me and to other players of my generation. I still find myself feeling frustrated and disappointed. The emotions are still there. And that isn't ideal from a psychological point of view. But you can't just wish away the past every time it revisits in the present. It haunts me a bit. Most people of colour still witness or experience racism almost every day. I do. What's different is that I see things more clearly now.

82

As far as making a playing career at Arsenal was concerned, I wasn't made to feel my colour played any part. 1981/82 was the season I broke through and became a regular. I played something like 35 games. That was great but, by then, the club was starting to slide. Liam Brady had left: this special, special player. Then, in the summer of 1981, Frank Stapleton joined Manchester United. Terry Neill made some signings which didn't work out. Our fans weren't happy. And some of that frustration got directed at me. The team wasn't a team, more a collection of individuals who lacked the togetherness you need if you're to achieve real success. But the supporters looked at me, a young player with a particular style, and decided I was the one who needed to adapt and adjust my game, in order to win them over.

The early years of my Arsenal career were difficult. I'd be playing at Highbury and hear people shouting: *Oh, Davis! What's he doing? Why's he in the team?* These were Arsenal supporters having a go at me. Groans if I gave the ball away, grumbles even if I did make the tackle. My confidence suffered; the team wasn't playing well, and we were losing more often than winning. One major factor was losing Liam: any team would have found that difficult. I remember thinking: *Something's got to change here.* Terry Neill was under pressure, too. We had some good players, but as a team it wasn't working. I realised the fans needed to see more of me chasing lost causes, flying into a few tackles and winning my challenges. *Up and at 'em!*

The Arsenal crowd began to see that I was trying my hardest. I'd run around and stick my foot in, making it obvious. The team wasn't doing any better, but I stopped being the player the fans were picking on. Instead, I think they began to recognise the things I was good at as a footballer: finding space, reading play, controlling the pace of a game, picking a pass. From then on, right through until I left the club 15 years later, out on the pitch at Highbury almost always felt like home. The supporters were fantastic with me. They still are now. I had a difficult time to start with but, once they were on my side, the North Bank wasn't ever impatient with my style, and never doubted how much playing for Arsenal meant to me.

Trying to find my feet at Arsenal, I was also trying to find my feet in North London. I'd had five years of trains and buses. I was driving now. And a professional, on enough money to get a mortgage. I hunted around and found a semi-detached house in Edgware, just off the A41, well-placed between the training ground and the stadium. I moved in, on my own, just 18 years old. This place had three bedrooms and a little garden, so I was rattling around in it a bit. I bought a bed for one room and left the others practically empty. In the lounge, I had a settee and a telly. Kitchen, a fridge and a cooker. Once I finished training, that'd be me: home alone. I wasn't even staying there at weekends. I'd go back to Mum's for West Indian Sunday dinner: fried chicken, rice and peas, yams and bananas, washed down with carrot juice. That was too good to miss.

My first real girlfriend was south, too. I had a solicitor, a big Spurs fan, named Zac Harazi, who loved his football and loved being around footballers. Zac helped me with contracts for more than ten years, although in the early days there wasn't much negotiating to do: Arsenal would tell me how much they were going to pay me, although Zac always did try to get the best deal he could. His office was in Brixton, and he had a legal assistant working for him, Maureen, a beautiful person with a lovely family who I got on very well with. We were together for four or five years. Maureen used to come to games at Highbury and then I'd see her in Streatham, where she lived with her parents, at the weekend when I was down by Mum's.

One way or another, my new home was standing empty quite a lot. As I travelled to and from games up and down the country, I suppose people got to know I lived there and would know when I was away. So, no surprise it got broken into. Must have been a disappointment for the burglars, though: the JVC TV was about the only thing they found in there to steal. In 1983, I sold that house and bought a one-bedroom flat in a new build in Islington, on a square just off Upper Street. Back into town, with a bit of buzz around me. Nobody broke into that flat, but I did come down to the car park one morning and find all four wheels had been stolen off my brand-new red Ford XR3i. I was gutted! Even so, I felt more at home there than I did in an empty semi in Edgware.

That same summer, Arsenal signed Charlie Nicholas from Celtic. Other clubs had been after him, like Liverpool and Manchester United. But he came to Highbury, and everybody was thinking: *Here we go.* He bought a place in Highgate, not too far from me. We'd go into town on Saturday evening after a game, to a wine bar or to Stringfellows nightclub in Covent Garden. He was given that image by the media: *Champagne Charlie.* He was loud and appeared to enjoy all the media attention. He and I were very different. But Charlie was a genuine guy, and we got on well.

Charlie wasn't scoring enough, though, and that's what Terry Neill had bought him for. The fans loved his style. Charlie was technically very good, flamboyant, and easy on the eye. He loved putting the ball through an opponent's legs. But he didn't score the number of goals he was expected to. To be fair to Charlie, he was never going to fix things on his own. The club wasn't in a particularly good place before he arrived, and didn't improve much after. There was a group of players who appeared to be the big earners at that time: Charlie, Tony Woodcock, Paul Mariner, Kenny Sansom, Graham Rix. I suppose we had a few cliques in the dressing room, and some players became very friendly with David Dein, who'd come in as a director at the club. These were our star players and I got on well with them, but we never had the unity and spirit, on and off the pitch, that I now know you need if you're going to win things together.

Some strange things happened in games, too. Graham Rix and Kenny Sansom were close friends. Kenny played left-back and was the best defender I ever played with; Graham played on the left ahead of him. Both very good players, England team-mates. They had a close relationship off the pitch. So close, I thought, it sometimes got in the way of what we were trying to do as a team. I played inside both of them, and I'd notice that they'd rather pass to each other than pass to me, even when I was in a better position. I wondered about it, but I knew better than to take it personally. It wasn't that they didn't trust me as a team-mate. They just couldn't help themselves; perhaps they weren't even aware it was happening, but I noticed it. As soon as one of them had the ball, his first instinct, almost always, was to look for his mate, even when passing to me would have been a better option. It didn't change my opinion of Kenny, though. He was the best left-back of his generation. Nobody wins 86 England caps without being a special player.

It all slid away quite quickly that season, '83/84. I remember one cold, wet night at Highbury, at the end of November. There were only around 20,000 supporters there to watch and we got beat 2-1 by Walsall in the League Cup. There were angry demonstrations by supporters outside the ground afterwards. Then, we lost 1-0 at home to West Brom to leave us 16th in the league. The following Saturday, West Ham beat us 3-1 at Upton Park. Terry Neill was sacked a few days later. Terry had given me my debut and the chance to establish myself as a first-team player, starting 35 or 40 games a season. But we weren't a team playing with any together- ness. And, off the pitch, things were no better: rumours about wild parties, three players on drink-driving bans at the same time, and even one player running over and killing a pedestrian on a zebra crossing.

Before he was sacked, Terry Neill had publicly criticised the players, saying they earned too much money and gambled too much of it away playing cards. That might well have been true, but that's a difficult part of being the boss: creating a sense of cohesion. Fixing that kind of situation is the manager's job. Terry, it seemed to me, didn't have the full respect of a few of his senior players. And we weren't winning games on a regular basis. While the club looked for a replacement, Don Howe was given the role of caretaker manager. Training was soon quicker, tougher and more demanding. Don wanted more from us, both physically and mentally. He got Charlie scoring, Tony Woodcock and Paul Mariner, too. Team meetings changed a bit: Don wouldn't mince his words and would get into all of us, insisting we could do more. There were players who'd have their say: I remember Brian Talbot used to get annoyed with what was going on around him. I did, too, to be honest.

I was young and I wanted to win things. I was in a team with very good players, but they didn't seem hungry in the same way I was. It seemed some were playing more for themselves than for the club and the supporters. Sometimes, after a bad performance, we'd have an inquest at Highbury on the Sunday morning, once tempers had cooled a little. Other times, it would happen in the dressing room right after the game. If things had gone really badly, it'd be both! I'd sometimes pick up the courage to have my say. Inevitably, that would mean criticising some senior international team-mates, something which didn't always go down too well, I suspect. Then Don would have us do punishing runs around the pitch, and up and down the terraces, until some players were physically sick.

I'd only ever known Arsenal. At the time, I got on with it, making sure I tried to focus on improving myself and my own game. Maybe football clubs were always like this. Looking back now, I realise how low a period those five years between 1981 and 1986 were for Arsenal. Everybody was frustrated, especially our supporters, who were watching some very good players but an under-achieving team. A team without an identity that was never in any danger of winning anything. Those difficult years were the making of me as a footballer in many ways, though. In '81, I was a youngster, hoping to get given an opportunity. By the time Don Howe resigned, in March '86, I was 25 and one of the more senior players. There was a group that had come up behind me by then, too, who had been given debuts by Don: Tony Adams, Martin Keown, Dave Rocastle, Niall Quinn, Gus Caesar and Martin Hayes.

All those players who came through the youth teams in the '80s will have good memories of Don Howe. Even the ones, like me, who found all the shouting hard to take sometimes. You listened anyway, knowing you would learn. Don was full of enthusiasm and passion, full of ideas, always had a joke or a great story to tell. He was known and respected for his coaching skills, but I'm not sure the manager's job ever fitted him quite as well. When Don left, Steve Burtenshaw was made caretaker manager. The club had spent a fair amount of money on transfers, but we were still way off challenging for trophies. Arsenal were drifting, even though there were some promising young players coming through. I remember media speculation about Terry Venables and one or two other big names coming in but, in the summer of 1986, the news broke that was going to change all our lives. George Graham was announced as Arsenal's new manager.

86

At the start of each new season, every player at Arsenal used to be given a little booklet: rules and regulations, what was expected of you in terms of timekeeping, behaviour, and everything else that went with representing the club. I've still got some of them: they're a dozen pages, and small enough to fit in your pocket. I'm looking at the ones for two seasons: '85/86 and '86/87, Don Howe's last season and George Graham's first. Just reading through those booklets, you can see George had arrived at Arsenal determined to do things his own way. There was only going to be one person in charge. In the '85/86 booklet, everything's about the club. Paragraph after paragraph, it's clear that the directors and club staff were the people you were answerable to. In the '86/87 edition, it's all about the manager. Every rule and every regulation, it's him laying down the law. Everything that had been up to Arsenal was now, it seemed, up to George.

The new boss straight away brought clarity. Right from the start, George made sure we understood exactly what he expected from us in training, in games, and in the way we conducted ourselves around the club. He wanted discipline on and off the pitch: we were representing Arsenal Football Club. The message was that things were going to be done a certain way and anybody who didn't buy into that wouldn't be around for long. George got us organised as a team and his training sessions were structured to make that happen. His first pre-season was different to anything I'd experienced before. We weren't just running and running for the first couple of weeks. Instead, the footballs came out early, within the first three or four days. I really enjoyed it. I think we all did. It was what we needed: a clean sweep. This was a great club, with some values and traditions that had been lost. George himself turned out to be exactly what Arsenal needed at the time.

George was very definite about how he wanted us to play. A back four, with two defensive-minded central midfielders who had to look after the players behind them. Wide players who could get crosses in to create goals, but who also had to track back. Get the ball into the two strikers as soon as possible, with those strikers expected to score goals and to work hard without the ball. George instilled organisation, desire, discipline, and camaraderie. And allowed for a touch of creativity, too. He could charm the birds from the trees but, at the same time, we knew he would do whatever was necessary to win games. George always looked the part and clearly enjoyed the media attention.

George's arrival was good for me, and he also gave younger players like Tony and Rocky, Martin Hayes, Niall Quinn, and Gus Caesar the chance to establish themselves. He recognised their abilities and also got his message across to the higher earning players. *Do what I need you to do, or you won't play. In fact, you'll be gone.* Kenny Sansom was outstanding – I enjoyed training and being around him – and he was club captain. But some players, like Tony Woodcock, who I also got on well with, were let go, while with others, like Graham Rix and Charlie Nicholas, there was a feeling their days might be numbered if performances didn't improve.

We started doing well pretty quickly. We didn't lose any of our first 10 games. George got a lot of things right: players enjoyed training, enjoyed playing. Enjoyed winning. You could feel, from week to week, the young players especially, growing closer as a group. We went on a long unbeaten run in the league and finished fourth. That was progress in itself, but that first season under George, '86/87, ended up being all about the Littlewoods Cup. For a start, there were three semi-finals against Spurs, which I'm sure no Arsenal fan will ever forget. They beat us at Highbury 1-0 in the first leg and then they went a goal up at White Hart Lane in the second leg, too. But, in the second half, Quinny and Viv Anderson scored to make it 2-2. It went to a third game, at their place again, on the Wednesday night.

Under the floodlights at White Hart Lane, the game was sold out: more than 40,000 inside and what seemed like the same number outside, unable to get through the turnstiles. The atmosphere was incredible, even more intense than when I made my debut there in 1980. It was a gripping game. Spurs scored first again, but Ian Allinson equalised with eight minutes to go, and then Dave Rocastle stuck in the winner in the 90th minute, just when we were all getting ready to go into extra time. And all in front of the end of the ground where the Arsenal supporters were standing. What an amazing, amazing night.

Full-time was the first time I'd ever had the feeling: *Is this what success looks and feels like?* It was only the semi-final, but it felt like we'd proved something, to other people and to ourselves, over those three games: that was a good Spurs team we beat. We were out on the pitch for ages afterwards, jumping all over each other, celebrating with the fans. George came out, in his black Crombie coat, looking a million dollars. We'd found this fantastic fighting spirit and confidence, which ended up taking that group of players a very long way. The game summed up what lay ahead for us all under George.

PAUL DAVIS – ARSENAL AND AFTER

You've got to credit George Graham with inspiring a winning mentality. The game at Spurs was a turning point for us and for him, even more than the final. The North London derby is different to any other fixture. That was always drilled into us as young Arsenal players: how important the game was and how much it meant to our fans. Great memories for me, personally, too: my debut and then the Littlewoods semi. I thrived on the rivalry, the atmosphere, and the pressure that came with those occasions. We all used to get fired up, but no one more so than Rocky. He exemplified what those games meant to us. It was fitting he was the hero that night in '87. We had some good, experienced professionals – Viv, Kenny, Ian Allinson, Dave O'Leary – but it was the younger, homegrown players who defined that Arsenal team.

David was another South London boy. He grew up in Peckham and was six years younger than me, so we didn't get to know each other until he started getting games for the first team in the mid-1980s. It turned out we were both travelling down south every weekend. I was seeing my mum in Stockwell. And he was doing the same, just a few miles away in Brixton. In fact, Dave was living there, too, until he bought his own place in Barnet. There were family connections. I got to know Linda, David's mum, and his brother Stephen, who was a footballer on Norwich's books for a while. The West Indian community in London has always had those threads of kinship running through it.

David was a special talent and a natural leader. He had something in his personality that drew people to him, and he was able to inspire them. He had a big heart and embodied the team. No other player was able to identify and connect with our supporters the way Rocky did. And his team-mates loved him. Michael Thomas and David were the same age, and were already close when I started getting to know them. Michael was from Lambeth. He played in all those Tottenham semi-finals, too, making his debut in the first leg at the start of his senior career. Everybody in the first-team squad got on well, but David, Michael and I spent quite a lot of time together. We all came from South London. I hope I was someone they could respect and rely on. I think they'd both followed what I was doing while they were youth-team players. The same way I'd watched Clyde Best all those years ago, maybe.

I was six years older than David and Michael but, when newspapers reported on our games, they would always lump me in with the younger players at Arsenal. Maybe it was because I didn't look any older, but I was never sure whether to take it as a compliment or not. The boys weren't having that. They started calling me 'Pops,' just so I wouldn't forget how much older I was! I took that nickname as a positive, though, with me being recognised as someone they felt was there to help and support them. Even though those South London boys could look after themselves and didn't need me to. George didn't take long to start moving out a few of the senior players. I soon found myself looking round the dressing room, realising I was older than almost everyone else.

The younger guys calling me 'Pops' stayed mainly inside the dressing room. But the nickname which stuck, for the fans, was 'Davo'. I'm not sure when that one started, but I remember Kevin Campbell and company singing it out at the tops of their voices: it came from a song by the famous singer and actor, Harry Belafonte. The hook line in that particular song is *Day-Oh! Day-ay-ay-Oh! Daylight come and me wan' go home!* The lads took the tune but changed the *Day-Oh!* to *Day-Vo!* Lots of people around football – and Arsenal supporters, especially – call me 'Davo' to this day, but probably have no idea why. Maybe it's good to let everybody know the story behind that nickname now!

In any winning team, there will be people from different backgrounds brought together by football, by being part of a successful group. At Arsenal, in the late '80s, that was true. There were a lot of big characters at the club, very different personalities, and very different upbringings, but everybody was pointed in the same direction. Quite a few of the players liked to drink. Some of them liked to drink a lot. That hadn't ever been part of my upbringing. It wasn't part of the culture I'd grown up in. But I knew how important it was to be part of the group within the team. I enjoyed being successful and winning games with these guys, even if I didn't have a lot in common with many of them apart from football. Our senses of humour, our music, our interests away from the game were different but, for the sake of togetherness and team spirit, I was always ready to go along with everyone else. I'd usually slip away early, before things got serious, though. I was okay for a drink or two, but not nine or ten.

Steve Williams was first choice alongside me in '86/87, but he was suspended for the semi-finals against Spurs. That was why George put Michael Thomas in. He was back for the Final, though. Steve was a unique character. I think 'unique' is the right word. Away from football, he was generous, easy to talk to. He'd go out of his way to help anybody. But once he crossed over that white line onto a football pitch, Steve's personality changed. He became this argumentative, aggressive, foul-mouthed beast of a player. Steve was a complete midfielder: he could tackle, he could pass, and he hated losing. He was one of the most self-assured players I ever played alongside. Confident and single-minded, he was always going to do what Steve Williams thought was the best thing to do. He and I would be sitting in during a game, defending in front of our centre-backs. That was what George wanted and what we worked on all the time in training. But then Steve would go off and do his own thing, leaving us outnumbered. I'd shout for him to stay alongside me, and he'd just let go a volley of expletives in my direction. He'd spare no-one if they said the wrong thing to him at the wrong time: his team-mates, the ref, or the opposition. It didn't matter who.

The Littlewoods Cup Final in '87 was great for all of us, and for me personally. It was my first time at Wembley to play in a final, and Mum and Sandra came: the club made arrangements for all the families to be there. A beautiful, sunny afternoon and a real sense of occasion. Liverpool had been the best team in the country for a while. *And they'd never lost a game when Ian Rush had scored.* That did go through my mind when Rush gave them the lead in the first half. But we played well. Steve Williams was outstanding and the two of us got stronger together as the game went on. Willo and I were similar players. Neither of us was particularly quick, but we both wanted the ball, wanted to pass, and didn't mind putting a foot in and having a scrap if we needed to. Usually, you'd want two players in there who had different qualities but, somehow, with me and Steve it worked. That afternoon against Liverpool, definitely.

They were big favourites. Liverpool were a good team with Kenny Dalglish as player manager. Kenny brought himself on as sub that afternoon. George was good at motivating us. He sent us out believing we could win every game and made sure that, whatever else happened, we were prepared and organised. So, even after Ian Rush scored, we kept going and started to get hold of midfield. Charlie Nicholas equalised and then, near the end, George sent on Perry Groves, who started running at them with the ball. Liverpool didn't know what to do with him. Our winning goal was scruffy, but we deserved it. Charlie had been at Arsenal for four years and he left in the summer when his contract expired. But he got both goals that afternoon. And all the headlines, too.

The Arsenal support was fantastic at Wembley that day. So many of us had come through the youth system, and our fans connected with that. Apart from Viv Anderson and David O'Leary, none of us had ever won anything. The win gave us confidence, the desire to achieve more. That was one of the manager's favourite words: *DESIRE!* George had changed the atmosphere around the club completely in no time at all. The whole experience was a first for me: climbing the Wembley steps to collect the trophy and our medals, passing our jubilant fans trying to kiss and hug you. So much joy around us. And then, back down on the pitch, everyone hugging and jumping on each other like schoolchildren in the playground. We had our pictures taken with the trophy by the newspaper photographers. And then we walked down to the end where all the Arsenal fans were standing to celebrate. I remember clutching my medal tightly, wanting to make sure I didn't lose it amidst all the excitement.

One-nil down, two-one up, and all that. I'd been at the club for ten years, but had never felt anything like this. Our first trophy. A job well done. I knew I wanted to have this feeling again. The dressing room afterwards was complete chaos. All of us, players, staff, directors, everybody together and so happy. Those moments are what you play football for. Even now, whenever I see any team lift a trophy, I'll think about what the players are feeling in those moments. George gave Arsenal back a sense of pride and purpose. Right through the club, players and staff, everybody knew their jobs.

Out at Colney, we'd work on things over and over again. I remember doing one particular drill with George almost every day, the whole time he was at the club. Half the pitch: goalkeeper, back four and two central midfielders. All the work was us defending against six forward players. *If the ball went into that player on the edge of the box, who was going to make the run to cover? If it got switched, who'd go across? Or would our full-back tuck in and the midfielder come in behind?* Defending the area, we worked out who was going to do what in all the different possible scenarios. And then George would mix it up by putting another forward or two in, so we'd be outnumbered. He wanted us to defend as one unit, not as individuals, to show our opponents into central areas. Our full-backs were instructed to defend ahead of our centre-halves, to help us deploy our offside trap.

We practised and practised, until it became second nature. It took a lot of hard work and discipline – as well as a lot of training sessions! – to get to the level we reached. It was based on structure and organisation; and it worked. These days, pretty much every team, out of possession, tries to show attackers outside, pushing them wide. We did the opposite under George. We'd always try to show the attacking team inside: push them towards where we were strongest. Nobody seems to play that way now. The only team I can think of who have used that approach in recent times are Atlético Madrid. George did a lot of work on distances between players, too. He wanted the back four to always be in contact with each other. He wanted his two central midfield players to be in the right positions in relation to each other, 10 or 15 yards apart, and for us to be the same sort of distance in front of the defenders. I always felt we were better organised than most teams we came up against.

Free-kick and corner routines which George introduced when he first arrived were still in place and working well six years later. The meticulous planning, and early success they brought, gave us more confidence in George's ideas. We'd work on something in training during the week, and then it'd come off for us on the Saturday: that helps players trust each other and trust what the manager's demanding of them. It happened a lot in George's first couple of seasons. That gave us faith in what we were doing. All the work we did on defending had a positive psychological impact on us, too. If we scored, we'd all feel secure: *It'll take a lot for the opposition to get anything at all out of this game now.*

George was good at being the public face of Arsenal in the media. And privately, inside the dressing room, he had the air of authority and confidence which Terry Neill and Don Howe didn't have. George wanted to restore some discipline and pride back into a club which hadn't won the league since 1971, when he had been an Arsenal player. I remember going on an end-of-season trip to Australia and George had us in our new club suits, collars and ties, on the plane the whole way. He wanted us to arrive looking the part 18 hours later, remembering who we were and who we were representing. As far as he was concerned, this was Arsenal, and this was the standard and the way to behave. All that suited George, anyway. He always dressed well. George had a few nicknames. 'Gorgeous' was one of them. Not that anybody ever called him that to his face. Another was 'Gaddafi,' which again we kept to ourselves.

George Graham rebuilt Arsenal and I believe he deserves enormous credit. He didn't have money to spend on players: his first summer, he bought Perry Groves from Colchester for £70,000, who had a fantastic career at the club. That was it. He worked with what he had. You could say he was lucky there was a good group of young players coming through, but George created a competitive atmosphere and environment. That helped Tony, Rocky, Michael and the rest believe they were going to get a chance to play, as long as they could give him what he was asking for. I'm sure George knew this was his big opportunity, coming from Millwall. You could see he was determined to make the most of the situation. And we all benefitted: players, supporters, everyone at the club.

Of course, George himself benefitted, too. Pretty quickly, it was rumoured that he was one of the best-paid managers in English football. The very first cracks between him and me, and in his relationships with the players generally, came from that. I think it was the summer after we won the Littlewoods Cup: a decision was made in the dressing room that we should go to George and ask for a collective pay rise. We knew we were on very low wages, especially the younger players, and felt we should now share in the club's success and be rewarded financially. There was a small delegation voted to go and speak to the boss: Kenny Sansom, the club captain, David O'Leary, Viv, and me. It was a job for the older players, I suppose.

It was a bit scary: you never knew what the repercussions might be if you were seen as challenging the manager or the club. We said what we had to say. George listened and told us to leave it with him. He'd speak with the club and see what he could do. We went back to the rest of the players. *We think George listened to us; he said he'll speak with the board and get back to us.* He never did. That didn't go down well with me, although the rest of the players weren't prepared to push any harder. When it was confirmed that George had signed a new contract with a big pay rise, though, you couldn't help feeling he'd looked after himself but hadn't fought hard, if at all, for his players. *So much for camaraderie.* That was the first time I can remember wondering how things were going to work out under George in the long run.

87

At the end of the '86/87 season, I was feeling good. Really good. I'd won something for the first time in my career. That summer I went to Jamaica, something else I'd never experienced. The idea came from Al Hamilton, who'd been born in the Caribbean but was now living and working in England, one of a very few black journalists at the time. He'd launched a football magazine called *Sports-Scene* and written the first-ever book about black footballers. I knew him through an event he'd set up in 1980: the Commonwealth Sports Awards. Al was a pioneer, for sure, and he was awarded an MBE in 2004. In '87, his plan was to take a group of 16 English-born players from West Indian backgrounds to play an exhibition game against the Jamaican national team, to put on a few coaching clinics, and meet people while we were there.

As soon as Al mentioned it to me, I said yes. What an opportunity to visit the country Mum had come from. But I remember it was complicated getting Arsenal to agree. Even though it was after the end of the season, the club were worried about injuries and insurance. We had endless conversations before they finally allowed me to go. I just kept pushing! I had my heart set on the trip. Jamaica was part of my heritage and I wanted to experience it. Being with this team of players with links to the island seemed like a huge honour. Back then, people described Jamaica as a 'Third World' country. This was a real adventure. I'd done a little travelling with Arsenal, but never in that part of the world.

When we got off the plane, the first thing I noticed was how basic the airport was. I picked up my luggage and went straight through Passport Control: a few steps and we were onto the street. The warmth and a bright, blue sky like I'd never seen before were the next things to hit me. And then, on the bus to the hotel, gazing out of the window: green, green countryside on the way into Kingston, but busy everywhere, people selling stuff by the side of the road out of little huts pitched together with corrugated iron. Fruit, tools, clothes, car parts: anything you could imagine. This was where Mum was from. This was my culture, my history, but it seemed alien to me at first, so raw, so basic. And poor. I knew what it felt like to not have much in London. That was how it was when I grew up. But, straight away here, I could see many people had next to nothing at all. That shocked me at first.

Within a couple of days, I started getting a clearer idea of Jamaica: how things worked, how people were with each other. I soon realised I felt very comfortable. Better than that: I felt connected to the place, to the country and to the people I met. This was a part of me, a culture I was familiar with from London, but which I'd never experienced full on. Everybody seemed to be telling stories all the time, living them out as they told them. It made me sound so English, so awkward, whenever I said anything. My London accent felt uncomfortable and out of place. And time: I was so used to being on time. School timetables, Arsenal training sessions, meeting Mum off the bus from Brixton Market when she'd been shopping so I could carry the bags. But, here in Kingston, time didn't seem to carry any importance. There was no rush for anything. A couple of minutes might be an hour or two. I had to get used to that.

People in Jamaica carried themselves so naturally, so unselfconsciously. That freedom of spirit made a huge impression. The trip was a big deal for me and for Jamaican football, too. The organisers really looked after us. We met dignitaries, visited schools, had a dinner with the local FA, and went to a couple of garden parties. Although it's a cricket island, of course, everybody seemed to be up to date with football. They knew the English teams and the English players, especially those players with links to the Caribbean: John Barnes, Bob Hazell, Luther Blissett, Brendon Batson, Vince Hilaire, Viv Anderson. People had obviously followed our careers. Claimed us as their own. While we were in Kingston, we all went on sports shows to tell our stories and explain why we'd come.

The trip was also an opportunity to spend time getting to know the other guys. We had played against each other, with maybe a nod of acknowledgement in players' lounges after games. But those were brief moments. We'd always be straight back to our clubs, into our own separate worlds, afterwards. We didn't really link up. The struggle with racism, we'd all been going through that on our own. There wasn't any kind of organised network amongst black players in England. The only time we'd ever be together as a group was at Al Hamilton's Commonwealth Sports Awards, which he put on once a year in London. Strange, really: it took a trip to Jamaica for me to start getting to know people like Cyrille Regis and Bob Hazell properly, guys I shared so much with in terms of our experiences as footballers back home.

For most of the trip, we were all together as a group. We all got taken care of, but John Barnes was the main man: he'd grown up in Jamaica, where his dad was quite high up in the army, and he knew everywhere and everybody. Everybody knew John, too. He was the king in Kingston, for sure. I had some time to myself, too, and a chance, at 26 years old, to meet extended family I'd known next to nothing about while I was growing up. Even though Mum had never talked much to me about my step-siblings, she gave me a couple of addresses before I flew to Jamaica. I got in touch with my sister and my two brothers, the children Mum had left behind when she travelled to England. Heading off on my own to meet family was the most fascinating experience of all.

I got in touch with Tasman first, the eldest son, and arranged to meet him where he worked. He had a good job at an insurance company, and I found my way to their offices. I climbed up the stairs – they were on the fourth floor – and Tasman was waiting for me, big smile and very warm straight away. He'd obviously told colleagues about me because he took me round to introduce me to everybody. *Oh, right! This is your brother! From England!* Tasman seemed proud of the fact that I was a player at Arsenal. And, in turn, him being proud meant a lot to me, even though we didn't really know anything about each other as people at all.

My sister, Sandra, had been out to Jamaica when she was 12 or 13. She went with Mum when our grandmother passed away, and met all sorts of extended family. Sandra was always better than me at staying in touch with them, too. So, from her, Tasman had heard a bit about me. He and I got on well. I visited him at home a couple of times. He lived with his daughter – her mum and Tasman were on good terms but not together – in a simple house, but comfortable and out in a nice suburb of Kingston. There we were: a fan going round above our heads to keep the warm air moving, Tasman telling stories, and the two of us talking football. I felt comfortable in Jamaica already. At home, you could say.

Tasman and I made a good connection. A couple of years later, he came to England for several weeks, stayed with Mum – his mum – in Stockwell, and saw for the first time how we were living. We hung out quite a bit. Tasman was bright, chatty. I really liked him. I remember sitting in the flat at Lansdowne Green together, watching the cricket. He came over to my flat in Islington, too. Tasman liked his football and I got him tickets for a couple of Arsenal games. That was his only time in the UK, but it was time we both valued. We spent so much time talking about Arsenal and about London, though, that I didn't ever find out as much as I could about our common roots. A few years later, Tasman was diagnosed with Motor Neurone Disease. He had a very tough time of it before, eventually, he passed away in 2005.

I met my step-sister, Carmen, who everybody called Queenie, in '87 as well. She was the one who I looked at and, in terms of physical features, saw myself looking back. That makes for a strange, powerful emotion when you meet a blood relative for the first time; we'd never known each other but, even so, with Queenie and Tasman especially, I had this strong sense of us being fundamental in each other's lives somehow. Queenie had a couple of kids and used to go backwards and forwards to America a lot because she could get better-paid work there as a nanny and send money home. I think, later on, she started working in hospitals in the US, too.

I was lucky Queenie was in Jamaica at the same time I was on that trip. She was older than me, of course, and decided I needed looking after. Even though I was 26, she mothered me a little. She wanted to know where I was, what I was doing and whether I was alright. She loved me being in Jamaica and, like Tasman, was proud of me, I think. In their eyes, I was doing well. I tracked down my other step-brother, too: Constant. He wasn't settled like Tasman and Queenie, couldn't find work and was on the hustle, really. Constant lived out of town, in the deep countryside, so I didn't see as much of him. We only met up a couple of times.

Constant's place was a distance from where we were staying, but Tasman took me out there. I hired a car. The further we drove, swerving round potholes, the greener everything got. Lush, lush vegetation. Where Constant lived wasn't even a village, just a scattering of a few homes and one or two shops beside the road. For so much of what people needed, they'd just go and help themselves to whatever nature provided. Life was lived outdoors, guys chatting, playing dominoes. No schedule, nowhere anybody had to be. It was something I'd never experienced before: people had so little but, still, they seemed so rich in terms of a sense of identity, a sense of self-worth. I felt a deep admiration for that.

Of course, we were on the trip in the first place to play football, to give the local FA a boost and help grow the game. We played against a Jamaica XI at the national stadium at Independence Park. The game was on a midweek afternoon and so the ground wasn't full. I don't remember the score, but I remember being surprised by how much talent they had in the Jamaican team. In many ways, the important stuff was the publicity and marketing we did around the game, and the coaching sessions we put on for young players. Football was big out there already, but the trip gave people the chance to see in person players they'd been following for years from afar. It helped raise the game's profile, got the media, sponsors and government interested. We were in on the start of something: 10 years later, Jamaica qualified for the 1998 World Cup, with lots of the guys being players like us, from the diaspora, who played their club football in the UK.

It was on that trip that I met Hope, too, who became very important in my life. On our last night, we were invited to an open-air party at our hotel, the Wyndham. Mad: I remember hearing these popping sounds, which I thought were fireworks. Someone put me right. *No, that's people firing their guns off into the air! That's part of the fun.* Hope was there with some friends, we got talking and exchanged numbers. It was a long-distance relationship for a couple of years, hours on the phone and handwritten letters. Eventually, she came over to England to visit a couple of times. Before her third visit, I told Hope I'd love her to stay and live with me in London. She was a high-flyer academically and early into her time at university in Jamaica. So, to leave at that point was a very big decision. I didn't fully appreciate the challenges Hope would face leaving home. It wasn't easy for her. We got married in Florida after we'd had our two sons, Du'aine and Jordan, in 1994 and 1996.

That first visit to Jamaica changed the course of my life. Certainly, it changed the way I thought about my background and my heritage. How much did I ever take in, Mum talking to me about Jamaica when I was a kid? Not much. It took going there myself to understand the journey she'd been on, the chance she'd taken coming to England and making a new life for herself, for me and for Sandra. For Tasman, Queenie and Constant, too, who she supported all those years, sending money home. Seeing where Mum had grown up, experiencing life there for myself, meeting my siblings, gave me a whole different perspective on my own journey.

Growing up, I'd been a part of the West Indian community in South London, with Mum's family and friends. I had one close friend of my own, Gary MacDonald, who I played football with, whose family history went back to Jamaica, too. Gary knew his dad, who was from Kingston, and he had older brothers who'd been born there before they moved and settled in Brixton. For Gary, his connection with the Caribbean was more first-hand than mine. He always had a warmth to his character that maybe came from that. I'm sure that's why Mum loved it so much when he came to ours for dinner on a Sunday. Around Kingston, years later, listening to the guys chatting, telling stories, laughing all the time, they reminded me of Gary. Maybe that side of Macca's personality was his own personal inheritance.

For me, though, Jamaican history and culture hadn't really been part of my everyday life, as a boy, going to school in South London and becoming a professional footballer with Arsenal. I was self-motivated and I was self-contained. Football, more than anything, was how I described who I was to myself. But then I went to Jamaica and was immersed in extended family and a different way of living. I came back to England a different person. I realised that South London, football, and the career I was trying to make for myself weren't the whole story. That trip was like opening a window onto stuff I'd never thought about before, Jamaica and the world Mum had left behind to join the Windrush generation. I've never forgotten it since: all that's my world, too.

88

George Graham changed a lot of things in his first year as Arsenal manager. And the changes worked. We won the Littlewoods Cup, finished fourth in the league. Now George was firmly in charge, in control of everything. We believed in him and, obviously, so did the board of directors. George was clear about what he wanted and about how to get there, so he didn't stop moving things around. Viv Anderson, Graham Rix, Charlie Nicholas and, a year later, Kenny Sansom all left. To replace them, George signed a new centre-forward, Alan Smith, and then players like Lee Dixon, Nigel Winterburn, Kevin Richardson, Steve Bould, and Brian Marwood. He gave Paul Merson a chance. All those guys ended up being important when it came to us winning the league in '89.

George knew about talent in the lower divisions, I guess, from his time at Millwall. He wasn't ever after the big or obvious names. He signed players who could do the job he needed them to do. I didn't know anything about most of the new lads, but they fitted in very quickly. The manager had a plan, and this felt like his club now. In '87/88, we had a good run in the autumn – ten straight wins – but, in the league, we faded away. We got to another League

After helping Arsenal become the first English club to win both domestic cups in 1992/93, and enjoying my football again after putting disagreements with George Graham to one side, we headed out to South Africa that summer in preparation for a season that would bring us more silverware, this time in Europe!

The earliest picture I have of me in my mum's arms aged around four years old and taken in Stockwell, South London

(Below) my sister Sandra and myself taken at Springfield Primary School. She would have been aged eight and I was aged 10

Playing Sunday morning football when I was aged 10 years old. The picture above was taken at Brockwell Park in South London and (below) all smiles with some early trophies

This would have been one of the first pictures taken of me after joining Arsenal. I'm in the home team changing room at Highbury in 1977

(Below) the moment I became all about Arsenal as Charlie George basks in the Wembley euphoria after scoring the FA Cup winner and securing the Gunners a first-ever Double in 1971

Being thrown in at the deep end on 7 April 1980 as I make my Arsenal first-team debut, aged just 17, in a North London derby at White Hart Lane – a game we won 2-1 after I'd been handed the task of stopping Glenn Hoddle getting on the ball for Spurs

At the end of my breakthrough season with the Arsenal first team, I had the pleasure of meeting Pelé, one of my role models growing up

(Above left) my international career never really got beyond the England B and Under-21 sides, but I was proud to help win the European U21 Championship in 1982. (Above right) my first ever tournament away with the Arsenal youth team was in Germany in 1977. We won the tournament but I badly injured my knee so missed the final

Not sure when this was taken but we all look relaxed. Some fine Arsenal players and staff here

(Above) the 1986/87 season was all about our Littlewoods Cup run, but it was the three semi-final meetings with Spurs that I first realised what success looked and felt like, with the atmosphere at White Hart Lane incredible as the final whistle sounded

Our 2-1 victory over Liverpool in the final itself was my first great achievement and climbing those Wembley steps for the first time owed much to the desire George Graham (right) had brought to the club

My moment of madness as I take a swing at Southampton's Glenn Cockerill during a home game in September 1988, breaking his jaw with a left hook after finally losing my cool with his persistent fouling. Although off-the-ball, the episode was caught on camera and cost me £3,000 and a record nine-game ban

My brother Tasman on his one and only visit from Jamaica to see Mum and myself. This was taken when we lived in Stafford Court, South London in 1991. I always looked forward to Mum's Sunday dinner. How I miss that carrot juice drink she used to make (next to the left of the Champagne bottle)!

One of my biggest regrets in football was never winning a senior cap with England, although I had joined up with the Three Lions and been on the verge of a first international appearance in 1988, but after the Glenn Cockerill incident, I was never called up to the England squad again

Cup final, though. Against Luton. We'd beaten Everton in the semi-finals, a strong side who'd won the league the year before. So, the final was a game we were supposed to win, weren't we? On the big day, though, we had problems even before we got to Wembley.

We were at the hotel and George announced the team on the morning of the game. I'd missed a couple of days training earlier in the week with a bug, but George put me in. Most of us expected it'd be Steve Williams with me in centre midfield. That was what Willo was expecting. Instead, though, Michael Thomas got picked to start. Steve wasn't happy at all. In the middle of the team meeting, he just got up, walked out of the room, and left the hotel. George let him go. The rest of us sat there, thinking the same thing. *This isn't going to end well for Willo.* George wouldn't stand for anyone crossing him. It was another chance for all of us to see how ruthless he could be. That was Steve done. He never played for Arsenal again. We all knew that, if you defied George, your days at the club would be numbered. He could be ruthless.

That afternoon, Luton scored first, but we went 2-1 up and felt like we were cruising, to be honest. We got a penalty ten minutes from the end which would have finished it at 3-1, but Nigel Winterburn's penalty was saved by Andy Dibble. It was as if the Luton players suddenly thought this might be their day and, a couple of minutes later, they equalised. Brian Stein got the winner just when we thought it was going to extra time. It was the first time Luton had ever won a major trophy. It was the first time I'd lost one. That defeat was even more disappointing because we'd been favourites. We'd let a fantastic opportunity to win a trophy slip past us. There aren't many worse feelings in sport than when you get into a strong winning position and fail to take advantage. That's exactly what happened to us that day.

We should have beaten them, but that was a good Luton Town team. Mick Harford and Brian Stein gave Tony Adams and Gus

Caesar a tough afternoon, and they had excellent players in midfield: David Preece and Danny Wilson. Their goalkeeper, Dibble, had the game of his life. The player that always stood out for me in that side, though, was Ricky Hill. Ricky was a couple of years older than me, from North West London. His mum was Jamaican, and his dad's family had ancestral roots in India. Ricky was the first British South Asian to represent England at senior level. Like me, Ricky had been born here and spent most of his career at one club, Luton. He'd been on the trip to Jamaica the previous summer, too.

Ricky was an outstanding footballer and played a few times for England: intelligent, articulate, a gentleman. I respected what he'd achieved in the game, and looked out for him, even after he finished playing. *Would he coach? Would he become a manager?* It's only in hindsight that I recognise it, but that Littlewoods Cup Final showed there'd been a shift in English football in the eight years since I'd made my debut. As a young professional, I'd often been the only black player in Arsenal's team. Now, in 1988, we had Michael and David and Gus playing alongside me. Luton had Ricky, Brian Stein and Mark Stein in their team. The game was starting to look different. It was like a door had been pushed ajar. A generation of players from backgrounds like mine were taking their chance. On the pitch, anyway.

The '88/89 season, which finished with a famous night at Anfield, changed everything at Arsenal. It changed English football, too. Two years after he'd arrived, George Graham had his team in place, a team in his image. The core of the squad were lads who'd come through the youth system at Highbury. George had added the players he needed, mostly from the lower divisions. Kevin Richardson was the exception: a central midfielder to replace Steve Williams – who'd been sold to Luton – and to put pressure on me. He was the only player we had who knew what it was like to win the league. Soft-spoken, but disciplined and tough, Kevin could play. He'd won the league and the Cup Winners' Cup with Everton in 1985. We signed him from Watford in 1987, and he played left midfield against Luton at Wembley. The rest of us had the hunger that came from never having done what Kevin had.

We started the season well. I started the season well. For the previous couple of years, every time an England squad was announced, I'd been hoping I'd be in it. I knew there were one or two outstanding midfield players ahead of me, like Glenn Hoddle and Bryan Robson. But I'd often look at other lads who were getting called up and winning caps, being given the chance to represent their country, and I'd wonder whether they were better than me. I was picked a lot for the under-21s as an over-age player and captained that team. But it wasn't until September '88 that I got called into a senior squad: England were playing Denmark at Wembley in a friendly. I was 27 years old.

Playing for England was the ultimate ambition for me, just as it would be for most players. When I got the call, I wasn't thinking I'd be there to make up the numbers. I really hoped this was a chance for me. Training at Burnham Beeches was great. I knew Tony and Rocky from Arsenal, of course, and had played against everybody else. There were experienced senior internationals around: Bryan Robson, Stuart Pearce, Peter Shilton, Terry Butcher. Bobby Robson, the manager, was such a charming man and made me feel welcome. Don Howe was his assistant and took most of the sessions. I was surrounded by people I respected and admired. I was more than hopeful that, if I made a good impression, I would get my first senior cap, and this would be the start of an England career, every boy's dream coming true.

The game itself turned out to be a bit of a non-event. There were only about 25,000 fans rattling around inside Wembley. I didn't make the starting XI. Neil Webb played alongside Bryan Robson.

Steve Hodge was on the left, Dave Rocastle on the right. I spent a lot of the time warming up, jogging on the touchline, hoping to get the call to go on. We were winning 1-0 and, late on, Paul Gascoigne got a run-out, but I didn't. I felt deflated and disappointed, naturally. But I was hopeful my opportunity would come again. Afterwards, Bobby Robson told me I was in his plans. All I needed to do was keep playing well for Arsenal. It didn't work out that way, though. One of my biggest regrets in football is that I never had the chance to win an England cap. I had a brief conversation with Gareth Southgate at St George's Park recently. *How many times did you play for England?* he asked. *None!* I replied. He apologised. *That's okay,* I said. *I was just getting over it until you brought it up again!* We both laughed. *That's life.*

Southampton at home, September 17th, 1988. I'd played against Glenn Cockerill many times and there had never been any issues between us. Which made what happened that afternoon even more difficult to explain. That game changed my life. From the first whistle, Glenn was trying to leave his mark on me. Every tackle, he'd be trying to physically hurt or intimidate me. Nasty stuff. At least that was my perception of events: high challenges and late challenges. If we were on the floor and the ball was somewhere else, he'd look to kick out or stamp on me. Or leave an elbow out when we went up for a high ball together. This was going on the whole of the first half and then on into the second. I couldn't work out what was happening. *Are you trying to put me off my game? Or are you actually trying to hurt me?*

The ref wasn't seeing any of what was going on. I wasn't getting free-kicks. It had a drip, drip, drip effect on me. I was getting increasingly frustrated with the injustice of the situation and took matters into my own hands. Professional to professional, what he was doing showed a complete lack of respect. If I'm honest, I remember making a conscious decision. *I'm not going to take any more of this. I don't know what's going on with you, but I've had enough of it.* We were attacking the North Bank, trying to come back from 2-0 down. There was a foul on Dave Rocastle over by the touchline, next to the dugout area and I found myself not far from Glenn, just the two of us in the middle of the pitch, everybody looking in the other direction. I walked over, closed my left hand and swung hard. I hit Glenn on the side of his face, the left jaw, the side where he wouldn't have seen it coming. That probably made it worse. He went down in a heap in front of me.

Straight away, the thought went through my mind: *Oh no! What have I done?* I tried to move away from Glenn, who was lying motionless in the middle of the pitch. I had no intention to connect as well as I did. But the referee, the linesmen, the other players, had all been focussed on the free-kick. As soon as Glenn got up, with me standing next to him, players started running across to us. There was some pushing and shoving, but nobody knew what had happened. The game was stopped. The medics came on to treat Glenn, and he walked off holding his jaw. The Southampton players knew by now that something had gone on. Once the game restarted, whenever I was on or near the ball, they were chasing me down, trying to give me a good kicking. I did fear for my safety from that point on.

A few minutes later, we got a penalty and, just as Lee Dixon ran up to take it and score, one of their players came up behind me and volleyed in the back of my calves. It hurt, but I didn't want to show him the pain I was in. It was Jimmy Case. No shrinking violet himself. He'd have thought, like I had before I punched Cockerill, that nobody would notice. And he was right. George could see what was happening by then and quickly took me off. I thought it was best to get out of the way to safety. The benches at Highbury were close to one another.

I went down the tunnel to the dressing room and sat there on my own. You could usually hear what was going on out on the pitch from the noise of the crowd echoing down from the East Stand overhead. For a while, though, in those few moments, with us chasing the game, it was quiet. I was hunched over, at the heart of this historic stadium, staring at the floor. *What just happened to me out there?* It was the strangest of situations: the hush of the empty dressing room, thousands of people just above my head, none of them knowing the full story of what had just taken place. Then, suddenly, a huge roar, cheers coming from the seats above me as our fans jumped out of them. Alan Smith had scored in injury time to get us a draw.

A couple of minutes later, I heard another cheer at full-time and then the clip-clopping of players' studs on the marble floors as they came down the corridor towards the dressing rooms. It never even crossed my mind that there'd be any fallout once the game was over. It had happened, the ref hadn't seen it, and that was that. Maybe I'd need to look out for myself next time we played South-ampton. But how wrong I was. The guys came in and sat down, happy to get a draw from a losing position. George said a few words to the team, then one or two asked me what had gone on. I told them. At that point, I still had no idea how badly hurt Glenn Cockerill was, that I'd broken his jaw. George came over and asked what had happened. I quickly explained, and he said: *Okay. Just don't say anything to the press.* He didn't seem concerned at all.

I was out that evening for a drink with some friends. That was when I heard: someone came up to me all excited. *Bloody hell! You're on the news. The 10 o'clock news.* I didn't know what he was talking about. *The 10 o'clock news. You hit that player on the pitch today! It's saying you've broken his jaw.* The conversation didn't go any further. The bloke had had a few drinks. But I left straight away and headed home. I'd already put the afternoon out of my mind but, when I got back to the flat, the answer machine was blinking away at me in the corner: 30-odd messages. I listened to them, and they were from newspaper reporters asking if I would call them. That's when it dawned on me. I hadn't even seen the TV pictures they were talking about, but I realised this was quickly turning into a serious situation.

Remembering what George had said to me, I didn't return any of the calls, but went out and bought the newspapers in the morning. There were some ugly headlines. Ugly about me, anyway: *Thug! Disgrace! Ban him!* My reputation was being pulled apart, and I felt powerless to do or say anything. On Monday, first thing, I met with George. He wanted to know every detail now. *What happened? Was it something he said?* A few pieces in the press had suggested Glenn must have said something racist to me to make me react in the way I had, in a way that was so out of character for me. I told George it hadn't been anything like that. I'd been getting kicked and intimidated all afternoon. I'd got frustrated and I'd snapped.

The pictures existed just by chance: the game hadn't been televised. Very few were in those days. But there'd been an ITV film crew there covering a different story altogether, and they caught my punch in the bottom left-hand corner of one of their shots. They must have thought it was newsworthy and passed it on. Sure enough, the images got replayed over and over in news bulletins for the next few days. When I could bring myself to watch the footage, it didn't look good. I became the story everybody was talking about, talked about even in the House of Commons. Everybody was expressing a view. It was football's first experience of trial by TV. Every time they showed the pictures, they looked worse. I didn't say anything to anybody but, the less I talked, the more the press and other people made up the story for themselves.

Within a couple of days, a week after I'd been on the bench for England, the FA announced they were going to charge me with bringing the game into disrepute. The papers had all been saying they had to. That I had to be punished. It was as if journalists had scented blood. The club stood by me, just as they had when I'd been accused of trying to steal a car as a teenager. George, especially. In those kinds of situations, more often than not, he'd back his player. He picked me for our next couple of games: a way of him saying he believed in me, I suppose, ahead of my appointment at the old FA headquarters in Lancaster Gate.

It was a Wednesday morning. We had to be at the hearing for 9.30am. I met George at Highbury. Ken Friar was with us, and a car took us down to Bayswater. There were photographers clustered round the steps when we arrived. All I could do was say what had happened. I couldn't deny what I'd done. But there'd been provocation. The club had tried to put video together to show me being fouled and stamped on and provoked all through the game. I wasn't going to say I wasn't guilty, but I wanted to explain why I'd snapped. But even though this whole thing was based on what had been shown on TV, they wouldn't let us show any clips. We were only allowed to present verbal evidence.

There'd been so much speculation about what the FA were going to do. So many people saying what the FA should do. All that was spinning round in my head while we waited for the hearing to begin. Here we were, in an oak-panelled room, smelling of furniture polish and deodorant, with three old boys in blazers and ties lined up behind their table: Bert Millichip, who was the FA chairman, and a couple of other middle-aged, white administrators who, I'm pretty sure, had no idea what life was like outside their own worlds. They asked questions. They listened to my answers, I think. After 45 minutes or so, they said we could leave. We squeezed out past the photographers and camera crews outside and drove back to Highbury. I went home not knowing what was going to happen next. All I could do now was sit and wait, and not answer the phone.

I had a head full of it, but it was strange: I drove into training the next day, and nobody asked about the hearing. The other players, I'm guessing, didn't really know what to say. Maybe they thought I wouldn't want to talk about it. But it was lonely: I hadn't spoken to anybody apart from George, Mr Friar and the FA. It felt like weeks – and it was definitely a few days – before the verdict came through. The club got in touch with me to say I'd been fined £3,000 and banned for nine games. Bearing in mind that, if the ref had seen what had happened, I'd have been sent off and suspended for three games, that seemed incredibly harsh to me. To the club, too. As far as punishments for on-field incidents were concerned, nine games was the longest ban in English football history.

The club and I considered lodging an appeal but, in the end, decided against it. The whole thing left me so low. That I'd be missing games, crucial games, with the team playing well, was only the half of it. I'd thought I was on the verge of getting a chance with England. But that dream now looked much further away: not just because I wasn't playing for Arsenal, but because of the way I'd been demonised by the media coverage. There were newspaper columns written saying the FA shouldn't ever allow me to represent my country again. I had played 11 games for the under-21s. I'd worked so hard to finally break into my first senior squad, only for this to happen. Bobby Robson hadn't been in contact. Those reports in the papers were harmful and hurtful. I was never called up by England again.

I just had to sit out the two months. I'd go in and train every day, but knowing there wasn't going to be a game for me at the end of the week. I didn't have any clear idea how this might play out long-term, either. Football's a competitive business. I worried about when – or if, even – I'd get back in the team. Once the ban finished, George wasn't keen to change a winning side. I couldn't argue with that. Kevin Richardson had taken my place and was playing well.

I'd started the season as a key player, but plans can change quickly in football. I felt like I was on the outside looking in, for Arsenal as well as for England. Completely isolated and alone, I was at the lowest point of my professional career.

I know now I should have talked to someone about how I was feeling. Instead, I think people around me, within the club and outside, felt like they should leave me alone. I didn't ask anyone for help. I bottled up a lot of my feelings. But it was on my mind constantly: what had happened, what was going to happen, what might happen. Nobody in the dressing room said anything. They either didn't think to ask, or they didn't know how to. Looking back, I think what I needed was someone to ask me: *How are you doing? Are you okay?* Those were difficult months. I'm left with regrets about that day, about how I reacted to Glenn Cockerill's provocation. I made a mistake and paid the price for it. The whole business damaged me: damaged my career and damaged my reputation. As things turned out, it wasn't just a matter of seeing out those nine games, either. The suspension was just the start of a season full of trouble for me.

89

It's the same for most players: it's hard watching games when you're not involved. While I was banned, I went to matches at Highbury and sat in the Paddock, the staff seats behind the two benches, in front of the old East Stand. When we played away, I wasn't invited to travel. I'd follow the scores on the TV sports shows or on Teletext. There weren't many games broadcast live back then. I seem to remember I had a hernia operation in the weeks after my ban ended, too. I finally got back in the team in the middle of January '89: Everton at Goodison Park. We played well and won 3-1. We were top of the league. I think everybody connected with Arsenal, including our supporters, felt as if there was something special going on at the club.

We got knocked out of the FA Cup by West Ham, though, and that meant we had a clear week at the end of January, when the fourth round games were going on. George decided to take us for some warm weather training, and we flew to Bermuda. The idea was to relax and recover: it would be nice to be out of our winter for a little while. One day, a few of us went down to the gym at the hotel, to do a yoga class. One stretch – I can still remember it

– I felt a little strain in the upper part of my thigh. I left the class straight away, but the next day, while we were training, I felt it pulling. Nothing serious, but it was my left leg, my kicking leg. I sat out the rest of the session, but never imagined that little strain was going to have such a major impact on my career.

Back in London, I got treatment on it: massage, ultrasound. It didn't feel like anything to worry about. It wasn't like a hamstring tear, an injury that actually stopped you in your tracks. This was in the front of my thigh, a little knot and tenderness in the muscle. Gary Lewin was a very good physio, and he got me to rest it, but I know he was under pressure, at first, to get me back and available. George wanted me playing. Which was what I wanted, too. Six weeks later, we all thought I was ready. I came back for Charlton at home and scored: a 50-yard sprint and a diving header. I felt pretty good. Then we were away at Southampton and won. All I wanted was to be involved. The thigh didn't feel 100 per cent, but we were winning, weren't we? Next game, up at Old Trafford, though, I felt the muscle go again. I knew straight away: that little tear had just become bigger.

It's one of the worst experiences for any professional sportsperson: the uncertainty around a chronic injury. This wasn't like a break, something you can fix and then set a timetable to recover from. Instead, it was a lot of time spent doing nothing: rest, treatment, and worrying. Then the whole process of rehabilitation, pushing yourself, wanting so badly to be back in action that you ignore warning signs, hoping you're ready. But you can't ever know, until you put yourself into a competitive game. I was into a cycle which was going to roll on for the best part of 18 months. Over and over again: rest, rehab, train, play, break down. Back to square one. I sometimes wonder whether we waited long enough before I played the very first time. I'm sure, like with many injuries, mine would probably be treated differently now. At the time, though, I know Gary Lewin and the medical staff were doing the best they could.

I had to face up to the fact that my season was more or less over. Arsenal were chasing a first league title in nearly 20 years, and it was a huge disappointment knowing I wasn't going to be a part of it. And then Hillsborough happened. April 15th, 1989. We were playing Newcastle at Highbury that afternoon and I was watching the game in the Paddock. Liverpool were taking on Nottingham Forest in an FA Cup semi-final the same day and, by half-time, people were talking about crowd trouble in Sheffield. Those days being what they were, 'crowd trouble' usually meant 'hooliganism,' and I think most of us assumed there'd been fighting and that's why the game up there had been stopped.

After our game, we all trooped up to the dressing room. News started coming in about what had happened – what was happening – at Hillsborough. Before long, we were all squeezed around a TV in one of the little offices on the opposite side of the corridor, watching the horrific pictures being broadcast by the BBC. They were already talking about how many people were feared dead. The numbers kept going up. It was hard to take in what was happening in front of our eyes on that screen. You could never imagine something like this: I'd seen plenty of crushes at football, but supporters always seemed to laugh and joke about it. I'd never seen anyone hurt. This was completely different. On a different scale. Straight away, you knew it was awful.

Words can't describe it: all I could think about was the people who'd suffered and their families. We'd won a game of football that afternoon, but nobody was celebrating. People were in shock. Even then, there was talk about the rest of the season being cancelled. *How could you play after something like this?* In hindsight, the tragedy was something that had been waiting to happen. Highbury was the only ground in the league that didn't have fences between the crowd and the pitch. We were supposed to play Liverpool at Anfield the following weekend. That game was postponed: the two clubs made the decision for themselves. But all the other fixtures went ahead. By the time the next Saturday came round, everybody knew nearly 100 people had died at Hillsborough, and that more were still in intensive care. But, a week later, players went out and played, and supporters turned up to watch.

Once Arsenal started playing again, I was just another fan, watching and hoping we could win the league. Hoping for a minor miracle and that I'd be fit enough to play a part in it. I remember travelling up to Middlesbrough with some friends and us winning 1-0. Terrible game but, driving home, we were feeling confident. *It's ours to lose now, right?* And then two games at Highbury in a week: Derby and Wimbledon. I was in the stand for both and can remember the frustration of not being out there, wanting desperately to be involved in games that meant so much. We lost 2-1 on the Saturday and then drew 2-2 on the Wednesday night. All of a sudden, it looked as if we'd thrown it away. One game left: 26th May, away to Liverpool, the game that had been postponed after the disaster at Hillsborough.

George told everybody – team, reserves, injured players: 18 players and six staff in all – that we would travel up together. Even though I found it difficult to watch if I wasn't in the team, I wanted to be with everyone else, to at least be a part of what might go down in English football history as the most amazing finish to any title race. So, the final game of the season: if Liverpool came out on top, they'd complete the League and Cup double. After everything that had happened to the club and the city since April, it felt as if the whole country wanted them to win. And if we won? By two clear goals? That's what we had to do to be champions. The closer we got to the game, the more I fancied our chances. We had nothing to lose. George decided we'd go up on the day of the game, which was going to be shown live on ITV. Everybody knows what happened. It was historic. Maybe the most dramatic game ever. And I'll never forget it, even though my experience of it was so different from the lads who actually played.

I met the team coach at Highbury, early. I remember sitting on my own, watching Tony Donnelly load up all the kit, hearing the crates being moved around underneath me. There was a little kitchen at the back of the bus, and the two guys who looked after us with food on the journeys were getting things ready. It turned out they'd even made sure there were some bottles of champagne on board. We picked up Niall Quinn at Southgate tube station. He was injured, too. And then everybody else climbed on at the training ground. I know some Arsenal supporters got held up on the M6 – in fact, they had to put the kick-off back to 8pm – but we were early and got to the hotel in Liverpool for lunchtime. We went through our normal routine for an away game: we ate, went to our rooms to rest, and then came down at around 5pm for our team meeting.

I felt part of it but not part of it at the same time. George's team meetings usually lasted 15 or 20 minutes. He'd name our starting XI and then run through what he thought our opponent's would be. This was the time for a few key messages and reminders about how we planned to win the game. Tactically, we set up to play with three at the back, in a 3-5-2 system which was different to our normal 4-4-2. We'd worked on a back three in the few days leading up to the game. The idea was for Lee Dixon – on the right – and Nigel Winterburn – on the left – to nullify two of their most important players, John Barnes, and Ray Houghton, in the wide areas. Everybody knew their roles and responsibilities in this new team structure.

Finally, George gave us his vision of how the game might pan out, a vision he repeated in the dressing room before kick-off. *We need to win by two clear goals, but we can't afford to let them score. If we get to half-time and it's still 0-0, that's okay. But don't give them a goal. 0-0 at half-time and then, if we can score early in the second half, they'll properly get nervous after that.* That was it. The meeting was over, and we walked through the hotel reception, which was buzzing with Arsenal fans asking for autographs and wishing us well. The team bus was waiting, with a police escort to Anfield. I could feel the excitement and anticipation. We stepped out into the cool evening breeze and climbed onto the coach.

We'd have wanted to get to the ground maybe an hour and half before kick-off. As it turned out, we were early and then found out the game had been delayed because of the hold-ups on the M6. I can't begin to imagine how fans must have been feeling, stuck in traffic, thinking they might not get to Liverpool in time for the game. Maybe being early was a good thing: we were nervous, excited, but now had plenty of time in the dressing room to settle down. Nobody got changed. The lads were just standing around, laughing and joking, or reading the programme. A couple of the directors, David Dein and Richard Carr, came down to chat with the players. An hour or so before kick-off, one or two of the boys started getting ready. That was when it got difficult for the injured guys who weren't involved: me, Quinny, Brian Marwood. Everything inside you is saying: *I want to be playing.* The adrenaline and nerves still kicked in.

I thought it was time for the three of us to leave the boys to it. I asked George about tickets. Nobody had thought about or mentioned where we'd be sitting. He said the benches were small at Anfield, so there wouldn't be room for us. We'd sit up in the Directors Box instead. When the tickets eventually arrived, though, they weren't the Directors Box. We looked at the little map on the back and worked out we'd have to go out into the car park, onto Anfield Road, and in again through the turnstiles over in the far corner. The three of us were all dressed smartly in our navy blue club blazers, white shirts, and red and white-striped ties. We wished the boys well and headed off. *Out of the dressing room. Right, right, and right again.* We found ourselves queuing up with the Arsenal fans waiting to get into the away section. People were looking at us. *Davo! Davo! How you doing?* It was surreal. A few minutes later, we were in our seats amongst our own supporters who couldn't believe we were there.

The atmosphere inside Anfield was fantastic. Once we kicked off, Niall, Brian and I were three more fans, kicking and heading every ball, as tackles flew in, and chances came and went. First half, Arsenal were kicking towards the Kop. Second half, they were kicking towards us and, a few minutes in, Alan Smith scored and all around us was mayhem. Us too. We all went crazy. Everybody jumping all over each other, celebrating. This was a much better place to be than the Directors Box. And then I remembered. *What did George say this afternoon?* It was so tense. Liverpool seemed nervous, caught between trying to win the game and defending the advantage they had. You could feel the pressure around the ground. Our supporters were shouting at us to get forward. But the longer it went, the more it looked like we were going to come up short. We were the better team, but we weren't exactly battering Liverpool.

It was great being amongst our supporters at Anfield that evening. As a player, you're trained to be professional about what you do. You have to try to take emotion out of it all. You never really understand the supporters' experience. That night of all nights, I was able to be in the middle of it, to share all their passion, feeling what the team and the club meant to our fans. I felt the same. Me, Brian and Niall were bouncing around, screaming, and shouting as much as anyone else. Even so, a few minutes from time, we decided we'd better get out of where we were, thinking there'd be a mad rush at the end. George wouldn't be happy if he wanted to get away quickly and got left waiting around in the car park for us three.

We decided it might be worth a go climbing over onto the track and walking round behind the goal. We went down to the stewards at the front and explained that we were Arsenal players. *Can we just get round the touchline this way?* Well, they weren't having any of it. *No, you'll have to go out the back of the stand, walk round and come back in again.* The Arsenal supporters around us realised what was going on and started having a go at the stewards: *They're Arsenal players! Let them get over the railings!* They really pushed them to let us go round behind the goal, and eventually we got our way. I'll always be grateful to those fans. If it hadn't been for them, we'd have been outside in Anfield Road and would have missed Michael's goal. Can you imagine? I'd have taken away a completely different memory of that famous night.

While we were walking behind the goal at our end of the ground, the ball was in the far penalty area but, as we turned at the corner flag to start walking along to the dugouts in front of the main stand, John Lukic threw the ball out to Lee Dixon and the move began. We were on the touchline, next to the pitch, when Michael scored, looking across at him and then at the Arsenal supporters behind him going wild. I couldn't believe we'd done it. I thought about running onto the pitch to celebrate, but thought better of it. We rushed down towards the benches instead. Pat Rice, Theo Foley and Gary Lewin were leaping around. There were a couple of youngsters there, too: Stevie Morrow, Alan Miller and Gus Caesar. George was still inside the dugout, trying to calm everyone down.

I watched the last few moments standing next to the dugout. When the final whistle blew, it all went crazy, everyone charging onto the pitch, hugging each other, punching the air towards our fans. It was mad: none of us had ever been involved in a game like this before. How do you take in what's happened? It took ages for them to set up for the trophy presentation but, once they did, I realised how lucky I was. It was a huge disappointment not being able to play, but George had brought us all up here as a group. Maybe for this moment. So that, if it happened, everyone who'd been involved during the season would be at Anfield to celebrate.

It was wonderful, looking at that stand where all the Arsenal supporters were, from where I'd watched most of the game. Thousands of delirious faces. People rushing down the stand towards us as we walked over towards them. None of us, players or supporters, will ever forget that night. It was electric. The euphoria was like nothing I've ever experienced, before or since. This was as good as it could possibly get. And full credit to Liverpool's fans: a lot of them stayed on inside the ground to acknowledge what we'd achieved.

We were in the dressing room for a couple of hours after the game. Liverpool sent through bottles of champagne. Some of it got sprayed around. Most of it got drunk. Our directors came down to congratulate George and the rest of us. Everyone was so happy. It didn't take long for a few people to get a bit drunk, a combination of the champagne and the shared excitement of the moment. Nobody was in any hurry to leave. All the Liverpool people were long gone. *Turn off the lights when you leave, eh, lads?* It must have been past midnight by the time we got onto the coach. Singing, shouting and partying all the way home.

Supporters in cars kept coming up alongside the coach, blowing their horns, standing up out of sunroofs and leaning out of their windows. We hadn't made any plans, but someone – I think it was Quinny – suggested a nightclub in Southgate: *I'll phone Winners. They'll stay open for us.* And they did. By the time we got there, it must have been about three or four in the morning and the club wasn't that busy, although I was amazed there were still a few dozen Arsenal fans there celebrating. I remember feeling a little disappointed that we hadn't organised something properly. But how could we have known what was going to happen? To this day, I've got no idea how or when I got home.

It was a night I was sure would never be repeated, and it hasn't been yet! It was only David O'Leary and myself who were the link back to the previous generation at Highbury. David had played so many games for the club and was a little older than me. But I was from the Terry Neill era, too. The season I made my Arsenal debut was a high-achieving season: runners-up in the league, two cup finals. David and I had been through all the time since then, when so many things had gone wrong, under Terry and then under Don Howe, as the club lost its way. In '89, most of the other lads were younger and didn't have that sense of perspective. Didn't yet understand, maybe, how special it was to achieve what we did at Anfield that night or the journey we'd been on to get there. I think about Tony and David and Michael, about Martin Hayes, Paul Merson and Niall Quinn. Maybe those young lads just assumed playing for Arsenal was always like this. That playing for Arsenal always meant that you won.

91

People sometimes say to me, even now, that they remember me as a player who used to get a lot of injuries. That hits a bit of a nerve with me. One, because I played nearly 500 games for Arsenal. And two, because I had very few injuries, really. But I had one bad one that ruined things for me for the best part of 18 months, the second half of '88/89 and then all the way through the following season. The tear in my thigh muscle just wouldn't heal. I played a few games early the following season and a couple more in the Spring of 1990. Even then, though, I was half-waiting for the thigh to break down at any minute. Out on the pitch, in the middle of a game, I'd be wondering if it would last the 90. Or, even worse, I'd train or play while trying to protect the injury. It definitely played on my mind.

People didn't really talk about depression in those days. Definitely not in a football environment. Now, perhaps, I'd be able to say: I was depressed, even though I always convinced myself that the next time the thigh muscle would fix itself. An injury sets you apart from the rest of the dressing room. The manager's focussed on the players he's got, not the ones who are unavailable. Supporters, too.

Every time I had a conversation with anybody, the first question was always the same. *When are you going to be fit?* The truth was that nobody really knew. Gary Lewin and the club doctor, Mr Sash, did their best to get me back playing. They were always available, always wanting to help. But psychologically, I had to find my own way to deal with the stress. It wasn't easy. I just kept telling myself to be positive. *Next time. Next time, it'll work.*

When the injury first happened, it had seemed so innocuous. But then it kept recurring. The problem was running and kicking. Well, that adds up to a footballer's job, doesn't it? I'm not sure exactly when the idea of an operation was first suggested. I was fearful: surgery is always a risk and can come with its own complications. But I'd been going round in circles for a long time. When the doctors and Gary suggested an operation might be the best thing, I was ready for it. I was desperate to be back playing again, for this to be sorted out once and for all. The op was very serious: they opened up my left thigh, an eight-inch-long incision, went in, sewed up the ruptured muscle and then stitched my leg back over the top of it. The scar's still clearly visible today: a permanent reminder.

I was never quite the same player after that operation. The muscle never felt as strong, and I was always conscious of that. The nerves in the thigh felt damaged, and I'd lost all sense of feeling in the area around the incision. I had to adapt my game. Before the operation, if I sprinted at more than 80 per cent or tried to hit long balls more than 80 per cent of my usual range, I'd feel the pain in my thigh. Afterwards, I didn't feel the muscle was going to tear again. But there were things I just physically couldn't do. I'd lost important parts of my game, lost confidence in being able to hit the ball consistently over 60 or 70 yards. I sensed those passes would drop short now. I was never particularly quick, but I realised that I couldn't push off into a sprint with any real power. Twisting, turning, accelerating, so much of the explosive power had gone. I didn't have the same feel for the ball, either.

The best way I can explain it is to imagine my thigh as an elastic band, which had snapped and then been knotted back together. It's never going to be the same as it was. However hard I worked at it, the power in my left thigh never returned. I'd come back and train with Gary in the afternoons, but I got to a point where I realised this was my new maximum, and that the thigh wasn't going to improve. I was 28 years of age – the age when most footballers hit their peak, physically, technically, socially, and psychologically – and here I was, struggling in every area. It wasn't a good time for me.

If I couldn't get back to being the player I'd been, I'd have to try and play a different game instead. In training sessions I had to re-learn what I could and couldn't do in terms of reaching tackles, tracking runners, finding out how hard and how far I could kick the ball. I had to find ways to compensate. At the same time, Arsenal was an incredibly competitive environment. I needed to get back in the team as soon as I could. There were other midfielders at the club, and younger players like Steve Morrow, David Hillier and Ian Selley coming through. George signed Siggi Jónsson from Sheffield Wednesday to play in my position, too, although Siggi had a back injury which meant his Arsenal career never really started.

Gary thought it might be useful to play somewhere over the summer of 1990, where the league ran through June and July. George had taken us to Scandinavia for pre-season in the past, and Arsenal had good links there. The possibility of a loan spell with a Swedish club called Eskilstuna came up. George was happy for me to go. I was ready to do anything I could to be sure of being fit for the start of the following season. I packed my bags and flew to Stockholm on my own. I was booked in to stay at a hotel in Eskilstuna, 80 miles west, a town in the middle of nowhere.

IFK Eskilstuna were the local semi-pro club and played in a regional league. It was quiet, with very little going on: that suited me. I was just there to train and to play. A bit of gym work at the hotel. Six weeks, with plenty of time to reflect and think. *Was my career slipping away from me here?* It felt that way.

Arsenal let me get on with it while I was in Sweden, but the people at Eskilstuna looked after me, always making sure I was okay. The manager of the club was called Svante Larsson. His five-year-old son used to come along to training sessions. His name was Sebastian: a lovely kid, and really keen on his football. Small world: Seb ended up signing for Arsenal ten years later, after I'd left, and had a fantastic career in England with Sunderland and Birmingham City. He played 133 times for Sweden, too, and captained them at the last Euros. I never got to know him, but I always looked out for Seb's career after meeting him when he was so young. He's back in Sweden now.

It was the first time I'd ever been away from home on my own or away from England for so long. The town was quiet, clean, open space everywhere and surrounded by forest. It was a very particular way of life there. Maybe it's the same in other parts of Sweden, too. During the week, everybody was low-key, going about their business and keeping themselves to themselves. But come the weekend, it was as if the whole town was out. Going to a bar was expensive – a beer cost £5, four times more than in England at the time – so people would get roaring drunk at home and then emerge from their homes to wander round town at 10 in the evening. Complete strangers, in this normally conservative community, would treat me as if we were old friends. But then, come Monday morning, everybody was back to normal: sober, serious, as if Saturday night hadn't happened at all.

I came back to London in time to start pre-season training with Arsenal. I'd been working hard in Eskilstuna, even playing in games, and so I was probably a bit ahead of most of the other players in terms of fitness. The trip had got me where I wanted to be: ready. I played our first game, away to Wimbledon. And then almost every other game for the rest of the season. For Arsenal, it was a brilliant nine months. For me personally, it was a strange nine months, though. On the one hand, I was still frustrated that I couldn't do many of the things I'd been able to do before my thigh injury, worried I wasn't the player I'd been or wanted to be. On the other hand: it was an incredible season, an almost invincible season. We won the League in '90/91 by a comfortable seven points, with Liverpool trailing in second.

George wanted his central midfield players to protect the back four. Whatever else you did, that was the first part of your job. That '90/91 season, I was probably more focussed on that than on any other part of my game. The keeper and the back four were the only guys who played as many games as I did. George saw me as a defending midfielder who could play a bit. But I saw myself the other way around, as a ball-playing midfielder who knew how to defend. But we were winning, so most people were happy. George once said to us all in a team meeting that our centre-backs would be able to play until they were 35 because of the work the midfielders were doing protecting them. Which left us midfielders thinking: *Great! So that means we'll all be finished before we're out of our 20s!*

If Michael was playing alongside me, he was the one who had more licence to get forward. Because I had doubts after the injury, the role probably suited me more. It's easier, really: sitting in and looking after the centre-halves, breaking up attacks, picking up knock downs, playing shorter passes to get attacks started. The longer I spent playing as a defensive player, though, the more frustrated I got. I wanted to do more. I'm naturally attack-minded. I'd been a striker scoring plenty of goals when I was nine and 10 years old, and I'm not sure that instinct ever left me. I'd rather win 3-1 or 4-1 than 1-0, even though I recognise that winning itself is the most important thing in professional sport.

We won the title and only lost one game, Chelsea away. I was an automatic first choice, from August right through till May. I wasn't over the injury, but I'd adapted to cope and developed a more conservative game. It was one of Arsenal's best-ever seasons. Even though I never felt I was playing at a level anything like my best, I'm so grateful that I was fit enough to be a part of what we achieved. When Tony Adams wasn't involved, I took over as captain. George had brought in Dave Seaman, Anders Limpar, Andy Linighan. Players like Paul Merson and Steve Bould were at their absolute peaks. Kevin Campbell and David Hillier were coming through and doing well. It was a team that had developed resilience, but it was also a team that scored lots of goals. '88/89 had been on a knife-edge to the last game. '90/91, it felt all season like we were simply better than everyone else.

We had to play seven months off a handicap, though, after the so-called Battle of Old Trafford. We'd had a few run-ins with Manchester United, going back to an FA Cup game against them at Highbury, when Brian McClair had missed a penalty and Nigel Winterburn had got in his ear. In 1990, we went up to play them towards the end of October and there was an edge all afternoon. Anders Limpar scored from a short corner in the first half. Then, in the second, he went into a challenge with Denis Irwin. Nigel Winterburn thought Anders was being bullied, and he flew in on Irwin. Nigel was on the floor and Irwin and Brian McClair started kicking him, pretending they were kicking the ball. So, a few of us went to protect our team-mate, something George had always encouraged us to do. Within moments, everybody on the pitch was involved, pushing, and shoving mostly, people trying to calm things down.

The whole incident only lasted about 30 seconds, and I don't think there was one proper punch thrown. Nobody got hurt. But, because the game was high-profile, being shown across the world, it kicked off afterwards and got more attention than it deserved. I got fined by Arsenal. So did a few of the other lads. George, too. The fines were an attempt to make sure the FA would see the incident had been dealt with by the club. But some of the media were doing what they do best: adding fuel to the fire. So, the FA were under pressure to make an example of us. A bit like they had with me over Glenn Cockerill. They docked us two points and United one. The only time in English football history a club has lost points over something that happened during a game. I'd already experienced trial by TV and been given a record ban after the Cockerill incident. Now I was part of a team being deducted two points in the same way. Anyone who didn't know me probably thought I was some kind of thug. Anyone who does know me, though, knows nothing could be further from the truth.

George had his ways of dealing with the press. He distrusted them. There were times, early on after he arrived at Arsenal, when stories leaked into the newspapers – team selections, injuries, that sort of thing – and he would ban all of us from talking to the papers. In the dressing room, it'd be like some kind of secret police investigation was going on. One week George would suspect Niall Quinn, the next it'd be Brian Marwood. *There's a story in today's paper, so who's going to get the finger pointed at them now?* It got a little paranoid at times, but it was useful for George, probably, when he needed to pull everybody together and build a siege mentality if he thought we were getting unfairly reported on.

After the scrap at Old Trafford, George got us all together after training, sat outside at Colney, and gave us a rallying speech. *Everybody's against us, they're trying to bring us down, but we'll stick together. We're second in the league, not second bottom. Don't worry about the press. I'll handle them.* It was powerful stuff, a classic George Graham ploy that he'd used many times before: *The whole world's against us, boys!* And it worked. The speech was filmed, something which wouldn't ever have happened without George's approval. In fact, it was probably his idea: it was like a scene out of one of those Amazon football documentaries. In hindsight, I realise that speech wasn't just meant for us. George orchestrated it all. The video of it got released to the media. It was George sending out a message to the world from inside the camp: he was a strategic thinker, no doubt about that.

The points deduction didn't stop us. It motivated us. That season, Anders was unplayable: the Super Swede. He did things in training I'd never seen before. In games, too. He was quick. He'd stop an opponent dead and then burst away from him. He was two-footed, so you never knew which way he'd go. Unbelievable power in his shots, with little or no back lift. And he was the first Arsenal player I ever saw who won us penalties. You'd think to yourself: *I don't know how he's won us that!* George did instruct all of us to go down in the box if we were touched. I remember Anders winning one against Liverpool at Highbury when we beat them 3-0. Mentally, Anders wasn't so strong. After a while, opposition teams started playing on that. He found George's psychological demands difficult to handle, too. But in '90/91 he was a match winner, a player who could produce a bit of individual brilliance from nowhere to win you a game. Anders and I got on well. I spent quite a bit of time with him, much as I had with another newcomer, Charlie Nicholas, all those years earlier. Maybe there was a connection with me having been in Sweden that summer.

Anders and I played together in Naples that season as well. We got picked for a Football League XI to play against a Serie A XI in January '91. Lawrie McMenemy was the manager. Lee Dixon and Michael Thomas were in the team, too. I felt proud to have been selected. The Serie A team didn't include any Italian players. They were all foreign stars, at a time when the Italian league was where the world's best players wanted to play. It was like a World XI, in fact, with guys like Aldair, Careca, Lothar Matthäus and Marco van Basten in their line-up. I remember Mark Wright had a difficult night and we ended up well beaten, 3-0. But being part of the occasion, at one of the World Cup stadiums from Italia 90 and against the very best players, felt special. Maybe more special for me because, unlike the other English lads in our team, I'd never had the chance to turn out for my country.

What we achieved at Arsenal in '91 was special. That team had many qualities, especially *camaraderie* and *desire*, two of George's favourite words. We were aggressive, organised and always ready to *Get tight!* And we had players like Anders and Merse who could do special things. We conceded only 18 goals in the league. And that was despite Tony getting sent to prison for drink-driving just before Christmas. He'd been arrested a few months before, but the case didn't get heard until mid-December. It came out of the blue. None of us players knew about it until we read that he'd been given four months. It seemed harsh. Maybe the magistrates wanted a high-profile case as a deterrent for people who might drink and drive over Christmas. There was a national publicity campaign running at the time. Tony served two months, but Andy Linighan came in at centre-half and did well. We kept winning games.

From outside, Tony being sent to prison was another stick to beat Arsenal with. From inside, it was another time for George to pull everyone together and make us believe we were fighting the world. The club said we wouldn't be able to go to Chelmsford to visit Tony. We should leave that to the family. But we could write letters, which I did. Just the obvious, really: *Try to stay strong. You've got my support. Looking forward to getting you back with us.* It was tough to lose him for that run of games. Tony was captain for good reason. But it was a lot tougher, I'm sure, for Tony himself and his family. That's a terrible thing to happen to anybody, although I wasn't aware that Tony had an issue with alcohol. I knew he was one of a few players who liked a drink, but no more than that. Maybe he didn't realise he had a problem himself at the time.

Steve Bould was exceptional while Tony was missing. He was exceptional all season. I always thought Bouldy was very under-rated, a player who got on with it, quietly and efficiently: no fuss, no dramas. Get the job done and be ready to cover for others. I don't think it was a coincidence that the only game we lost that season, at Chelsea, was when he had to go off injured at half-time. We gave away a couple of soft goals. I know it's ifs and buts, but maybe the only thing that stopped us going unbeaten in '90/91 was Steve not playing that second half at the Bridge. Otherwise, he didn't miss a league game. Hardly missed a tackle or a header all season, either. And comfortable on the ball. I always felt reassured playing in front of him. He and Tony worked centre-forwards out: the physical ones, the technical ones, the quick ones. Between them, they always came up with a plan.

The one big disappointment in '90/91 was the FA Cup semi-final against Spurs. It was played at Wembley, which I thought was wrong. Wembley should be for the finals. Still should be now. Semi-finals, traditionally, were always played at Villa Park or Old Trafford or Stamford Bridge. Even at Highbury, sometimes. Spurs had a good team and, in the week building up to the game, I remember George getting a bit over-concerned about their players, especially Paul Gascoigne. I remember wondering why we were focussing on their players when we had talented players of our own for them to be worried about. George had Michael do a man-marking job on Gazza, and follow him all over the pitch. Michael wasn't keen: he wanted to be the player getting followed, not the one doing the following. It cost us. That decision took something away from our game and, of course, Gascoigne scored with a fantastic free kick anyway, and they beat us 3-1.

I hated losing any game to Spurs, and that afternoon at Wembley was worse than most. I had some great battles against Paul Gascoigne, though, starting in his early days at Newcastle. Even then, he used to take charge of games and would throw a few choice words in my direction. He was always a handful: strong, skilful, audacious, cheeky, someone who played the game like an extremely gifted child might. He was a very good dribbler and would look to put the ball through your legs if he saw the opportunity, and then look to do it again as you tried to recover. He was also physically strong. Paul was an entertainer, but an effective footballer, too. Without doubt, he was the outstanding English player of his generation.

I used to see a few of the Spurs boys out in North London: Gazza, Paul Stewart, Mitchell Thomas, Paul Walsh, Gareth Crooks and Chris Houghton. On the pitch, Gascoigne and I had some fierce battles, but we could also enjoy a laugh and a joke together during the game. We were quite different personalities, obviously, but we had a connection and a mutual respect. Paul and I played under-21s for England together. Even then, he was always up for pranks, out after curfews. But Paul had such a good heart and was so genuine. We loved being around him, although some of the stuff he got up to he'd never get away with now. The summer of 1990, at the World Cup in Italy, he became the biggest star in English football, as a player and as a personality. Everybody wanted a bit of Gazza.

The semi against Spurs didn't do us any lasting damage. We won the league a couple of weeks later. It was a Sunday and Liverpool were away to Forest before we played Manchester United at Highbury. We got to the ground quite early, and Liverpool's game was on the TV. Some of the lads watched on the little telly in one of the rooms off the corridor, while the rest of us were in the dressing room getting ready. Forest won, so we knew we were champions before we kicked off. It felt strange to win it like that. You'd always like it to happen out on the pitch, but it meant that, by the time we went out to warm up, there was already a party atmosphere inside the stadium. A weird situation, but it was great. All the pressure to win was no longer there, and we could enjoy the celebrations.

I liked that we still did the job properly, though, and beat United 3-1, especially after what had gone on at Old Trafford earlier in the season. Afterwards, the directors came down to the dressing room. Champagne was sprayed around. We had the windows open so we could hear the supporters out in the street, singing and cheering. Avenell Road was jammed for hours after the game. I'd had 18 months with the Cockerill suspension and then my thigh injury, where I'd been on the outside of things: even at Anfield in '89, I'd been in the crowd instead of on the pitch. But '90/91, I played pretty much every game. All the great stuff that went on amongst that group of players, and between the team and the supporters, what we achieved together, I was right at the heart of it this time. And that felt very good.

92

I'm happy I played my football when I did. The financial rewards for playing professional football were nowhere near those of today. We certainly weren't multi-millionaires like current Premier League players will be. At our peak, top earners would have been on between £150,000 and £200,000. A year, not a week! Average earnings would have been around £60,000 or £70,000, with bonuses, although wages weren't discussed in the dressing room, so none of us really knew what our team-mates were being paid. In the early days of my career, bonuses were only paid to the players who played on a Saturday, which sharpened the competition amongst us even more. When I was playing, a club retained control of a professional player's registration so, even at the end of your contract, they could demand a transfer fee for you. It wasn't until the mid-'90s that the Bosman Ruling changed all that and meant a player could move between clubs for nothing once his contract ran out. That helped start the trend towards higher and higher wages but, by then, I'd already retired. If only I'd been born ten years later!

Seriously, though, I have no regrets. Back in the '80s and early

'90s, Arsenal players and supporters had a close and very special relationship. That wasn't just because the team was doing well. It was because it was possible: everywhere we went, up and down the country, there'd be fans waiting for us when the coach pulled in, wanting a wave or a chat or an autograph. And we could do that. There were thousands of our fans in every away end, season after season. At Highbury, supporters would be clustered round the gate at the back of the Clock End. You'd get to know faces. You'd even get to know names. I was local, too, living in Islington. The relationship with the fans was personal in a way that the profile of modern Premier League football has made more difficult. We had freedom, socially. The fans were more than just an anonymous crowd.

I used to go out with the Arsenal boys, but usually ducked away before the drinking got serious. Their idea of a night out wasn't really mine and, for sure, they wouldn't have wanted to go to the places I did: clubs where they played good R&B and Lovers Rock and I could dance, make new friends and enjoy the scenery. I'd go out in the evening around London and be able to enjoy myself, without getting hassled and without having to worry about camera phones or social media. I could go for a drink at Browns in Covent Garden, or to see a band at the Jazz Café in Camden, or to dance on a Wednesday night at the Café de Paris in Leicester Square. I'd go and have dinner at Dover Street Wine Bar in Mayfair, where the owner, George, would always make sure I got looked after. Anywhere around town, you'd have a chat with supporters who recognised you, but that was always fine. There was never any aggravation. Footballers hadn't become movie stars yet, a process that only started with the Premiership rights being bought by Sky in 1992. I often wonder how the guys deal with the intensity of attention they get nowadays. Personally, I like to think I'd be able to cope!

I also got friendly with one or two people from *EastEnders*, who were Arsenal fans. That was the big TV show at the time: only four channels meant 20 million people used to watch every episode. The actors were household names. I ended up helping them out, coaching the charity team they'd started: the Walford Boys Club. They played all over the country and got big crowds turning up to watch on Sunday afternoons. There were stars like Nick Berry and Jason Watkins playing, one or two ex-pros, like Tony Kay who'd won the league with Everton back in the '60s, and some close friends, like Gary MacDonald, who'd gone into acting since we'd been youngsters playing Sunday football for Tamla together. With such a variation in their abilities, it was one of the hardest coaching assignments I've ever had! Discipline, on and off the pitch, wasn't the best. It was just fun for them. And maybe I took the challenge a little too seriously! The ones who listened weren't the better players; the better players felt they could go off and win matches on their own. The concept of football as a team game was one a few of the boys struggled to understand! But we did have some good times and raised a lot of money for charities. And I like to think I got the Walford Boys Club a little fitter, at least.

That summer, I had my testimonial: July 30th, 1991, against Celtic at Highbury. It marked 10 years plus as an Arsenal player. Before the days of Premier League wages, a testimonial counted for a lot in a player's career. Hope, along with a good friend, the businessman Harvey Sharpstone, and the rest of my committee did a fantastic job organising the six or seven big money-raising events during the season, including a dinner for 800 people at the Grosvenor Hotel in London. The testimonial year finished with the match against Celtic. All the events got a fantastic response from Arsenal fans, and I'll always be grateful for their support, during that season and throughout my career. The match got squeezed into the calendar a couple of months after we'd won the

League. Everyone who had a testimonial always wanted Celtic as the opposition because they brought down so many supporters. Liam Brady was the manager at Parkhead and, eventually, we managed to work out a date for the game.

It was such a fantastic night. It rained all day, but supporters still turned out. There was a crowd of around 35,000, and I remember the whole Clock End was green and white with fans who'd travelled down from Glasgow for the day. Charlie Nicholas was in the Celtic team and Arsenal fans loved seeing him back at Highbury. And, because it was just a couple of weeks before the new season started, George took the game seriously. He put out his best team, and Celtic did the same. It was a competitive game and finished 2-2. I had all my family there: Mum came, Sandra, all my nephews and nieces. Melissa, Dave Rocastle's daughter, and my sister's oldest boy, Anthony, were the mascots. So many people helped to make that testimonial year a success, and I'll always be grateful to Arsenal for granting it and finding a date for the game. Like I say, I'm happy I played when I did. Not many players are at a big club like Arsenal long enough to earn a testimonial.

During his first four or five years as Arsenal manager, you couldn't fault George Graham on recruitment. He brought in players from the lower divisions who nobody recognised, but who he knew he could improve and fit into his system. Even the big signings weren't superstars. I remember when we signed Alan Smith, my first reaction was to wonder why. *Wasn't Niall Quinn the same kind of centre-forward? Didn't he deserve a chance?* Quinny was sold to Manchester City and went on to have a very good career, but Smudge won titles and cups and Golden Boots with Arsenal, and you quickly understood what George had seen in him. Same with our goalkeeper: I thought John Lukic had done well for us. *Why were we buying David Seaman, summer of 1990?* To be fair, John left us and, later, won the league at Leeds. But training and playing with David, you realised how exceptional he was. George had been right. He knew what he was doing: 18 goals conceded in the league in '90/91 told its own story.

Seaman and Smith on the one hand; Grovesy, Lee Dixon, Nigel Winterburn, Steve Bould, Andy Linighan on the other. You thought you knew the kind of players George signed. Most of them had long Arsenal careers, too. But in the autumn of 1991, the manager broke the mould. Broke Arsenal's transfer record, too. We signed Ian Wright, in the days when £2.5 million was a lot of money in football. Wrighty was already an England international, already a star. And he was about as close as you'd ever get to a sure thing when it came to guaranteed goals. George knew he wanted Ian. He kept pushing until the transfer happened, and then managed him really well once he arrived.

Wrighty was like a force of nature. He scored on his debut at Leicester in the League Cup. It's one of my favourite photos: me, Rocky, Michael and Ian celebrating his goal at Filbert Street. In that zig-zag yellow and blue away kit. Then, come the weekend, away to Southampton, he got a hat-trick in his first Arsenal game in the league. Before he came to Arsenal, I'd never met Wrighty. He reminded me a bit of how Charlie Nicholas had been when he first arrived. The big difference was that Wrighty started scoring straight away. From the first training session, you could see this was a guy who just lived to score goals. Arsenal? He was up for the challenge.

Ian gave us pace, directness, finishing ability. He brought with him a personality and a vibrancy the club had not had for a long time. There was nobody like him around the place. Before almost every game, Ian and I would have a quick chat. He'd remind me and Anders Limpar: *Put your passes in behind the opposition's defence. And I'll do the rest!* Often my first look up, before I'd even received the ball, would be to check where Ian was. *Can I get him in with the right weight of pass at the right time? Sometimes I wouldn't even need to look.* I remember games when we were losing at half-time, and things weren't going well. After George had given the team his directions for the second half, Ian would shout: *Get the ball to me, in behind, and I'll guarantee us a goal.* And he usually delivered. Wrighty had complete self-belief.

We had some strong characters and personalities in the dressing room. Many of us had come up through Arsenal's youth system. We had the club's DNA in us. But Wrighty came in fresh, an explosion of energy. Our supporters loved him: not just for his goals, but for the way he involved them in his celebrations. He took no time to settle in. *This is me, guys. Love me or loathe me. I'll score goals and win football matches!* The way we played changed almost immediately: Ian was so direct, so determined, so quick. We were looking for him all the time, and the other strikers suffered a bit. Before he arrived, most of our goals came from crosses. Fewer of those meant Alan Smith's goal supply dried up a little. Kevin Campbell was doing well, but was still young and new to the team. I felt Kevin was a little overawed by Ian's personality and that affected his game at times, which was to be expected. Ian had come late to professional football. He had no time to waste and wanted to grab his opportunity with both hands.

Ian and I are so different in our personalities. By nature, I'm a quiet person. Ian's the opposite. There were times, I'm sure, we got on each other's nerves, but we managed to make it work. Ian would come into the dressing room, shouting and being dramatic about something. I'd be thinking: *Wrighty, can you just give us some peace and quiet for one minute, please?* At the same time, I'm sure my personality annoyed him at times: *Davo! Why haven't you got the same energy for this? What's the matter with you?* Most teams are made up of a variety of personalities, all needing something different. Add to that the complex emotions and the pressure which are part of the game. Great teams and managers harness those different personalities and abilities, finding ways to connect them for the common cause: winning games of football for the club. When Ian was having a great time, scoring goals and enjoying the adulation, he wanted everybody to be feeling the same. When things got difficult for me with George later, though, Ian appeared oblivious to what I was going through. But then he wasn't there to be my therapist, was he?

Ian didn't sign in time to be registered, but winning the league meant Arsenal went into the European Cup in '91/92. It was the first season English clubs were allowed to play in Europe after the Heysel Disaster in 1985. David O'Leary and I were the only ones who'd ever been there before with Arsenal: we were both in the team that got properly beaten by Spartak Moscow, 5-2 at Highbury, in the UEFA Cup in '82/83. Our only experience since had been in pre-season tournaments, like the Makita Trophy at Wembley. Those were friendlies, but made me feel my game might be suited to that style of football: everybody comfortable on the ball, passing and possession rather than running around and jumping into tackles all the time. I regret those six years when English clubs were banned from Europe. We were in our prime, but couldn't play because of the violent behaviour of some English fans during the '70s and '80s.

Arsenal had only ever played once before in the European Cup and that had been 20 years previously, when George Graham was still a player at the club. So it was something special. There were two knockout rounds that season, and then a group stage, which guaranteed six more games and a lot of revenue for the club. We were all looking forward to a different kind of challenge. I think George was looking forward to it more than anyone. He loved the tactical side and wanted to play against all these different systems. First game, we beat Austria Vienna 6-1 at Highbury. Smudge scored a hat-trick, and we thought we were going to be alright in this company. We lost the second leg, but that didn't matter. We were through and the papers were talking us up. We fancied our chances, too.

Next round, though, we drew Benfica. They were a good team, managed by Sven-Göran Eriksson. The first leg was in Lisbon, in the old Estadio da Luz: a big, open bowl with a 120,000 capacity. I'd never played anywhere like it before. The atmosphere was incredible leading up to kick-off and even louder after they took the lead. Benfica gave us a bit of a chasing: they had a Brazilian attacking midfielder, Isaías, who scored and was running the game. They were so good at keeping possession. We probably got taken by surprise. Kevin Campbell equalised but, at half-time, George told me to go man-to-man on Isaías, their most influential player. I hated being told to man-mark an opponent. Basically, you're being told he's better than you, and that the best you can do is follow him around and stop him playing. I always felt I had more to offer than that. But, second half, Isaías didn't get on the ball as often. We were comfortable and good for the 1-1.

The atmosphere at Highbury for the second leg was special, too. Everyone thought we'd done the hard work, that Benfica wouldn't be as good away from home. We tried to blitz them, and Colin Pates scored, but they came back and beat us 3-1 after extra time. Isaías got a couple of goals out of nothing. He looked like some player. Even during the game, I caught myself thinking: *These are playing the game in a completely different way.* You'd have to say they were better than us and deserved to win, but it was a massively disappointing night. We'd been looking forward to Europe so much and, just in that half hour of extra time, we got bundled out. It was a very flat dressing room afterwards, and I think that defeat changed how George approached our big games from then on.

In hindsight, the Benfica defeat was a turning point in my

relationship with George, too. We played this rigid 4-4-2, getting it forward quickly, and our central midfielders really being two extra defenders, looking after the back four, and getting onto second balls. I'd spoken to him about it. He knew I wasn't comfortable with how we were playing and what he was asking me to do. I don't think he liked that I'd said as much to his face. Around the same time, after being pretty much ever-present since the start of the previous season, I was dropped after that Benfica defeat and I didn't take it very well.

We'd had an amazing few years under George, but there were issues around bonuses and contracts, which didn't just affect me. I thought the club – and the manager – were taking us for granted, despite the fact we'd won two titles. It felt to me that George was looking after himself. I believed we should all be rewarded for our success. I wasn't prepared to accept the situation and made my feelings known. Of course, a manager can do whatever he thinks is best: drop players, manipulate situations, be straightforward and honest, have some integrity or otherwise. My relationship with George changed. I felt the club had given him too much power and control, I suppose because he had brought success back to the club so quickly. By now, they were letting him do pretty much what he wanted. Looking back now, maybe it all started with things being said publicly which would, under normal circumstances, have been better kept private.

My frustration got to a point where I did a piece with a newspaper in December 1991, explaining my situation: I resented being left on the sidelines and the way I was being treated. That blew our relationship apart. George had always hated stuff being out there in public. He started leaving me out without any regard for me as a person or as an experienced professional. George was in a position to decide how things developed from there. I'd lost much of the respect I had for him. I didn't feel I could speak to him, obviously. Instead, he unceremoniously discarded me from the first-team set-up. Second half of the season, I didn't play once. I wasn't involved at all. To make matters worse, George sent me to train with the youth team. I was no longer part of his plans.

I wasn't the only player having a problem. Michael Thomas, like me, had been unhappy with what was expected from Arsenal's central midfielders. He had his own run-ins with George, too, around being pressured to play when he was carrying injuries. While I got sent off to train with the youth team at Colney, Michael got sold to Liverpool for £1.5 million. Probably a coincidence, but that was what people said it cost the club being knocked out of the European Cup. I felt disappointed about Michael leaving, of course: he was another South London boy who'd come up through the ranks, who'd made his mark on Arsenal history, only to be kicked into touch by George without any kind of explanation, public or private. It was so bad for Michael, though, that I think he was happy to go. By the turn of the year, I'd asked to leave Arsenal, too.

Once things turned sour with George, I wasn't surprised by how he dealt with me: I was completely isolated. I'd seen it before. He'd done the same to player like Graham Rix, who he either felt he needed to make an example of or who he wanted out of the club. So, I was expecting a similar backlash. What shocked me, though, was how long the stand-off lasted. And how much it hurt. A grudge that's carried for the best part of a season and a half? That was on another level. Although George told the papers, whenever they asked, that I was out because of an injury, I was fit the whole time. Didn't miss a training session with the kids. I always kept myself available for selection.

I always had a feeling with George that, although you had to respect him as the boss, he managed us all by fear. During those months I was away from everything to do with the first team, my mind went back more than once to a conversation I'd had with Andy Cole a few years before. George had asked me to talk to Andy. He couldn't get through to him at all. *Just get him to listen, Davo.* So, I sat down with Andy. *The manager is what he is. He won't change. Just play the game. Don't make how you feel about him so obvious. That'll only work against you.* But Andy wasn't having any of it. He thought, even at 17, that he should be in the team and that George didn't treat him with any respect. Andy went on to have an amazing career. Unfortunately, it wasn't at Arsenal. He believed in himself and knew how he wanted to be treated. Andy had a very determined streak, an unshakeable self-respect, which I've always admired him for. George's loss was, eventually, Sir Alex Ferguson's gain.

I have that same sense of self-respect I saw in Andy. Something in our culture, maybe: you've seen and had to put up with a lot, one way or the other, and there comes a point at which you run out of ways to channel your frustration and deal with your pain. Enough is enough. You explode. George Graham, for his part, wasn't ever one to back down. You can argue the rights and wrongs of it. Either way, I'm still convinced George's treatment of me was completely out of proportion. I didn't like the way he wanted me to play, or the way he treated me as a person. What left the bitterest taste, though, was that George did his best to turn Arsenal supporters against me. I wasn't playing, and there didn't seem to be any likelihood of me getting a game. Neither of us were talking to each other. I took the heart-breaking decision to ask Arsenal for a transfer. I could not see another way out. I wrote a note and then hand-delivered it to George personally. He said he'd put my request to the board of directors. But then he told the press that I was only asking to leave now that I'd picked up the money from my testimonial. That wasn't the case, of course. And he knew it. The suggestion hurt: it was George's way of making life as difficult as possible for me.

I was lucky – grateful – in one respect. I think the supporters weren't that happy about the way we were playing. And I think they had a good enough idea of my character and personality to know that what George was saying about me wasn't true. They'd been watching me represent their club – my club – for ten years now. I didn't have Arsenal fans giving me a hard time about my battle with George. They just wanted a winning team and couldn't understand why I was out in the cold. George and I were too stubborn to sit down and try to sort it out together. He had his way of dealing with players like me. *Forget him. The rest of us will just get on with it.* In the meantime, over on the youth pitches, I'd try to find the motivation to give my all in every session and to help the younger players.

I had nothing to do with the first team for months. I didn't train with them, wasn't part of meetings, didn't travel to games and, obviously, didn't play. The only contact I had with my team-mates was at London Colney. Weird: I still changed in the first-team dressing room. But, when we went out to work, I'd walk over to the youth-team pitches, while the lads trained elsewhere. That made the situation even worse. It was a daily reminder of how isolated I was. I needed someone to show some empathy or understanding. It was tough, psychologically, week after week, month after month. I had no idea how long it was going to go on. George had all the power which, by definition, left me with none. I didn't feel I could do anything to change the situation.

I was a senior player at Arsenal, nearly 30 years old. Only David O'Leary had been there longer. I knew I should still have a role in the team, but George did anything and everything he could to avoid having me involved. He pushed Dave Hillier on before he was ready to carry that responsibility; he played Rocky in central midfield; looked to rush youngsters like Steve Morrow and Ian Selley into the first team. I knew how this was running when, despite injuries to other players, George preferred to play David O'Leary and Colin Pates ahead of me in my position. That was painful. We lost to Wrexham in the FA Cup, a low for the manager and for the club. It seemed as if George would rather the team suffered than for people to catch any sign of weakness in him. Wanting to punish me – and refusing to back down – had become important out of all proportion. George was cutting off his nose to spite his face. I suffered. He suffered. And Arsenal did, too.

By the end of '91/92, it felt like things had changed around the club. I'd been isolated for the previous six months. Michael Thomas had been sold. And then, that summer, George let Dave Rocastle leave. That was a huge shock to all of us. Rocky represented so much of what the club was about. He was absolutely adored by our supporters. He'd played almost every game that season and had this fantastic relationship with Wrighty, on and off the pitch. Then, all of a sudden: *By the way, David's going to Leeds.* None of us had any idea the transfer was in the air. It came as a complete surprise to Dave, too, that the club didn't want him. I saw him in the car park at Colney after training, and he was holding back tears. *It looks like I'm leaving, Pops.*

David never wanted to go, but he had no option but to agree personal terms with Leeds. He had a knee injury and there were rumours, later, that was the reason Arsenal sold him. It was tough for David. All he'd ever wanted to do was play for Arsenal, even more so now Ian was at the club. So, I was training with the kids. Michael and David had been moved on. George brought in a couple of new players besides Wrighty: two Scandinavians, Pål Lydersen and John Jensen. Even though he signed John as my direct replacement, George still wouldn't agree to let me go. In hindsight, I wonder if those months were when the interests of the club and the interests of the manager started getting confused. The Lydersen and Jensen transfers, after all, ended up costing George Graham his job.

93

Last game of '91/92 was against Southampton at Highbury. I watched standing up, on one of the corners of the North Bank: they were pulling the old terrace down straight after the game, the end of an era. During the summer, Hope and I moved out of Islington and up to Hadley Wood. That was the start of something new. With me and George, though? Nothing had changed. I did some pre-season training at Colney but, when it came to pre-season games, I was left behind to play for the reserves. I didn't know whether there was a way back in for me or whether, eventually, he was planning to move me on. There was nothing I could do but wait it out. Either way, I decided I needed to stay fit and be ready for whatever came next.

We were poor in the league that season and finished tenth, the lowest we'd been for a very long time. We were just defending and hoping for the best. Getting the ball up to Wrighty and seeing if he could nick us something. The supporters weren't impressed and the atmosphere at Highbury wasn't helped by there being a mural where the North Bank had been, which had to be repainted, I remember, when someone pointed out that every single supporter on it was white. I didn't notice that until it was mentioned. But, once it was pointed out, it got me thinking. I'm pretty sure whoever painted that mural didn't make a decision to leave out black faces. It just never occurred to the painter or the designer to include them, which was the result of us all living in a 'white' environment. It was what we now know as unconscious bias. The more aware of it I became, the more I started to notice it. Anyway, Arsenal were building a new stand behind the mural all through '92/93.

For the first seven months of the season, I was looking on, knowing I could have helped and knowing I was ready to. It was a miserable time. Leaving me out now felt like the manager was intent on proving a point at the expense of everything else. Spring of 1993, though, my world got turned on its head again. I ended up playing 11 games for Arsenal between then and the end of the season. I wasn't on the losing side in any of them. And three of those games, as it turned out, were cup finals. The first week of March, we were away to Norwich. On the Monday, I was training with the youth team as usual. Out of the corner of my eye, I saw Stewart Houston, George's assistant, walking towards the pitch we were working on. Stewart started calling my name, gesturing to me to come over. Pat Rice was looking after our session, and he waved me off. Stewart said: *The manager wants you to join in with us now.* So, I followed Stewart across and trained with the first team for the rest of the morning.

That was it. I was in the team a couple of days later. Completely out of the blue, not a word said to explain what had been going on or what had changed. It was as if the previous 15 months hadn't happened. I joined the session, and it was just George going over the preparations for Norwich, as if all this was a normal thing after he'd spent so many months trying to grind me down. I'd got to a point where I'd stopped thinking about being involved with the first team ever again. I still don't know what changed George's mind. Players out injured? His team getting criticised by the supporters? Or, with us still in the League Cup and the FA Cup, was he aware there was still plenty to play for that season? Maybe he just decided I'd been 'punished' enough. I'll never know why I got back in when I did. Anyway, I played that Wednesday evening. We drew 1-1 at Carrow Road.

The next couple of months were quite eventful. The Saturday after Norwich, I played in the sixth round of the FA Cup at Ipswich and then, the following Wednesday, in the second leg of the League Cup semi-final at home to Palace. We won both, which meant we had a couple of visits to Wembley to look forward to. I didn't play against Spurs when Tony scored the winner in the semi-final, but started the League Cup Final, the FA Cup Final and the FA Cup Final replay. I was happy to be back. Confused, but happy. George said nothing. I said nothing. Maybe you could look at it and say neither of us had lost face. I just got my head down and played. Even though the football wasn't great, people still remember '92/93, the first time any team won both domestic cups in the same season.

Maybe George and I will get the chance to talk it all out one day. Maybe I should make sure that happens. It does feel like unfinished business. I'd like to ask: *Why?* Those 15 months out in the cold, I really suffered. But we'd had three or four good years before the relationship started to fall apart. As a club, we had some good times afterwards, too, even if things couldn't ever be the same between me and George. I was still being asked to do the same job for the team, but there was a lot of chopping and changing, as if the manager was looking for something that worked. But everything I won in football, I won while George was at Arsenal. It's also a fact that George didn't win anything at Highbury – two League titles, two League Cups, an FA Cup and a Cup Winners' Cup – without me in his team. I was at the club when he arrived, and

I was still there when he left. It was an important and very successful time for Arsenal. And George and I were wrapped up in it together from start to finish. Because of George's vindictiveness, though, my career was probably short of at least 60 games. I still think about that even now.

At the end of '92/93, I was back playing and that was the most important thing for me. All I've ever wanted to do is play and enjoy my football, even if – as a professional – the fun can sometimes get lost in worrying about winning and getting the next contract. That season was just about the trophies. The manager and I were done arguing now, but it had all become very serious, straight-faced, around the club by then. George had always been hard on us. In the early days, Theo Foley was his assistant. Theo was a funny guy and knew how to take the tension out of situations, the only person I've met who could somehow be involved in two or three conversations at the same time! He was particularly good with the younger players, but didn't come back to the club the summer after we won at Anfield. Stewart Houston replaced him. None of us ever knew why that happened. Stewart was quieter, more serious, and didn't get close to the players in the way Theo had.

Behind the scenes, a lot of the players recognised that Gary Lewin played an important role in what we were trying to achieve together. He genuinely put our well-being at the forefront of everything he did. He was a bit like glue, holding us together in ways we never knew about in detail. He was great at his job, of course, and ahead of his time. But Gary was never just the physio. When players had issues away from the club, personal problems or situations which got out of hand, he'd be the one who made sure things got fixed. He needed to because there would often be medical implications, but he was always completely discreet. He looked after us. I spent a lot of time with Gary while I was out injured. He was a really important part of Arsenal's success.

By the time I was brought back into the team, something seemed to have changed within the squad. George had made a few signings that weren't working. But we were playing in finals at Wembley, and those didn't come round all that often. I wanted to enjoy the occasions. All that mattered in those games was that we won. Nowadays, particularly at the bigger clubs, there's a demand on players to entertain, too. In '93, I put any doubts I had about the manager and where he was taking the club to the back of my mind. We beat Sheffield Wednesday in the League Cup final and then beat them again, after a replay, in the FA Cup. There wasn't anything memorable about those finals as games of football. It still felt good winning, of course, but there wasn't the same kind of excitement or joy as there had been at Wembley in '87, just after George arrived.

The following season, I was in and out of the team in the league. Maybe George was saving my legs or looking for a way to not have to rely on me. I know how desperate he was to make a mark in the Cup Winner's Cup, though. Arsenal had only ever won one European trophy, and that had been a long time ago: George was in the team when we beat Anderlecht in the old Fairs Cup in 1970. 1993/94 finished in Copenhagen, and I played almost every minute of every game on the way to that final. I felt like I wanted to play all the time and there was never any explanation, from one week to the next, why I was being left out for league matches so often. Maybe George had a plan for me and for Arsenal that season. If he did, it might have been good if he'd told me what it was! Instead, it hurt every time I was left out of the team. I'd want to know why but never got any more from George than: *Paul, I feel this is the team to win this particular game.*

We did play differently in Europe that season, with three in midfield, five when we didn't have the ball. It worked: we beat some good teams on the way to the final, like PSG with George Weah and David Ginola in the semis. Those Cup Winners' Cup games were great to be a part of. Flying out of Luton or Stanstead the day before, travelling to grounds we'd never been to, the different atmospheres and the challenge of facing different players and styles of play. I enjoyed training in those empty stadiums the night before games, too. However well George prepared us, we never knew quite what to expect. We went to Liege and won 7-0, which wasn't what we were doing to anybody. None of us had experienced a run like this in Europe. It was exciting for the players, exciting for the club. You forgot how we were struggling at home in the league. George loved those games, too. He was a different man on European nights that season.

By the time we got to the final in Copenhagen, though, we had so many injuries. Experienced players like John Jensen, Martin Keown and Dave Hillier were out. And Wrighty was missing through suspension. Things weren't looking good. We'd been all set up to keep clean sheets and for Ian to get us a goal. '93/94 was when that *1-0 to the Arsenal* song started. Now, everybody was wondering what kind of team we were going to be able to put out for the biggest game of the season. I'll be honest: when we flew out to Denmark, it was hard to fancy us getting any kind of result. Parma had a team full of great players: half the Italian national team, plus Faustino Asprilla and Tomas Brolin. And we were scratching around for a starting eleven. I'd been more confident about us beating Liverpool at Anfield back in 1989.

The one thing we did have going for us that night was our supporters. One end was full of Arsenal, and all the Danish fans were supporting us, too, because of John Jensen. There were hardly any Parma supporters. When we came out for the warm-up and saw red and white everywhere around the Parken Stadium, that gave all of us a lift. We needed it. Steve Morrow, Ian Selley and I were in midfield. I felt an enormous amount of responsibility that night to try and support the younger players. The first quarter of an hour, I don't think any of us touched the ball, except in tackles: Parma should have been two or three up. They were making chances, playing their football, shots flying wide, Dave Seaman tipping others over the bar. Parma blitzed us: I couldn't get my breath and felt like I was second to almost every ball. I remember thinking, though, that if we could get past this first 20 minutes, we might have a chance of clawing ourselves back into the game. We kept our shape, dug in as a team, and managed to get a foothold.

We had the goalie and the back four. And massive credit should go to Steve and Ian, too. They were young, but they didn't buckle. The two of them stuck to their jobs the whole 90-plus minutes. They were brave and they were incredibly disciplined. The whole team was. We'd learned how to hang on and survive when we were getting outplayed in games. If one of those early chances had gone in for Parma, I'm not sure we'd have had the firepower to score two or three goals to win the game. But they didn't. We started seeing a bit of the ball and Kevin Campbell had a couple of chances before Alan Smith scored. Then, for the next 70 minutes, we showed all the characteristics of a George Graham team: organisation, cama-raderie and desire. A goal ahead, the midfield set up to protect the back four, and everyone doing their job. Beating a team that we all knew, man for man, was probably better than us.

What Parma didn't have was thousands of Arsenal supporters singing from start to finish. Our fans played their own part in the victory that night. The football we played those last couple of seasons under George wasn't very special. But Copenhagen was a very special night. After being presented with the trophy and our medals, I remember going over to our supporters and celebrating with them for a long time. I couldn't make out any single person up in the stand: just this sea of happy faces and countless Arsenal scarves and banners. The whole squad was on the pitch, like we had been after winning at Anfield, jumping all over each other, delirious with joy.

And it carried on down in the dressing room, like it had at Anfield. The directors, and Dennis Hill-Wood and David Dein, the whole squad, all of us together. With a few bottles of champagne. I remember just sitting there for a while, looking at my medal, socks rolled down to my ankles – boots off, shirt off, shattered! – thinking about the game: *How the hell did we manage to win that?* We'd stuck together, dug deep, made it difficult for Parma. *But really, how did we win it?* And then: *Who cares, though? We did it. Now, where's the party?* We started singing *1-0 to the Arsenal, 1-0 to the Arsenal,* the song that had followed us around Europe all season long.

That night was one nobody who was there will ever forget. I swapped shirts with Gianfranco Zola, who later achieved so much in English football with Chelsea. It's amazing just how small the shirt is, almost like a kid's size. But it represents a big memory for me. I've still got it tucked away – unwashed! – yellow with Zola's blue number 10 on the back. What I don't have, though, is the winner's medal I was given that night. Years later, I left it behind in a little wall safe, after we moved out of the family home in Barnet. By the time I realised it was missing and remembered where I'd left it, the house had been demolished.

I assumed that was the last I'd ever hear of it, imagining the medal must have been buried under rubble. Then, two and a half years later, I got a call from a number I didn't recognise. *Paul Davis? Yeah, I've got your Cup Winners' Cup medal.* I couldn't believe it. Then, there was a pause. *How much will you give me for it?* This guy wasn't re-uniting me with my medal. He was trying to sell it to me. I told him I didn't think that was right and that I wasn't prepared to pay anything. That was it. He hung up and I never heard from him again. I still wonder sometimes who's got that little gold disc, won on one of the very best nights of my football career.

95

The summer after Copenhagen, George signed Stefan Schwarz, who'd played for Benfica against us in the European Cup in 1991. Stefan was a Swedish international, a left-footed midfielder, and a very good player. And younger than me. Him arriving felt like a turning point. Stefan had obviously been bought to replace me. 1994/95, I hardly played. Stefan and John Jensen were the first-choice pairing. Ian Selley and Steve Morrow were getting more games than me. At a club like Arsenal, you were always looking over your shoulder anyway. You couldn't ever relax or feel too comfortable: there'd always be another player coming to challenge for your place. In the back of my mind, I still felt my thigh was an issue and maybe George was aware of that, too. My days at Arsenal were probably numbered. I wanted to see what would happen, whether there was still a place for me to fight for at Highbury.

What I'd never have imagined was that I'd still be at Arsenal at the end of the season, when my contract was up, but that George Graham wouldn't be. I suppose I was fearful of what was going to come next. *What happens after Arsenal?* Nobody mentioned the possibility of a new contract being offered and I was scared to ask, worried I'd get the answer I didn't want to hear. It was very unsettling. Arsenal had been my life, the life I'd dreamt about since I was a boy. And here I was, 34, and perhaps it was coming to an end. To be honest, it was a frightening prospect. But then rumours started to circulate in the press – just a few lines at first, but then big back-page headlines – about George having taken illegal payments from an agent to get players in at the club: John Jensen and Pål Lydersen.

In those days, overseas transfers were still quite unusual: a few months before, we'd won the Cup Winners' Cup with 10 English players and Steve Morrow, an Irishman, in the starting line-up. I had my own history with the manager, of course. George had been happy to accuse me of being greedy and letting the club down. I understood from my own experience the degree of control he had at every level at Arsenal. My instinct was that he'd be capable of doing what he was being accused of, whether you wanted to call the money that changed hands a bung or an 'unsolicited gift'. I was interested to know what the other players thought. Whether they felt loyal to the manager, or whether they were just naïve, I don't know. But all of them seemed to believe George's denials.

My thoughts on the situation were completely different. I believed the story right from the start. The whole business unfolded in the papers and on the TV news over the next couple of months, more evidence becoming public about what had gone on between George and a Norwegian agent, Rune Hauge. Arsenal sacked George, even before an FA inquiry found him guilty. There were always rumours that certain managers were taking illegal payments to make transfer deals happen. Maybe George was a scapegoat. But he got caught and was punished. None of it really surprised me, and I didn't have any sympathy for what I saw as greed, plain and simple. Whatever the details, this added up to stealing money from Arsenal.

As well as being sacked by Arsenal, George was banned from football by the FA for a year. George even gave the £425,000 back but, by then, the deed was done. He'd achieved great things for Arsenal, as a player and as a manager, and had made sure he was well-rewarded for our success. But George never looked after the players in terms of fighting for us to share in all that success financially. I felt strongly that was wrong, it lacked integrity and was mean-spirited. When Arsène Wenger arrived at the club, he looked at some of the homegrown players' contracts and started to change things. That was too late for me, though. I'd left Arsenal two years before Wenger arrived.

The club hadn't been in a good place when George came in as manager. In all honesty, it wasn't in a great place when he left. We were in the bottom half of the table. The core of George's success-ful team was still around, but the squad was also full of players who you couldn't work out why they were there. Glenn Helder arrived as a new signing the day before George was sacked. The players soon found out he was on a very good contract. That didn't go down too well: some clubs will always try their best to short-change homegrown players, but then overpay for a random signing who has no real connection with the team he's joining.

Stewart Houston was put in charge of the team. Pat Rice was moved up to work alongside him. Terry Burton, a very good coach who'd been at the club a long time, was also involved. Arsenal started looking for a new manager. We still had three or four months of the season ahead of us. My contract was then set to expire. If I'd been unsure about my situation before George was sacked, I had absolutely no idea now that he'd gone. I didn't even know who to talk to. Who'd be making decisions about contracts now? I wasn't playing – I didn't get included to travel to Paris for the Cup Winners' Cup final against Real Zaragoza – and that was maybe all I needed to know.

At the end of the season, we went on a seven-day tour to China, the kind of commercial enterprise most of the bigger clubs had begun doing. I used to enjoy those trips, but this one was different: I felt low, anxious and unsure about where I stood. Instinct told me this would be my last trip with Arsenal. I sensed my time at the club was probably over, even if I didn't want to hear that said out loud. All through my career, I'd been conscious – at some level – that this day would come. I thought I'd prepared myself for it. When it came, though, the harsh emotional reality was that I wasn't prepared enough.

I actually played a couple of times in China but, when we were getting ready to leave the hotel to fly home, I got a telephone call: Stewart wanted to see me and asked if I would meet him in his room. As I walked along the corridor, I remember thinking: *This is it.* As soon as he let me in, Stewart confirmed it: *I'm sorry, Paul. The club won't be renewing your contract.* If he said anything else, I don't remember hearing it. I just remember feeling lost, feeling empty. Over 20 years since I'd been a quiet, nervous 12-year-old schoolboy arriving at Highbury for the first time. The club had been my life and I didn't know anything else. I was 34 and, even away from football, life wasn't in a good place at the time. And now this.

The flight back to Heathrow was horrible. I couldn't sleep. I didn't feel like I could talk to anyone. The rest of the lads were in party mood, they were having a great time. The season was over and they were having a few beers and enjoying a laugh and a joke, looking forward to their summer holidays. I sat on my own, pretending to be asleep, hiding tears that had started rolling down my cheeks. There were lots of questions racing through my mind. But one big one: *What happens now? After Arsenal?* Once we landed, players started heading off in different directions. Not everyone was taking the team bus back to the training ground. There were only eight or nine of us on it, going to Colney to pick up our cars.

I still hadn't spoken to anyone, and I don't think anyone had noticed how I was feeling. Feelings, anyway, are something which, as a sportsperson, you often believe you have to push to one side in order to get to the top. I've seen that in myself and in others. But, as we drove round the M25, it crossed my mind that I wasn't going to see these guys again. Not as a team-mate, anyway. *I'd better say something, hadn't I?* Just before we got to the training ground, I stood up at the front of the bus: *Lads, can I have a minute, please?* The laughter and high spirits settled down. Instead, there was silence. I was fighting back tears. *I thought I should tell you that I won't be here with you next season. My contract isn't being renewed. I just wanted you to know.* And that was it. Nobody said anything. Probably, nobody knew what to say. And then we were back at London Colney, and everyone was off in their cars: like always, it looked like a scene out of *Wacky Races.*

I got off the bus and looked around. And I saw home. Those pitches; those changing rooms; the canteen and the medical room. *All done.* I was aware I was seeing this place, as an Arsenal player, for the very last time. The players and staff I'd worked with were ghosts now, weren't they? They were history. And it was hard not to feel like I was history, too: so much of who I was had been tied up for so long with those people and these places. At the end of each season, everyone would go their separate ways. The club would then write to you after a few days, informing you when you needed to report back for training. What weight you should be on the first day of pre-season. The schedule the manager had planned. Driving home – of all the things to dwell on – I felt heartbroken that I wouldn't be getting one of those letters ever again. My career at the Arsenal was over.

Over the weeks that followed, life at home came under strain as I began trying to adjust to having finished at Highbury. I spoke to Harvey Sharpstone, who'd helped me with my testimonial, and asked if he could help me again now with finding another club. Harvey had contacts with a few clubs and very soon told me he'd spoken to a small second division Norwegian side, Stabæk, who were based outside Oslo. The season in Norway was about to start because, in Scandinavia, football shuts down for most of the winter. Before I knew it, I was there, feeling like I was back in Sweden. Stabæk reminded me a lot of Eskilstuna: the peace and quiet, the landscape, the personality of the people. I'm not sure what they were expecting from me. Or vice versa. I guess it was a trial for both of us. The idea was I'd be there for a month or two and we'd see where we were. I trained with the team and even played a game or two, but I think everybody realised quite quickly it wouldn't work out.

I flew back to London, knowing I needed to clear my head before I decided what to do next. I'd gone to Norway because my nature has always been to move forward, to take the next thing on. If nothing else, those few weeks gave me some football but, in all honesty, I wasn't in a good state, mentally or physically. No disrespect to the club: they were giving me an opportunity. But, in my head, I was thinking: *From Arsenal to Stabæk? How did that happen?* It didn't make me feel any better when it became clear that they'd been expecting more from me and were prepared to let me return to England. I wrote letters to a few clubs, letting them know I was available. I didn't have an agent and, anyway, thought it gave a better impression if the contact came directly from me.

Two clubs were keen: Southampton, who'd actually finished above Arsenal in the season just gone, and Brentford, who were in the Second Division – what's now the Championship – and had just been beaten in the play-off semi-finals. While I'd been in Norway, I'd realised I didn't want to leave London. Hope and I had a young son – Du'aine was maybe a year old – and I wanted to be around for him. I knew from experience what it was like not having a dad there, and I wanted to do everything I could to make sure it wasn't the same for my children. Every son needs his father, but black boys in particular, need that support, because of the extra challenges society's going to put in their way. I knew that for fact.

I went across to Griffin Park to speak to the Brentford manager, Dave Webb. He explained what he wanted from me and his vision for how he wanted the club to develop. He said he needed an experienced head in midfield to control the pace of games, and to help introduce a more possession-based approach. *You've been at Arsenal. You'll be able to guide the younger players.* I'll be honest: I really liked the sound of it, liked the fact that Dave had a plan for me and the team. And I liked the club. Brentford were rooted in their local community. This wasn't a club with Arsenal's status, of course, but they were ambitious and people around the place were great with me. *You're just the sort of player we're after.* I agreed a two-year contract pretty much there and then.

I was excited by the challenge. I turned up for pre-season training. Arsenal was all I'd ever known. I'd never had to take my own kit home before and get it washed and ready for the following day. Naturally, the stadium and the training ground weren't what I was used to, and the drive around the North Circular was a chore. I soon learnt I needed three hours in the morning to make sure I was on time for training. I didn't enjoy the commute, but at least I was getting home to see Du'aine every evening. It just took some adjusting to. I was the oldest professional at the club. There were some good players, but it was a very young team. In pre-season, all the work we were doing was around developing a new style for the club, a passing game. That's what Dave had signed me to help with. But once we got started in Division Two, results weren't great. Almost straight away, Dave announced that he wanted to scrap everything we'd been doing. *Forget all that. We just need to get the ball forward as quickly as we can.*

The plan had been for me to play in central midfield, as a focal point for building attacks. Once the manager decided we were going to play from back to front as quickly as we could, though, my position became redundant. Dave wanted young legs running around in the middle of the pitch. So, after half a dozen games, I was dropped from the team. And then dropped from the squad. I think Dave hoped I'd walk away from the club and the contract we'd agreed. I was frozen out: it was like the situation with George Graham all over again. I was thinking: *I really don't need this!* I was back training with the youth team, just a couple of months after signing a two-year deal. *Oh, no. Not again! I can't go through all this a second time.* I asked myself: *Why are you in this position again, Paul? Is it down to you?* But I dug my heels in. It was embarrassing. Even the kids I was training with were coming up to me and asking what was going on. *You're Paul Davis. You're Arsenal. How can the manager be treating you like this? It's not right!*

Later in my career, especially, it would have been good to have had an agent. Late '80s, early '90s, though, there weren't so many around, and I'd never really seen the need. All I wanted to do was play football. For Arsenal. I wasn't ever looking for sponsorships or commercial things on the side. As far as I was concerned, it was negotiating contracts and I could get a lawyer or an accountant to help. But I'm all in favour of agents as an idea. It's important that players are looked after and have someone on their side they can rely on. It would definitely have helped me at Arsenal during the stand-off with George Graham; and at Brentford, too, when Dave Webb decided he wanted me out. I've never been scared to fight my own battles, but maybe situations would have been handled differently if I'd had someone working on my behalf. An agent might have saved me some heartache.

I trained with the kids at Brentford for about seven months, every morning and some afternoons. I wasn't playing any games. Again,

I've no idea how I stuck it out. It was another terrible situation. I keep telling myself: *You've been here before, Paul. Don't lose your cool. That's just what he wants you to do.* I stayed until the end of the season, when we worked out a package that was fair to all parties. I'd found it difficult to adjust to a new club, but I'd done my best. At the same time, I understood that I wasn't able to give Dave Webb what he wanted from me, especially after he decided to go back to a long ball game.

It was a tough season for Brentford. They lost their top scorer, Nicky Forster, to an injury in October and were in a relegation scrap until the Spring. I got to know everybody at Griffin Park, though. Brentford was a very friendly, welcoming club. There were some good people there. A few years later, I ran into a lovely guy by the name of Peter Gilham – who's still at the club now, working as Player Welfare Manager – and he actually took it upon himself to apologise for how I was treated. Not that Peter had anything to do with what happened to me! I'm very happy to see how far the club has come now, in a new stadium and promoted to the Premier League.

Maybe everything that happened at Brentford was what I needed to push me into a decision. Summer of 1996, I decided that was it. I didn't want to take another step down through the divisions just to get myself a contract. I was tired, mind and body. Eighteen years of professional football had taken their toll. I was done. It was over. I felt my level of performance was a long way off what I was happy with. I had a reputation I wanted to try and protect. The after-effects of the thigh injury weren't going to get any better. I still sometimes wonder whether having the operation was a good idea. I look for it in players now, whenever I see someone coming back after a bad injury. *Are they struggling to adapt? Are they having to play within themselves? Do they look like they're worried about their game?* My experience is that it's a difficult process and not one that gets talked about much. In football, you're either supposed to be fit or you're not. The psychology of recovering from a serious injury isn't ever addressed.

I'd done my first coaching qualification when I was just 17 and coaching had always been on my mind for after I finished playing. When I was sent off to train with the kids at Arsenal by George Graham – and again at Brentford by Dave Webb – every session was part of a learning process for me, I think. I made sure I helped the young players whenever I could. The youth teams had their own coaches but, while we were out on the pitches, I felt as if it was part of my responsibility to support the boys I was training alongside. It was about trying to set the right example, by being professional in my behaviour, no matter how difficult things were for me personally at the time.

In '96, I knew I wanted to stay in the game, as a coach or a manager. I felt I'd had an outstanding football education, having worked and played with some of the best coaches and players of my generation. I'd already started on my qualifications. I'd taken an interest all through my playing career. So, getting a job coaching somewhere shouldn't be too difficult, right? At the same time, though, I was aware of what had happened to other black players, some of them after stellar careers. I was under no illusions about how difficult it would be to get a full-time coaching role. I was ready to do whatever was necessary, though, to carve out my opportunities.

But when I looked out across the landscape for black coaches – looking for a potential role model – things appeared bleak. It seemed like there was always an easy explanation. *Football is a level playing field. The best coaches will get to the top. Black players aren't interested in coaching. Football hasn't got an issue.* I listened to those things and even wanted to believe some of them but, deep down, I knew it was all BS. Some of it is the same BS that's still with us today. I realised then that I would have to recognise untruths and half-truths when I was being told them, recognise ignorance and a lack of awareness when I encountered them. The harder I looked, the more convinced I became that I was going to have to trust in my own impressions and my own experiences from now on.

96

My first visit to Jamaica, in 1987, had a huge impact on me. I'd never thought before about what that side of my family history might mean to me, but I felt a connection with the country and the people straight away. Meeting family was a part of it, I'm sure. Something in me felt a kind of belonging. Being there, experiencing it for myself, I got a very different sense of Jamaica and Jamaicans to the one I'd absorbed growing up. Sandra was always better at staying in touch with Tasman, Queenie and Constant, and she travelled back to Jamaica more often than I did. I'd met Hope in Jamaica, and she came over to London a year or so later and stayed. A few years after that, in the early '90s, my eldest step-brother, Tasman, was in London to visit. That was the one time any of them came over to England.

I used to see my step-siblings whenever I went to Jamaica with Hope to visit her family. And, by the mid-'90s, I had another big Caribbean plan to work on. Mum had got married. She and my step-dad, Rupert, were talking about a plan to retire and go back to Jamaica. That was always the dream for many of the Windrush generation. I felt drawn to Jamaica and I got involved in looking for a house over there. I was happy to buy somewhere for them to live, which could also be a holiday home for my family. I did the trip to house-hunt on my own, with Tasman driving me around when he wasn't at work. It felt like the right thing for Mum and, now I was finished as a footballer, like an adventure for me.

I found a place in Ocho Rios, a little harbour town on the north coast, 50 miles from Kingston. It was beautiful: surrounded by lush countryside and close to Dunn's River Falls, one of the island's big holiday attractions. Picture postcard stuff. The house was up in the mountains, an older three-bedroom bungalow with its own little swimming pool. You needed a car to get to it, and there were just a few other houses dotted around nearby. It was a lovely spot, looking out onto the Caribbean Sea. That was what did it: the view. I couldn't send pictures home, but Mum and Rupert knew the area and I told them all about it. I made the decision there and then that this property was the one. I agreed on a price and then the arrangements were made from back in London, juggling time differences and waiting for solicitors' letters to travel back and forth.

The whole process seemed to take a while but, in August 1996, I took ownership. The house was just waiting for Mum and Rupert to decide when they'd move. Except it suddenly went quiet at their end. They didn't seem too interested in talking about arrangements anymore. Mum finally got round to saying it: *Do you know, Paul, I'm not really feeling like I want to go back to Jamaica now.* An empty property waiting for her in Ocho Rios, but now she'd decided she didn't want to leave London, where she felt so at home. *Maybe you could have said something before now, Mum? I only bought it for you!* Rupert, though, still wanted to go. I think moving back to Jamaica was maybe his idea all along. And maybe Mum thought it was never going to happen. Now that it had, she'd made her decision.

Rupert went off and looked after the house for 18 months or so.

He got to know all the neighbours and had a good time, hanging on to see if Mum would change her mind. But she didn't. She was happy with her life in England, with church, her friends and her neighbours. Mum had retired from work and saw England as home. She had a gym membership, had started to learn to drive and announced one day that she was going to give up smoking: I never saw her with a cigarette ever again. I was still visiting her at Lansdowne Green most Sundays.

Then, Rupert had to come home to have medical treatment: the early stages of the cancer from which he eventually died in February 2000. So, the house was empty, and I decided the best thing would be to rent it out. The woman who took it was a presenter for a radio station, quite a well-known name locally. She was a good tenant for several years and there were no problems until I received a phone call to say she'd been held at gunpoint and robbed at the house. That was a huge shock and horrible for her, although she wasn't harmed physically. Nothing like it had ever happened in the neighbourhood before. She'd been targeted: whoever robbed her must have known exactly who she was.

I flew out immediately. My perfect tenant had left and, understandably, wasn't coming back. The house was empty again. The rental agency thought it'd be difficult to let after what had happened. It was obvious Mum had no intention of ever going home, especially on her own. She'd become quite pessimistic about Jamaica, fallen out of love with the country she'd grown up in. Maybe she'd left in '59 with an idealised picture of the island in her mind but then, while she was in England, all she ever heard was bad news coming out of the place. I knew that the bad news wasn't the whole picture when it came to what Jamaica was really like, but she wasn't convinced. So, I decided to sell up. I had to find an estate agent and solicitors who I could rely on.

I was on my own with it now. Tasman passed away, young, in

2005. He had multiple sclerosis and, by the end, couldn't walk. I remember visiting him in hospital and we travelled out for his funeral. All through the years I had the house in Ocho Rios, I didn't see much of Queenie. She seemed to be away in the US working most of the time. She'd left her kids in Jamaica and was sending money home like Mum had for her back in the day. There was a situation with her work permit and, if she had left the States, she wouldn't have been able to go back. When Queenie died, Mum and Sandra and I went out and made the arrangements. The funeral and cremation were in Florida, but we took Queenie's ashes back to Jamaica. She's alongside her brother, Tasman, now.

That leaves one stepbrother, Constant, who I've only ever seen if I was in Jamaica and went out to the countryside to find him. He and Sandra are still in touch, but I haven't spoken to Constant in a long while. Both Sandra and I have stepped back a little from our connections with relatives in Jamaica. Nobody used to say anything out loud, but there was always that expectation, with us being in the UK, that we should be looking after people back home, Sandra especially, because everybody knew her better. Car insurance, medical bills, that kind of thing. Coming to England was Mum's decision, but it felt almost as if her commitments were being passed on to us. Sandra still goes back to visit. Her partner, Patrick, was born in Jamaica and the two of them go to see his family. I've still got family there myself: Mum was one of eight children, so there'll be uncles and aunties and cousins. But I'd never got to know them, and the time for that maybe has passed. The sale of the house in Ocho Rios went through in 2012.

97

Hand car washes are everywhere now. You see one every few hundred yards around London. At all the big supermarkets, you can get your car washed while you're doing your shopping. But 25 years ago, they were a new thing. So, I had a plan to do something outside football: a mobile car wash business. Harvey Sharpstone liked the idea and helped. I went to talk to a few retail outlets: we'd offer their customers a car wash service while they went round the stores. The Galleria shopping centre in Hatfield were very interested and wanted us to do it in their car parks. I was pretty sure if we could make it work at one location, other places would buy into it. It wasn't easy, though. The real problem was finding reliable staff and then hanging onto them. I'd never really intended to be out washing people's cars myself, so the business depended on guys turning up every day for work.

While I was struggling with establishing the business – maybe I was a bit ahead of my time with that! – I wrote to David Dein about doing some coaching at Arsenal and Liam Brady got in touch. He'd just started back at the club, running the academy, and had taken on another ex-player, David Court, as his assistant. He'd seen my letter and wanted to know if I'd be interested in working with young players. I jumped at the opportunity. It hadn't been much more than a year since I'd left. I went in to meet Liam and he explained what he wanted. It was a part-time position, working with the younger age groups, under-12s and under-13s. Liam wasn't offering any kind of contract, and there wouldn't be much money. It was just a case of being paid by the session, £60 for a couple of hours, as I remember. But money wasn't what mattered. I was just grateful for what I hoped would be the start of a coaching career. I was happy to have a chance to be back at Arsenal, too. I believed I had something to offer the club and the players I'd be working with.

I started a few weeks later, the first former player of my generation to return as a coach. I was excited. I was at Highbury, early evenings, working with the under-12s on the Astro in the JVC indoor training centre, behind the Clock End: boys who were the same age as I'd been when I'd first arrived at the club in the 1970s. Like me, the players came in after school for sessions twice a week. I understood how they might be feeling. I was given that team to look after, which meant taking the boys for games every Sunday. I was surprised how far we travelled for some fixtures: Ipswich or Bristol seemed like a long way away for these lads. I was even more surprised one day when I was asked if I'd drive the minibus to a game. I wasn't sure at all. I didn't think I should be doing it, not least from the point of view of the safety of the players. I pushed back, and the club found someone else to drive.

I enjoyed the coaching and supporting the young players in their development. We took them away to tournaments, around England at first and then, later on, to places in Europe. Those were great experiences for the players themselves and for me, too. I was conscious of this having been where my journey began as a 12-year-old turning out for the Arsenal. But this was a different time. Everything was more structured, there were clearer processes in place. More than anything, this was an opportunity to help young players learn. And for me to learn, too. How much administrative work was involved came as a surprise, but I knew I had a chance to develop and started working towards the next level of qualifying as a coach.

I learned a lot from a guy named Roy Massey, who came in just after me and was responsible for all the coaching for the younger age groups. The overall programme was set out by the club, and Roy gave me some templates to work from, but I remember designing a lot of my own sessions, too. I had my own experiences to draw on, sessions I remembered from coaches I'd worked with. I found ways to adapt those now for younger players. I talked a lot to the more experienced coaches in the academy, like Neil Banfield and Steve Leonard. All that mattered was good ideas; it didn't matter where the ideas came from. I read books and coaching manuals, too. It was about digging up whatever I needed from session to session. I did a little media work, too, with TalkSport and BBC London: watching games and talking about games. It was all part of what I knew I wanted to do.

As well as taking training, the job meant getting to know the boys themselves and, with that, some of the parents, too. From very early on, I was involved in discussions about who'd be kept on and who'd be released. I'd sit in on the meetings with Roy and Liam and David Court, even though it wasn't me who was making the decisions. I had to meet parents four times a year and talk about their sons and how they were progressing. It was something else I had to learn: how best to communicate when there are so many emotions involved. The boys' emotions and their parents' emotions, too. I soon realised it was about finding a balance. I had to be aware of people's feelings but, at the same time, I needed to be as honest as I possibly could.

The other lesson I picked up very quickly was that every boy was an individual, with his own set of circumstances. One thing that stood out was how much more the club, the staff and the coaches knew about the young players they were working with. It was our business to find out as much as we could about what was going on in the rest of the players' lives. It made me think back to when I was a schoolboy at Arsenal. Although trainers and helpers like Alf Fields and Pat Wiskin would offer some guidance or encouragement, the club knew nothing about me, other than what they saw in training, in games and around the building. You'd call it pastoral care: that side of youth development has advanced so much.

So, part of my job as a youth coach was to identify what might be holding a young player back, or what might become a problem in the future. *How could I help them all develop as players?* In a single group, you might have one boy who was just bigger and stronger than his peers and so didn't work hard enough at the weaknesses in his game, which would become obvious once other boys caught up with him physically. You might have another whose mum or dad would want to tell us how we should be developing their son. *Why isn't my son playing this week? Why did you take him off? Why did you play him in that position?* To the point sometimes where the player himself might be embarrassed and end up leaving. You might have a boy with ability whose confidence was being undermined by his parents: his dad, perhaps, giving him a hard time on the way home after a game or a training session.

And then, in that same group, you might have an Ashley Cole or a David Bentley or a Fabrice Muamba: players most people could see had the potential to have good careers at Arsenal. Those boys had talent and, also, a single-minded determination to do whatever it took to make it as a professional. I wanted to help all the boys I worked with at Arsenal get as far as they could in football. They were growing up as young men as well as young players. That feeling of having played a small part in a boy's development is incredibly satisfying. I loved being able to help move a young player's career forward, however far the game might eventually take him. I was happy being able to stay in the game to do that. And grateful that I got the opportunity to start doing it at Arsenal so soon after I finished playing. At the time, it felt as if I'd come home. I wanted to stay with the club and become the best coach I could be.

My ambition was to be working, eventually, at the senior end of the club. Working with the youngsters at Arsenal made doing my qualifications much easier to organise. As you progress through the FA's qualifications, it's helpful to have a group of players to practise with. I qualified for my 'B' licence – 'B' for 'Basic' – within eight months of starting at Arsenal. The 'A' licence, though – 'A' for 'Advanced', the 'Full licence' as it was called back then – was more of a challenge. I had to go up to Lilleshall, where the FA's centre of excellence was based then, for two weeks. There were 40 of us from around the country, a mix of former players and people from different backgrounds, such as teaching: Bryan Robson was part of that cohort, Brendan Rodgers, too.

The 'A' licence course was 60 per cent practical and 40 per cent intensive theory work, which wasn't easy for someone who'd left school at 16 to play football and hadn't done anything remotely academic since. When it came to putting on practical sessions, everybody wanted the former players to be involved, so their work would look better in front of the FA assessors. People like me and Bryan ended up being asked to take part in everyone's sessions, helping to make sure they ran as smoothly as possible. There was a bit of pressure: everyone else was relying on us. At the end of the two weeks, I was physically and psychologically shattered.

Every morning, we had lectures. The course leader was the late Dick Bate, who was – and still is, 30 years later – recognised as one of our most respected and influential FA coach educators. If you were being taught and assessed by Dick, you knew you would be passing your course the hardest way. His lectures went into the most incredible detail. He'd be talking about Italian players, like Baresi and Costacurta, names from across Europe as well as in England, explaining how and why they played the way they did. He had statistics to back up every idea. I'd never been exposed to anything like this before. It was a residential course: we would start at eight every morning and usually finished at around eight in the evening. My head would be spinning at the end of each day.

After the two weeks at Lilleshall, we had to go away and keep practising a variety of different sessions. We had specific things to focus on. The 'A' licence material was for coaching 11 v 11 senior football and players, so I had to adapt and adjust my sessions to make them work for the under-12s I was coaching at Arsenal. A year later, we went back to Lilleshall for another week, to receive more training and, this time, to be assessed. We were each given two sessions to plan and deliver in front of our peers and the course tutors. One attacking session; one defensive session, each 45 minutes long, with some clear guidance as to what you needed to improve on in between the two sessions. And then you were assessed.

I can see now there were two elements to what we were doing. We were being taught what to coach: the content of our sessions, the ideas we needed to get across. But we were also being taught how to coach: the FA wanted us all to deliver in a very specific way. And that wasn't a method that sat particularly well with me. Sessions had to be very regimented and follow a set formula, which left very little room for the coach's own personality to come through, or for the players to put their own characteristics into the work we were asking them to do. Instead, it was about telling players what to do: the coach was, in the main, expected to be 'in command', extroverted, and loud. I wasn't very well-suited to that style of coaching. It was the norm back then, but it never felt right to me. I found it hard to study for those qualifications. If you didn't do everything in that very particular way, you weren't going to pass. No room for anything other than what was seen as the norm.

I failed my first attempt at getting the 'A'. Out of 42 of us, only two passed that year. It was tough failing, after all the work I'd put in. But the tutors were hard on most of us. The feedback was difficult to take. The assessors expected us, as learner coaches, to be able to demonstrate what we were doing, which wasn't easy for most of the guys who hadn't come from playing backgrounds. I was fine with showing players how to do things, but some of the other stuff didn't come so easily. We were assessed on planning, preparation, organisation, observation and communication, as well as the technical content of our session delivery. I was told that I needed to be louder. I didn't shout enough. Also, some of my technical content wasn't good enough. That disappointed me because I felt it should have been one of my stronger areas. I'd had nine years with George Graham, who was always so insistent on teaching players exactly the same stuff we were covering now on the course.

Whatever my misgivings about the 'A' licence, though, I've always been ready to put the work in. I've never wanted to cut corners or be given anything on a plate. I can't understand when I see players looking to do that with their courses now. I wanted Liam and Arsenal to know that I was serious about my future in coaching, too. I went back to Lilleshall the following year, better prepared, knowing exactly what the FA wanted to see, and I got my 'A' licence. I remember driving back to London feeling very proud. It hadn't been easy.

That was another time: the courses run by the FA now are very different and represent a different culture. In the '90s, you still had to learn coaching like you would learn your times' tables at junior school. Any of your own ideas, or any personal approach you wanted to bring to what you were doing, had to wait until after you'd got the qualification. The 'A' licence course taught me a lot, though: about organisation, structure and communication. I learnt that playing and coaching demand two different sets of skills, that having been a good player doesn't automatically make you a good coach. I knew I had to study and put in the hours to make a success of this new career. And I was definitely ready for that.

00

Around the time I was working towards my 'A' licence, I got involved with England and the FA for the first time. The Arsenal role was only part-time. I'd been back at the club for three years and was starting to get a little frustrated at what I saw happening – or not happening – in terms of my career progression. So, I looked for other opportunities to develop as a coach. I wrote to Howard Wilkinson, the FA's technical director. *Was there a way for me to get some experience in the England set-up?* Howard wrote back saying there wasn't anything suitable but that he'd get back in touch. He said he'd like to get young coaches like me involved if he could.

Howard was true to his word. I got invited to work as an assistant coach with the under-20s, who were managed by Martin Hunter. I did a few games with that group over the next couple of years. It was unpaid work but a fantastic experience. I needed to get that sense of developing as a coach, which I wasn't getting with the under-12s at Arsenal. With England, we took teams out to compete at the Toulon Tournament in France, playing against teams from around the world. I'd do a little on the training ground but, it was an opportunity to be with an England team, to get a feel for how it all worked at that level. The level of planning and preparation was incredibly high.

During that whole period, working at Arsenal and doing my licences, I was happy at first to be giving something back to football and finding my way after retirement. But I also became aware of the economic choices that came with coaching as a career. I went into coaching because I loved doing it and loved the game. That's why I jumped at the chance to go back to Arsenal. But, at some point, you have to think about whether you'll ever be able to make a living from it, working at the youth levels.

If you've got a mortgage to pay, coaching under-12s, even at a top club, isn't going to cover it. In fact, unless you're working around a senior team, very few coaching jobs are going to make financial sense. That's a big issue. *I love coaching; but can I afford to be a coach?* I'd already made my decision. I wanted coaching to be a career, not a hobby or voluntary work, not something I had to subsidise. I'd been a professional player and I wanted to be a professional coach. I felt strongly that, if given the opportunities, I had what I needed to make a success of it.

I had the impression that Liam, as head of the Academy, wasn't particularly interested in coaches' continuing development. The message was never: *Yes, go and get your FA qualifications. And yes, of course, we will fund you.* There wasn't that kind of encouragement or support being offered, which surprised me. We were looking after potential Arsenal players of the future. If we were trying to develop them properly, why wouldn't we be trying to develop our coaches, too? They certainly didn't push me in that direction, but I knew I wanted to do things the right way and get my qualifications, even if that meant paying for the courses myself. I was committed to improving as a coach, and so I made my own arrangements.

Liam's policy, developed with his assistant, David Court, was that coaches stayed with a group for two years. That meant I took boys from under-12s through to under-13s. I'd then hand the team on to the under-14s coach, before going back to start again with a new group. That was how the system worked, but I was aware that it wasn't really moving me forward. Even though it was a different group each time, I realised that, after a couple of those cycles, I was just on a treadmill as a coach.

I saw coaches being hired to look after older age groups who I wasn't convinced had anything more to offer than I did. I'd done my 'A' licence off my own back. I'd already done several years working with the younger groups. I'd had nothing but positive feedback from parents, players, and coaches from other clubs. Liam himself seemed happy with my work. Nevertheless, people were coming in at Arsenal who were far less qualified, had far less of an Arsenal affiliation, but were getting ahead straight away. *What was going on here?* I wasn't even getting interviewed for those jobs.

I started to get a sense that, no matter how well I was doing with the younger players, I wasn't going to be trusted with any of the older age groups, despite the good feedback I was getting. It felt like I had hit a ceiling. *We trust you with the younger age groups, but not with the older boys.* It was disheartening and frustrating. I believed wrong decisions were being made: wrong for me and wrong for our young players. I didn't know how to handle the situation. I remember it crossing my mind that this would have been a moment when drawing on a father's experience would have helped me. I needed someone to discuss my thoughts and feelings with, but had nobody around me who I thought might understand.

I didn't sulk, though. I just got on with it, waiting to see how things developed. At the end of each season, I'd ask for a meeting with Liam. He'd say everybody was happy with what I was doing. But there was never any mention of a pathway. Liam never talked about how he saw me being able to progress. I did make it clear in those conversations that my ambitions were to work with the senior groups, the under-17s and under-18s. I reminded him I'd been working part-time for five years. But there never appeared to be any kind of plan for me. My session fees went up from £40 to £100, which was above the average rate. Most coaches in similar roles at other clubs were earning £25 a session. The money, though, wasn't the point.

The oldest Arsenal age group I got the chance to work with, a little later on, was when I was put with the under-15s for a short period. That, though, was only to support my former team-mate, Steve Bould, who'd just retired from playing and had been invited by Liam to work with the young players, just as I had six years previously. Steve was working his way through his 'A' licence, again just as I had done. I continued to do what was asked of me, helping Steve to the best of my ability, even though I had five or six years more coaching experience than him. I worked, I watched, and I listened rather than saying anything.

Thinking back, my career progression wasn't the only thing that got handled badly during my time with the academy. There was also a strange stand-off between the youth and senior set-ups. It felt as if they were two different organisations, being run with different philosophies and values. I remember Arsène Wenger arriving at Arsenal in '96, right around the same time I joined the academy as a coach. He had an incredible impact: Arsène won the Double in '98, brought in exciting young players from abroad, and coached using revolutionary methods. Of course, I wanted to see what he was doing first-hand.

I thought it made sense that every coach in the academy should watch this guy at work, and then use what they learnt when it came to coaching our younger players. Wenger was changing the game as we knew it in this country. Suddenly, Arsenal became a byword for exciting, attacking, forward-thinking football. I was part-time, working either at Highbury or out at Hale End in the evenings, so I thought I could go over to Colney now and again during the days to watch the under-18s, the under-21s and the first team working. It would be a chance to see for myself where the club was going and apply anything that was useful to the younger age-groups.

The response I received came as a surprise: I got no encouragement at all. Nobody from the academy was allowed to go over to Colney without an invitation. There seemed to be some tension between Don Howe, who was head youth coach, and Arsène. Which was a crazy situation for a club like Arsenal. These were two great coaches, albeit from very different backgrounds and with very different methods and ideas on how the game should be played. Sadly, I feel that some younger players didn't get the opportunities they deserved because of the lack of communication between the academy and the first team. I think Liam found himself in the middle of it all, trying to keep the peace between the two sides of the club.

I persisted and eventually managed to get in. I was the only academy coach able to go and watch Wenger's sessions. I'm sure Liam must have understood why I was so keen. He agreed, and I wrote to Arsène, asking if he'd be okay with me being there. I started going in once or twice a week. I'd watch the sessions, and take notes. I've still got pages and pages of ideas and drills tucked away in my files. And there were quite a few things I was able to adapt and try with the under-12s and under-13s. Arsène even let me film sessions on my camcorder. *Paul, you can bring your camera, but don't let anybody outside see what I am doing!* It's worth remembering that everyone wanted to know what Arsène was up to, producing football as good as we'd ever seen in this country. No wonder he was a little guarded. It was like trying to get in to see the Queen! To this day, I've shown no one those videos.

What stood out for me with Arsène's coaching was how clear and clean everything he did was. You could see each session was meticulously planned, with a clear idea of what he was looking to get from his time with his players. Everything was so clearly worked-out: equipment, timekeeping, his instructions. The sessions were precise, immaculate. Even the grass the team trained on had to be perfectly prepared. Arsène knew exactly what he wanted, but he was so quiet. The work was intense: lots of small-sided games with very clear objectives. He talked every now and again, but never raised his voice. He'd walk over to chat with the players rather than bawling at them across the pitch. He'd use his whistle to stop play when he wanted to make a point. Training was tranquil. Arsène nurtured and trusted his players, and the players loved it.

It was always clear what Arsène was trying to achieve in a session, and it was easy to see why the players enjoyed themselves. Even the very best players need to be engaged by what they're being asked to do. The sheer quality of the play was like nothing I'd ever seen before, but the sessions were simple and uncomplicated. It's a pity more of the young players we had coming through didn't get a chance to experience working with Arsène. I couldn't help but imagine how I might have bloomed even more as a player, working under a coach like him. Of course, quite a few of the lads who were still in the first team had been my team-mates: Tony, Lee, Nigel, Bouldy, Dave Seaman, Ray Parlour, Martin Keown. We'd say hello and share a joke, but I tried not to be involved beyond being an observer.

Apart from the once. One day, I was filming a session and, suddenly, Arsène gestured me over. He needed a defender alongside the other centre-half – a human mannequin, basically – and he didn't have the numbers to hand. So, I got my chance. *Paul, will you just stand there, please?* I had to 'mark' Dennis Bergkamp, and I can still see the look crossing his face as I jogged over. *What's going on here? Who's this guy?* I don't think Dennis had any idea who I was. He didn't know, of course, that I'd played almost 450 games for the club, and I'm not sure he was very impressed with me even sharing a pitch with him. After all, I was just the guy with the camera who usually stood over there.

03

What was really disappointing was how Bouldy's appointment came about and how it was handled. Steve Bould and I played together, of course. We always got on well. We had – and still have – a warm and respectful relationship. But for him to be handed the under-18s role right after he'd finished playing, before he'd completed his coaching qualifications? And after I'd been asked to help him settle in as a coach? I'd already spent six years gaining coaching experience and working hard to get my qualifications, but there'd been no discussion about plans for my progression at Arsenal. I wasn't even interviewed for the job Steve was given.

Most of us knew the under-18s position was going to be available at the end of the season. We'd heard that Don Howe was going to retire. And then Steve was appointed. Just like that: no application process, no opportunity for anyone else. I couldn't believe it. I was frustrated and upset: all the preparation I'd done, but I couldn't be trusted to work with and develop our under-18s. When I stripped it back, I found myself asking: *What's the difference between Steve and myself?* This wasn't fair and it wasn't right. What was the thinking behind the decision? *How could this happen to me at my club?* I needed a reason, needed to ask Liam why I'd been overlooked. Angry and feeling let down, I asked for a meeting.

I made an appointment and went across to Colney to see Liam the following day. The way I saw it, after the time I'd been working in the academy and the effort I'd made to qualify as a coach, I thought I'd deserved an opportunity – at the very least – to be interviewed for the under-18s role. In my mind, I believed I should have been offered the job. I was experienced now, I was capable. The only thing I could see to explain why I'd been overlooked was that football – and that included Arsenal – couldn't see a black coach looking after senior players. They couldn't see past the 'norm' and couldn't see the impact someone like me might have. That, and the fact I wasn't shouting and bawling at players all the time. Not that Steve Bould was, either.

My voice was raised in that meeting with Liam, though. Not like me, maybe, but my emotions were running high. I was still angry and frustrated when I went into his office. I don't know if Liam expected me to react as I did. What's certain, though, is that the reason for me being passed over didn't wash: all he said was that he believed he was making the correct decision in appointing Steve. No why. No because. I was given no valid explanation as to why I didn't get the opportunity even to interview, and that really hurt. And it got me thinking. I started wondering why it was that the senior levels of football didn't reflect either society or the playing side of the game when it came to diversity?

Steve and I were in an incredibly difficult position, and I knew I didn't want that. We had been team-mates and had been through so much together. I think we understood each other on a personal and professional level. We were friends. And I don't believe he had anything to do with Liam's decision. Bouldy wasn't the type who'd try to get ahead at a colleague's expense by stabbing him in the back. We hadn't spoken to each other about the situation: we didn't know ourselves what was going to happen until the decision had already been made.

I felt, being the more experienced person, it should be me who started what was a difficult conversation. I said I was surprised that we'd found ourselves here. But I told Steve that I thought I understood what had gone on and didn't feel he'd had any part in it. *I would hate for this to undermine our friendship. You've been handed an opportunity here and I wish you well.* This was a bad situation for me, but I didn't want it to be a bad situation for Bouldy. He didn't say much in reply, but that was fine. I just didn't want any ill feeling between us, I just needed to let Steve know where I stood. I'm so happy I had that difficult conversation. Bouldy and I still see quite a bit of each other, and I've followed his coaching journey. In fact, I've recently been his tutor on the Pro licence course.

Liam told me he was putting me with the under-14s. I told him that wasn't something I was prepared to accept, given everything that had gone on. I was coming up towards seven years working in Arsenal's academy, and that felt like a long time to have spent making no progress: still part-time, still no contract, and still no sense of a pathway. I loved working with the kids and had learnt a lot, but I felt I was more than capable of moving into a more senior coaching role at our club, working with young professionals at London Colney. If I wasn't any good at the job, I would have been found out or Liam would have let me go by now. I was just being overlooked, undervalued, taken for granted, it seemed to me. As far as I was concerned, my only option was to leave.

Maybe I shouldn't even look at the notes and correspondence from the time: I've got everything laid out in front of me now, the details of what went on between me and the club after I resigned from my coaching role at Arsenal. It's painful to re-visit and raises all sorts of questions that are still unanswered in my mind, rekindles memories and emotions that are buried inside me still.

So many people got involved, and that meant there were so many opinions. When I went to Liam, I spoke my mind. I told him I thought the decision he made to promote a less qualified coach, with less experience, over my head was wrong: the wrong way to deal with me, the wrong way to deal with any employee. Even all these years later, I believe Liam made a bad decision. The issues were about fairness, opportunity and injustice.

I'd been overlooked on other occasions, but had always tried to be honest with myself and looked for reasons to justify those decisions. Steve Bould being promoted ahead of me, though, was a final straw. I deserved more of an explanation than the one I'd got from Liam. I contacted David Dein, Arsenal's vice-chairman at the time and someone I have a good relationship with to this day. I wanted to know if the under-18s appointment had been a club decision or a decision by just one person. *Did the club even know what had gone on? And how were appointments like this supposed to be handled?* I wondered what David knew. I wanted to let him know how I felt. I got the impression that he didn't know what had happened or why. He said he'd speak to Liam and come back to me. His suggestion was that the best thing, perhaps, would be for the three of us to meet up and work things out.

As far as I was concerned, it was too late for a meeting like that to matter. Liam had made his decision, hadn't he? I didn't want or expect him to change his mind. There didn't seem any way back from here. I tried to explain things for myself, to myself. Liam didn't see me as good enough to coach the under-18s. He can't have rated me, even though I'd been told everyone was happy with my work. Perhaps my interest in wanting to go over to Colney and watch Wenger work had made him uncomfortable. Did Liam feel I wasn't one of his guys? Did he think I wasn't loyal to his side of the divide that existed within the club at the time? All I knew for sure was that the reason I was given wasn't any kind of reason at all.

The subject of racism hadn't come up between Liam and me. It didn't come up when I spoke to David Dein, either. But it did come up in the press. I hadn't said anything to anyone. Only Hope knew about my frustrations. I certainly hadn't spoken to any journalists. But, one Sunday morning, it was all over the papers: headlines saying I'd left Arsenal, suggesting it was because I felt that racism was why I hadn't been promoted to a more senior position by the club. I'd never said that so, obviously, there weren't any quotes from me. The quotes the journalist had were from Liam and David, fiercely denying that the club was racist, and saying that the best person for the job had been given it. I suspect a journalist went to Arsenal or Liam with no more than speculation, and their response had been what turned it into a story.

From that point, the whole issue became increasingly sensitive. Defences went up. Arsenal, as a club, were in a very uncomfortable position. And I was, too. People outside Highbury were putting pressure on me to take the club to court over unfair or discriminatory employment policy. Kick it Out, and Show Racism are important organisations. I supported them back then and still do. I've worked with both over the years. I felt I'd been unfairly treated by Arsenal, but did I want to take my club to court, even though I was sure I had a strong case?

The Commission for Racial Equality and others were urging me to take the club through the courts. *How could it come to this?* I'd never witnessed or heard anything of a racist nature from Liam in all the time that I'd know him. That said, he and Arsenal clearly hadn't complied even with the pretty loose regulations that surrounded employment practice back then. I put in an official complaint to the club and to the FA: the way I'd been dealt with contravened equal opportunities regulations at the very least. That term – 'equal opportunities' – summed up how I felt: all I've ever wanted is to be treated fairly, given the even chance I deserved. I didn't want anything that I hadn't worked hard for.

Some upsetting things happened during the few months my situation was being discussed. I was given to understand by one of the club's directors that carrying on with this process would mean cutting myself off from any kind of relationship with Arsenal forever. It was like an 'offer you can't refuse' moment out of a *Godfather* movie. Also, negative comments about me from the club started to appear in the press. It looked as if this was turning into a very public affair. I'd been at Arsenal since I was 12. I didn't want 30 years to end with me taking the club to court. At the same time, though, I wanted an acknowledgement that I'd been treated badly and a commitment to doing things differently – and better – in future.

I also had to consider my own future: taking legal action against Arsenal might make other clubs wary of ever employing me. I felt as though I was damned if I did and damned if I didn't. I've never been one to run from bullies. Perhaps me being a quieter person gives the impression people can get away with threatening me. But my instinct is always to challenge bullying: it's something I despise. As soon as that phrase – 'equal opportunities' – came up in my solicitor's letter, Arsenal did everything to make sure I didn't take my complaint any further. My complaint meant the club's reputation was at stake now, and more people within the club got involved in trying to smooth things over.

In the end, I did meet with David and Liam. They said they wanted to find solutions. *What about a scouting role?* I wasn't interested. In fact, I felt insulted. I wanted to coach. I felt I was an asset to Arsenal, in terms of my reputation as well as in terms of what I'd achieved in the game. If Arsenal couldn't see that – after 30 years – then the best thing was for me to leave. That was my attitude. I'd have rather just had an explanation as to why I'd been overlooked.

Despite people telling me I should go to court, that I had a strong case, I didn't want to have a very public battle with Arsenal. A few thousand pounds for winning the case wouldn't have been worth that. The more discussions went on, the more I realised this was simple: Liam had made his decision. I never got a reason why. Everything else was just the club backing a senior member of staff, their academy director. In the end, Arsenal did rewrite their equal opportunities policy. Too late for me. I'd decided I needed to get on with my life and find a new home for myself somewhere else in the game.

04

Leaving Arsenal for the second time was almost as painful as the first. The difference, though, was that this time it was me saying: *enough is enough.* I valued what I had to offer more than the club did, obviously, but I didn't have a clue what I was going to do next. *Where do I go after Arsenal?* I'd made a commitment to a coaching career and had all my qualifications already, apart from my Pro licence. I knew I wanted to stay in football – it had been my life, after all – but I'd lost some faith and didn't trust the industry's employment practices, especially when it came to opportunities for black former players. If things could finish how they had at Arsenal, what chance could I expect to be given by people who didn't even know me?

It's the same for most players: football's what you know and what you love. It's maybe the biggest challenge any of us have to face in our professional lives. *What do I do now?* When you're a player, it all comes to you, doesn't it? *Will you do this? Can you be at this place at this time, please?* To start making things happen after retiring, and now again after leaving Arsenal, I was having to write letters, make phone calls, ask for what I needed. And that wasn't easy. I needed a new frame of mind and I had to decide what it was, exactly, that I wanted to do.

It was a difficult time. By now, we had two sons: Jordan was born in 1996. Life at home wasn't easy, not least because my income wasn't close to covering the bills. I'd been sensible with my money over the years, a habit I'm sure I picked up when I was a boy, watching Mum struggling to get by. The money from my testimonial had helped us through seven years of part-time coaching, which I'd had to make financial sacrifices for since retiring as a player. Now, though? For the first time in my life, I didn't have enough money coming in to cover what was going out. And that didn't sit well with me. I felt stressed and anxious. I'd seen so many footballers struggle with the transition. It's a challenge, even if you can somehow take money worries out of the equation.

Soon after, I received a call from a friend, Gary Karsa, who was running youth development at Barnet FC, round the corner from where I lived. Gary wanted to know if I'd be interested in coming in to work with the age groups up to under-16 at Underhill. It was a part-time role again, of course, and very different to the set-up at Arsenal: another world, in fact, when it came to the facilities. But Barnet seemed like my only way to stay in the game. The boys weren't the elite players I'd been used to working with, but they were good kids and wanted to learn. This wasn't where I'd expected to be at this stage in my career as a coach. I believed I should be in and around first-team football by now. It seemed I was the only person who saw my situation that way, though.

I was at Barnet for a while, until Gary moved to Orient. He asked me to go with him, but to do a different job. He asked if I'd help to develop the youth coaches at Brisbane Road as well as working with their young players. Again, it was part-time but, looking back, I realise those months at Orient were my first practical experience of the kind of roles I've worked in ever since: coach education and coach development. Gary's background was very different from mine. He came into the game through working on Football in the Community programmes. That was how he'd got started at Barnet. After Orient, he went on and worked at some good clubs: Wycombe, Colchester, Norwich, Villa. He's now in charge of academy recruitment at QPR. Gary was a friend, but it was never a case of him doing me a favour. He knew I could help at Underhill and at Brisbane Road. And, from my point of view, working with Gary kept me involved as a coach.

I was exploring possibilities, I suppose. While I was at Barnet, I remember wondering whether I really wanted to put my future in the hands of people whose motives I couldn't trust. My experience at Arsenal had shown me how the game worked in terms of making progress as a coach. I wanted to be somewhere I felt what I had to offer was recognised, and where I'd be valued and respected. I'd written to Gordon Taylor at the PFA, asking about coaching opportunities with the union. I'd been the PFA rep at Arsenal in the 1980s and had known Gordon since we'd first been in touch over the Glenn Cockerill affair. He invited me to the PFA's London office, and I had talks with Bobby Barnes, who was Gordon's Deputy Chief Executive.

I knew the PFA were involved in coach education, and I wanted to know more. From the PFA's point of view, Gordon and Bobby wanted to hear about what had happened at Arsenal. There'd been a lot of noise, one way or the other, and they wanted to get things straight in their own minds, I suppose. And they wanted to find out what I could offer the union, why I was thinking about moving from coaching into coach education, and where my ambitions lay. I made it clear I wanted to stay in the game.

I coached for seven years at Arsenal, at Barnet, and at Orient, probably assuming all the while that was where my future lay. But, whenever I stopped to think about my prospects and looked at the landscape in football, I couldn't avoid seeing how things worked, how and why people were getting jobs or weren't getting them. None of it seemed right or fair to me. Did I really want to look forward to 15 or 20 years of frustration and disappointment? I decided I couldn't and wouldn't put myself or my family through that. Life at home was in a difficult place as it was. And I'm sure that was partly down to what had been happening to me in my professional life.

From my own experience and the experiences of people I knew – Cyrille Regis, Luther Blissett, Ricky Hill and others – I wasn't comfortable at all about what seemed to me to be bias at best, or outright racism at worst, across the whole game other than out on the pitch. I'd become convinced in my own mind that equal opportunities in the football industry weren't being made available to black players. And I began to ask why. I slowly came to the conclusion that trying to pursue a future in club football would probably be disheartening and painful, for me and for my young family, with the odds stacked against me as regards a coaching career.

What can I say? *I was aware that some of us weren't really welcome.* Certainly, we weren't competing on a level playing field when it came to getting jobs and progressing in our careers. I loved football. I wanted to be part of it and knew I had plenty to offer. But, at the same time, I knew I had to be careful who I discussed my feelings with. I understood that making claims publicly would mean my words being taken out of context and dismissed. *That's not true. Prove it. You can't say that without evidence.* And, of course, I had no evidence other than the numbers, which I didn't think added up, however much people tried to deny the truth of what they represented.

I got used to hearing the lazy, stereotypical responses. *Black players aren't interested in coaching or management. If black players put the work in, they'll get opportunities like everyone else. The best jobs will go to the best people.* Those ideas added up to the received wisdom in football, but I didn't believe them or recognise them from my own experience. But I knew if I came straight out and said what I thought was going on in football, I'd be labelled a troublemaker. That I'd be sidelined, marginalised and squeezed out. That's what I was sure would happen if I questioned the status quo. It's what still happens if you're courageous enough to ask the difficult questions.

Did I want to be at the beck and call of decision-makers who employed people, in the main, who looked and sounded like them? And were so quick to sack people who didn't? The uncertainty, the randomness, the uneven playing field: I had come to realise that football management wasn't going to be for me. I needed to find an environment where entrenched attitudes, history and culture might be open to change, somewhere I could believe I'd have an equal chance to make an impact and succeed. I didn't know for sure that the PFA and coach education were the answer, but the union was at least ready to accept that the game was getting it wrong. And they seemed to recognise that I could help and support a process of change.

I met with Bobby Barnes again and with Simone Pound, the Head of Equality and Diversity at the PFA. It was effectively a job interview. I spoke about what I wanted to do and what I thought I could bring to the PFA. They told me there was a regional coach education role if I was interested, supporting young players who were working towards their FA qualifications. *Take it on part-time at first, and we can see how we feel about it in six months' time. We'll get you trained up and qualified.* They were prepared to invest in me and in my development. I had an idea what coach education involved but, at that point, couldn't be sure whether it was something I'd be suited to. I was grateful for the opportunity to find out, though, and said yes.

What struck me very early on was how few people worked for the union: only around 60 between the two offices in Manchester and London. I got to know the staff, some incredibly hard-working and effective people, like Carol and Jim Hicks, who are still doing outstanding work on behalf of the players. My colleagues in the coaching department were all former professionals. Geoff Pike, who'd been at West Ham, and Dennis Mortimer, who'd played in midfield for Aston Villa, were two I'd met during our playing careers.

A couple of things struck me straight away. One was that the FA's coach educators – who were delivering 'B,' 'A' and Pro licence courses or were training new coach educators like myself – came mainly from academic backgrounds. The other was that there was hardly any diversity in coach education either. I found myself in a lot of classrooms, sitting in on a lot of meetings. I knew that was all part of my development, all part of finding my way in a very different environment. I was one of ten regional PFA coach educators nationwide.

As well as studying, gaining qualifications and working with young players, I met a lot of senior professionals, who were either starting their coaching careers or thinking about doing so. Many of them didn't enjoy being taught by people from academic backgrounds who didn't have experience of the professional game. They didn't want to hear the game being talked about in ways that made it seem more complicated. Personally, I didn't mind where my learning came from. But I did think it was a shame that coach education didn't seem to be a path which many high-profile former players had taken.

Perhaps one explanation was it being a role where you supported and guided, rather than one where you were the centre of attention as a coach or a manager. Most players get used to being that centre of attention during their careers and enjoy it. For me, though,

Michael Thomas clinches us the 1989 Division One title in the most dramatic finish to a top-flight season, although myself, Niall Quinn and Brian Marwood had to watch events unfold with the Arsenal fans at Anfield

There was no chance of me missing the title celebrations in 1991, and it was even more special to enjoy the moment with Michael and Rocky (below), then later with my mum, sister Sandra and step-dad Rupert (right)

After 10 years at Arsenal, I was honoured with a testimonial match against Celtic on 30 July 1991, a fantastic and well-organised occasion that I will forever be grateful for

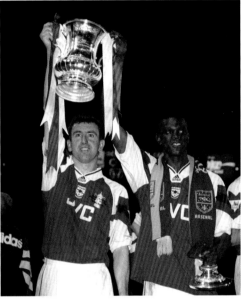

The summer of 1991 also saw me meet up with the great Nelson Mandela as Arsenal enjoyed some pre-season games in South Africa. A few months later and Ian Wright would join us and soon get off the mark with a scoring debut against Leicester (top right). With the team coming together under George Graham, we went on to lift both the League Cup and FA Cup in 1993, becoming the first English side to complete that domestic double

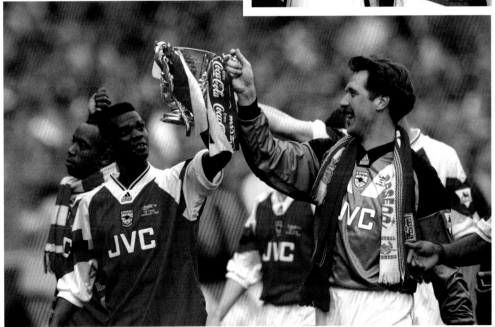

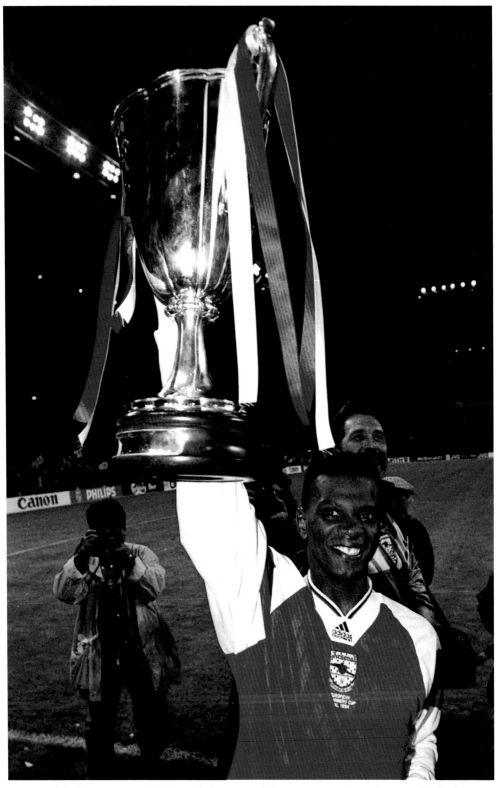

Hoisting aloft the European Cup Winners' Cup in 1994 after overcoming Parma's star-studded side 1-0 – a great achievement for the club and for me, having played almost every minute of our European campaign

Introducing my mum to Arsène Wenger – the man who would go on to revolutionise Arsenal and someone I was keen to learn as much as I could from as I began my coaching career with the Arsenal youth teams

(Right) I'm proud to have picked up some great medals and memorabilia during my 15 years at Arsenal, although I'm not sure if I'll ever be reunited with my European Cup Winners' Cup medal from 1994!

After tutoring Paul Gascoigne on an FA coaching course and making a good impression on the former England star, he asked me to join him as his assistant at Kettering Town in 2005. It was a short-lived venture after Paul's relationship broke down with club owner Imraan Ladak

Images from my time at the PFA. I'd been the PFA rep at Arsenal and after I left the club, they were prepared to invest in me. Of all the organisations I've been involved with, the PFA has been the most forward-looking in terms of diversity and trying to achieve tangible change

A few of the first players invited to be members of Arsenal's 100 Club with Janet Rocastle in the middle

In my role at the FA as Senior Professional Game Coach Developer and National Coach, taken in 2021. (Below) at Loughborough University in the same year

(Above) at Leeds Beckett University after gaining my Postgraduate Diploma in Coach Development in 2021

(Left) with Mikel after mentoring him through his early coaching qualification in 2015. I was at the PFA and he was in his final year as a player at Arsenal

Family time. (From left to right) Natalie my niece, sister Sandra, Tarraine and Taiyon my grand-nephews (Natalie's sons) and my nephew Anthony

(Above) Du'aine, Mum and Jordan pictured on a trip to New York

(Above) with Angela enjoying a charity cricket event at Lord's and (right) sons Jordan and Du'aine on holiday in Portugal

coach education seemed a good way of staying in football. And, just as important, I felt the PFA was an organisation which treated me with respect, somewhere I could develop. I had more trust in the job and in being able to progress. I had a little more faith in the PFA as an organisation that tried to do the right things.

Of all the organisations I've been involved with, the PFA have always been the most forward-looking as regards diversity and trying to further real and tangible change. Conversations that are only now being had around football were being had by Gordon Taylor and his colleagues in 2003, when I first started as a coach educator. Gordon realised very early on that there was an institutional problem in the industry and identified me as someone who could play a part in looking for a solution.

At the same time as I was going out to talk to players in clubs about coaching qualifications and pathways, he asked me to have conversations, particularly with senior pros, about their ambitions and their experiences. The numbers told their own story, but the PFA were the first to look past the lazy answers and ask the obvious, but difficult questions.

As far as the coach education itself was concerned, I worked alongside Geoff Pike, who was going into clubs across the South East of England to work with their young players. For the first six months or so, I shadowed Geoff so I could watch and learn what the job involved, from scheduling and liaising with the academies through to delivering the courses. Every academy scholar takes a Level 2 coaching qualification and the PFA delivers those courses on behalf of the FA. The idea is that, at 18, if a player isn't offered a professional contract by his club, he'll still have taken the first step on an alternative pathway if he wants to stay in the game. The difficulty for us, of course, was that most young players don't really grasp the importance of having that alternative. They're completely focused on earning a professional contract at their clubs.

So, the role of coach educator, I discovered, wasn't just about teaching the players how to coach and achieve their basic qualifications. You also had to motivate students who didn't really want to be there. *I don't want to be a coach. I'm here to become a player! What's the point of this?* They'd never say as much to me, but it was clear that was the attitude for many. I found that difficult to deal with at times. I'd always urge them to take every opportunity that was on offer. It was a challenge for me. Boys who were dreaming about making it didn't really want to hear the truth, which is that they probably wouldn't. It was hard work trying to convince them that, even if they did manage to make careers as players, a basic coaching qualification might still be a useful thing. I knew how small a percentage of them would go on to become professionals. It seemed vital to me that those youngsters had something else to fall back on.

Eventually, I was given my own group of five or six clubs to look after, in and around London. I'd arrange to go in and work with the clubs and their academy education officers to help their boys get their Level 2s. Each course would run over a season, for anything between 10 and 15 first- or second-year scholars. Every club was different in the way they wanted to run the course, and that meant I had to be flexible. I'd introduce the course, explain what we'd be doing and then, over the coming months, deliver all the different modules, a combination of classroom work and practical sessions. I learnt so many new skills and developed my own style of delivering the courses. The football element was easier for me than the theory sessions: I'd not been in a classroom environment since leaving school at 16. Learning how to use an overhead projector was a whole new ball game for me!

Geoff Pike had mentored me well, and we had regular PFA and FA training days. Even so, there was a lot I had to pick up as I went along. There was plenty to get through: as well as football, we had to cover subjects like the laws of the game, first aid, and health and safety. It was intense: teaching as best I could at the same time as trying to learn as much as I could! Presentation skills, communication, planning and logistics and administration: more than ever before. But it all had to be taken care of so I could get on to what I really enjoyed: the football and teaching these young scholars the basics of coaching.

What was fascinating for me, having spent so much of my career at just one club, was going into different ones, getting an idea of how each worked. Or, sometimes, how they didn't. It was a little strange going into Spurs. People looking at me as if to say: *What's he doing here?* But they were good to me. Each football club has its own personality, its own culture: going in over the course of a season to work with the scholars gave me a real insight. As a player and as a coach, you go into a dressing room, out onto a pitch, back into a dressing room again, and then you're gone. Delivering these courses gave me the time to build relationships and get an understanding of what the individual clubs were about.

I worked largely with the younger scholars, but I'd also get senior professionals wanting to talk to me about taking their coaching qualifications, wanting to find out what would be involved. The older players knew who I was, remembered me as a player, and I think were surprised to see me doing what I was now. Some were curious about why I was there working with the youngsters. *Why aren't you coaching in senior football? That's where you've been all your career. Why aren't you managing?* At the time, I was the only black coach educator going into professional clubs.

At that time, you didn't really need anything in the way of qualifications when it came to applying for coaching and management roles. It seemed plenty of people who were being appointed didn't have them. But, at the same time, former-players and young coaches I knew were still being told they needed to do their qualifications. It was as if some of us were being sent off down a blind alley. Some ex-players were doing the work, preparing professionally for coaching careers, while others were getting offered jobs without having put in any of that effort. *Why bother putting in the work when it seemed to make no difference when it came to getting jobs?* That was what I was being asked almost every day.

I had those conversations and then, over the summers, I'd deliver Level 2 courses for some older players. I think many of the guys I came into contact with felt comfortable with me in the role, and at ease when it came to talking about their experiences and their ambitions after football. Those were exactly the conversations Gordon Taylor and Simone Pound were so keen for me to have. I felt appreciated,recognised as someone players could talk openly to about how they were feeling regarding their prospects in coaching and management.

Once I started going into clubs on my own, the job became full-time. The PFA were concerned by the obvious lack of black coaches in proportion to how many black professionals were playing. I was pulled into meetings with Gordon, Simone and other PFA staff. *What can we do about this?* We decided we needed to find out exactly why black players weren't going on to do their coaching qualifications after they retired. And why they weren't being hired for senior positions in the same proportion as the white teammates they'd played alongside. We needed to gather more data and to start a serious discussion around the subject within the game.

Speaking to black players, those still playing as well as those who'd retired, became a part of my job description. I asked for their stories; I sought out opinions; I spoke to a lot of people and heard a lot of very similar things repeated time and again. At times, those conversations were awkward for me. I was going into clubs to encourage players to get qualified. But those same players would then ask me what I really thought. *Why are you encouraging me, Paul, when you know the opportunities aren't there?* I understood fully what they were telling me. And I knew that – qualified or not – it would probably be very difficult for them. *Why spend all that time and money? It won't make any difference.* What was I supposed to say in reply?

Deep down, I knew the game had a problem and that the way of dealing with it was usually to deny the problem even existed. Racism can be difficult to prove: if someone says they're not racist, then what? All these years on, I've reached a point where I no longer give situations 'the benefit of doubt'. I can't say *I just don't know* any longer. Those in power in football make decisions based on 'experience' – and unconscious bias – which undermine the prospects of black and ethnic minority candidates when it comes to positions other than on the playing side. I thought that back then. I'm even more sure of it now. I've asked myself the important questions over and over again, wanting to be sure I've considered everything. I'm still looking for any other answer as to why we have so few black coaches at the senior end of the game.

The same narratives, the same frustrations and disappointments, came up time and again in my conversations. That's the key to understanding this. Take one person's experience and you can find reasons, excuses. *Oh, he didn't interview well. He didn't have the experience. He wasn't a good fit for the club.* But then you hear the same stories over and over: different coaches, different clubs, but the same outcomes. Well-qualified, able, and hard-working people not getting opportunities. Usually, not even getting an interview, or the respect of an acknowledgement or explanation. When it's so many people having the same experience, then you start to realise it's something more fundamental. You can tell me why one guy didn't get a job. But you can't tell me why hundreds didn't. Not without telling the truth. I'd heard every excuse now: they just added up to denying there was an issue around race in our game.

I've met a lot of decent people during my time in football. But I've also met some I wasn't so sure about. A friend of mine recently showed me an article they'd come across on the internet. *Paul! You worked for this bloke, didn't you?* The story was about a guy named Imraan Ladak. He'd been sentenced to six months in prison in Birmingham for contempt of court, but had gone missing. Now, the local paper was reporting that the police had tracked him down to a Travelodge in Milton Keynes and that he was about to go to prison. I recognised the name: I had indeed crossed paths with Mr Ladak. It was while I was working for the PFA. At the time, he owned his local non-League football club. He was young, already a wealthy guy, and a big Tottenham fan. In October 2005, he appointed Paul Gascoigne as manager at Kettering Town.

I knew Paul from our playing days, of course. I loved those Arsenal versus Spurs games, and we had some great battles on the pitch. We developed a mutual respect before he went to Italy, joining Lazio to play in Serie A. After he retired as a player, though, Paul was looking at coaching and came up to Keele University to do his Level 2 qualification on a fast-track bespoke course run by the FA, designed for former players who had a certain level of international experience. It was a combination of the Level 2 and Level 3, delivered to a small group of five or six players. I'd been trained up and was one of the tutors. With fewer guys involved, it was a chance to get to know them all and, in the case of Paul, a chance for us to get to know each other a little better.

I'd followed his career from a distance and had seen how complicated Gazza's life had been. But, up at Keele, he seemed really motivated. It was obvious he wanted to learn. Paul knows football and he was a good student: his work was very detailed and thorough. On the last day of the first block of training, he pulled me to one side. *Davo! I need your phone number. If I get a job somewhere, I'll want you to come in with me.* I gave him my contact details. *Sure. It'd be good to stay in touch.* I was happy someone had seen enough in me to think about offering me an opportunity in club football again. I liked his attitude towards the course. In fact, I liked Paul. It was hard not to. Everybody on the course took to him. The course finished. The idea then was that the group would go away and get practical experience, putting what they'd learned into practice.

A little time later, the phone rang. It was Paul, saying he was on the point of going in as manager at Kettering Town, a non-League club playing in the Conference North. True to his word, he wanted me to come with him as his first-team coach. He was so excited, but I needed to know more about the club, about the contract, about what he'd need me to do. In truth, I wasn't sure. I was just establishing myself at the PFA. I even had the word 'Executive' attached to my job title and had taken on more responsibilities. I spoke with the PFA to see if they'd be happy with me helping Paul alongside doing my job as a coach educator. I remember Gordon asking me: *Are you sure?* Kettering were part-time, so I thought the arrangement could work. Paul was so enthusiastic, so ambitious.

Whatever you want, Davo! Whatever you need. I'll pay your wages out of my own money if the chairman won't give you enough! The chairman. That was the guy: Imraan Ladak.

Paul was staying at Champneys, at Henlow Grange, which was owned by a friend of his and a keen Arsenal fan, Steven Purdew, who I knew too. It was only about 30 minutes from where we lived, and so I drove up to talk to Paul a few times. He was very clear about the role: he'd manage, but he needed me to handle the coaching side. He seemed in good shape. He assured me that his problems with drinking were behind him, and I trusted what he was telling me. He was fired up at the prospect of being the manager at Kettering. He wanted the club to go full-time and have a proper go at getting into the Football League. I was keen on the challenge and agreed to give it a go with him.

Within a few weeks, we were sitting in front of the press and the TV cameras at Rockingham Road being introduced to the world. Imraan didn't know a great deal about football, but he seemed committed to supporting Paul, desperate to have him at his club. He was enthusiastic. From how Paul was speaking about him to me, I thought the relationship would need to be managed if it was going to work long-term, but Imraan was promising to back Paul financially and seemed respectable enough when I met him. I was looking forward to it: a new challenge, coaching senior players, coaching to win games.

Being around Paul while we were at Kettering was like nothing I'd ever known. The whole world knew who he was, wanted to talk to him, to be in his company. Anywhere – everywhere – people would want a bit of him, and Paul was always willing to make time for them. It's hard to explain: Paul enjoyed that attention, but I soon realised it wasn't as simple as that. Even when he wanted to be left alone, Paul seemed under pressure to show up, duty-bound to give people what they wanted. It was like he felt he owed it to the public to play up to the Gazza image and give them what they expected from him.

We spent quite a bit of time together. I got to know Paul better. I got to know about him, too. I hadn't realised how tough his life was at the time: we spoke about how he'd fallen out with friends and with his dad. He'd phone me up all hours, really excited about something, and I'd drive up to Henlow Grange, and we'd chat. About football most of the time: Paul absolutely loves and is fascinated by the game. People were saying he wouldn't last long at Kettering, but he insisted he was fully committed, looking forward to working at this level of football. So, we got on with it. I took the training, twice a week at the stadium. He did all the managerial stuff: dealing with players, the media, and picking the team.

It was Gazza, so there was a lot of interest in the club and in him. The highest-profile footballer of his generation and here he was working in the sixth tier of professional football. I think the media attention was just what Imraan Ladak had been hoping for when he offered Paul the job. We did okay: in our first nine games, we won three, drew three and lost three. The players were fine with us, although it's the same at any level: players will often look for weaknesses. They respected what Paul had achieved as a player, but they'd read the newspaper stories, too. They saw a guy who didn't dress or behave or communicate in a conventional way as a manager. I don't think most of them could believe that Gazza was in charge at their club.

What really cost Paul at Kettering, though, was his relationship with the owner. Imraan was new to football. He wanted to know everything, wanted to be involved in everything. *What's the plan? Who's in the team? I know a player who can improve the team.* All that really got to Paul. He thought this was an owner interfering. Imraan was around a lot. He would turn up at training unannounced.

Paul resented it, and maybe dumped all his own insecurities into that box. I tried to calm things. We weren't going to change the guy. He owned the club. Best we could do – the best Paul could do – would be to let Imraan have his say, let him ask his questions, and then make our own decisions. But Paul couldn't let it go. He became completely obsessed about it. *Why won't he leave me alone to manage the team?*

The relationship with the chairman started to go downhill almost from day to day. It became a massive distraction, and dawned on me that their relationship wasn't going to work out. The whole thing unravelled in no time. Paul was only in the job for eight weeks. I couldn't understand why he'd become so fixated on the relationship with the chairman. Paul told me Imraan was on the phone to him all the time, wanting to pick the team. He couldn't handle it and stopped answering his calls. When it happened, it happened quickly. Mr Ladak sacked Paul and then asked me if I'd be willing to take over as caretaker manager. I said no. *If Paul's going, then I'll go too.* And that was that: an extraordinary experience; an extraordinary couple of months.

I had no idea that Paul had been drinking while we were together at Kettering, so I can't say how true the allegations Imraan Ladak made afterwards actually were. I know from having played with Tony Adams and Paul Merson – they've talked publicly about it since – that addicts are good at finding ways to disguise what they're doing.

I thought it was wrong, anyway, for the chairman to tell the media that Paul had been drunk on the job. That was spiteful, with no regard for any mental health issues or personal problems Gazza had. Being shamed publicly never helped anyone. I do know Paul brought people through the turnstiles and attracted attention to the club like never before. Maybe that's what it had been about from the start. Imraan knew Paul's history like everyone else, and had grabbed an opportunity to get some publicity for Kettering Town.

I stayed in touch with Paul, and he talked to me about one or two other jobs he'd been offered, one in Qatar and one in the North East. I'd really enjoyed working with the Kettering players. They were part-time and there was a certain amount of patience required because of that, but it was senior football. With kids, it's largely about development. This was more like the mindset from my days as a player. It was about winning. I enjoyed being with Paul, too: he's a vulnerable, generous, open-hearted man. I thought he had something to offer football. For all that, though, I wasn't ready to repeat the experience we'd had together at Rockingham Road. Later on, I know Paul's life got really complicated: arrests, rehab, reality TV and everything else. He changed his number and, since then, we've simply lost touch.

06

I did my first coaching qualification as a 17-year-old. I did my 'B' and 'A' licences while I was coaching at Arsenal. The next step was the Pro licence. The Pro is an 18-month course, and passing it means you're recognised as being competent to work at the very highest level. It's difficult to get onto in the first place: there are around 400 applicants for 25 places each year. The PFA, though, have one place on each intake set aside, which they can nominate a candidate for. In 2006, that candidate was me. I still had to apply: the previous year I'd been put forward, but hadn't been successful.

The Pro was difficult for me in that I didn't have a regular group of players I could use to put theory into practice. It's a course focussed more on leadership and management, and I wasn't leading or managing anyone but myself. Dick Bates was the lead tutor, who I already knew from my 'A' licence, and who I later worked alongside as an assistant delivering the 'A' licence courses. I learned a lot from this highly respected and demanding man. I learned from other candidates, too. I studied for my Pro alongside some very established coaches: Steve Clarke, Kevin Bond, René Meulensteen, Kenny Jackett, Martin Ling, Martin Allen, Peter

Taylor, Chris Ramsey. John Collins, the former Scotland international, too.

For one part of the course, we had to partner up with another person for a study visit, to look at a subject of our choice, and then present on it together to the other candidates. John had played at AS Monaco and still had good contacts at the club. Still had an apartment in Monte Carlo, too. He suggested we go there and put together a presentation on Monaco's coaching methods. *Good idea, John!* Off we went to the south of France for a week: watched training, talked to their staff, and put together our piece. Great place to go and be a student and get so well looked after by John and his lovely family!

Several of the Pro licence course modules were based around working with senior players in club environments. A lot of the candidates were already working at the highest level: Steve Clarke, for example, was José Mourinho's assistant at Chelsea. I was working as a coach educator rather than as a coach, though, which didn't make it any easier. The challenge was to find ways to adapt what I was learning to what I was doing for the PFA. I made it work and got my Pro. I learned a lot, especially on the theory side, and got used to spending time back in the classroom so many years after leaving Beaufoy at 16 to join Arsenal. I was exposed to the very best practice in leadership and management: both from the tutors and from the candidates I was studying alongside. And I've come full circle with it. My current role at the FA is tutoring on the Pro licence.

I felt valued and secure at the PFA. I could see the purpose of what I was doing. The union has some very good people and I respected the organisation itself, which was forward-looking and diverse, practising what it preached. I enjoyed the practical side of what I was doing: coach education, going into the clubs, talking to and working with young players. I also found myself getting more and more involved with the push against discrimination and racism. I'd been the person going out and meeting black players and coaches, listening to their stories, trying to gather some data and look for possible solutions. I wanted to do that work around diversity: it was important to me personally, and I recognised that I was probably the right person at the PFA to take on the extra responsibility.

Not long after I started full-time with the PFA, we'd gathered a group of football's black players together at a hotel in London to share experiences and discuss what the union could do to help. Just getting these guys to sit around a table was a step forward. Until now, none of the game's stakeholders could see there was an issue which needed to be addressed. That first get-together led to other meetings, including – eventually – one with representatives from the Premier League, the Football League, the League Management Association, and the FA. It was the first time the governing bodies had ever been brought together to listen to us. The PFA deserves credit for getting the ball rolling. Since those meetings in the early 2000s, progress has been painfully and frustratingly slow. Imagine the resistance and push back we faced then, when we first stood up and said: *The game needs to change.*

Ricky Hill and I had stayed in contact after we'd been on our Jamaican trip together in '87 and his Luton team had beaten us in the Littlewoods Cup final in '88. I'd always known how much he wanted to stay in football after he retired. Ricky was a student of the game and had completed all his coaching qualifications, even before you needed any of those qualifications to get jobs. He did everything he could to carve out opportunities to go into management, but eventually had to go to the States and then the West Indies to find work. I'd watched and wondered why nobody was pointing out the obvious. It wasn't rocket science to see what was going on.

I felt frustrated and disillusioned when I saw how he and Chris

Ramsey were treated after Ricky was appointed manager at Luton in 2000. He was sacked just a couple of months later. I'm sure Ricky felt hurt, and I felt disappointed for him. Following Ricky's career from the '90s onwards, I'd seen things happening that opened my eyes for the first time to how the game worked, how and why some people got given a chance and others didn't. It always seemed harder for Ricky – and for guys like Cyrille Regis and Luther Blissett – to get opportunities, compared to other coaches who I often thought had far less ability.

Ricky attended one of the PFA meetings and told us about an anti-discrimination policy he'd learned about when he'd been in the States, managing the Tampa Bay Rowdies: the 'Rooney Rule'. None of us had heard of it, but Ricky explained how it worked: for every senior coaching role in the NFL, franchises had to interview at least one candidate from a minority ethnic background. It wasn't a quota system. There were no job guarantees. But it was a fair foot in the door when appointments were made. It seemed to be working in America. Ricky suggested the Rooney Rule might be a way for us to move forwards, and we decided to look into it.

We contacted the civil rights attorneys who'd done the study in the US which had led to the Rooney Rule being implemented in 2003: Cyrus Mehri and Johnnie Cochran, two very prominent US lawyers. Cyrus came over to talk to us and I looked after him while he was here. By now, we were thinking we needed their help and support to get something similar implemented. To try and gauge whether that might even be possible. The fact Cyrus had come to the UK generated a bit of media coverage. He and I did a few radio and newspaper interviews together, trying to highlight that we had an issue around racism in the game. Cyrus and Johnnie followed English football. They couldn't understand why we hadn't implemented something like this already. But putting something like the Rooney Rule in place was never going to be easy. We knew that.

Affirmative action – positive discrimination – was legal in the US. It was the law, in fact. Here, equal opportunities legislation made things more complicated. Those conversations with Cyrus and Johnnie were the start of something, though, and we at least got the subject onto the agenda. Eventually, more than a decade later, governing bodies like the FA and the Football League began to put a very watered-down version of the Rooney Rule in place, which a few clubs volunteered to sign up to. Then, as now, many people still felt there wasn't an issue: *Everything's fine. The best people rise to the top if they put the work in. The system's fair here.* That's what I kept hearing. Anyone who spoke up against those stereotyped responses was seen as having a chip on their shoulder or 'playing the race card'.

There was real controversy around the Rooney Rule. Controversy that, in my opinion, shouldn't have existed. Resistance to the idea was driven by ignorance. Or worse, by wilful misrepresentation of what the Rooney Rule actually was. Large sections of the media – and a lot of people in football – presented it as tokenism: guaranteeing jobs to candidates from ethnic minorities even if they weren't up to standard. That wasn't ever the reality, but it was how a lot of the media chose to present it to the public. The Rule only ever looked to guarantee diversity in the interviewing process, and the people pushing back knew that full well. They weren't stupid. But they were intent on protecting the status quo at all costs, even at the expense of the truth.

Listening to and reading those misrepresentations, I began to see things even more clearly for what they were. Like never before, I questioned what I was being told and became determined to trust, instead, what my own eyes and my own thoughts were telling me. I began to recognise the ways that institutions and structures, inside and outside football, were insidiously racist. It was frustrating to see how people could be misled by statements which presented a twisted version of the truth at best. Or were outright lies at worst. I'm almost certain now that those misrepresentations were a conscious attempt to keep things as they were – and to avoid change for the better – for as long as possible. *If not, why have we waited so long for real change?*

There were a few journalists who had the courage, empathy and intelligence to understand what was going on. Henry Winter, Oliver Holt, Darren Lewis and John Cross spring to mind, but there were others, too. And credit to them: they used their positions of influence to come out and say what they saw. But it was demoralising to see how many people could be so easily misled, even people in the black community. At the time – and to this day – black players and ex-players could be divided by what I see as a sleight of hand. It all seemed so subtle, so skilful and sly. I even sometimes wondered whether the people defending the status quo were aware of what they were doing. Maybe those attitudes were just buried that deep within them. That whole period had a real impact on me personally. It challenged my faith in people when so many of them – people I'd always thought of as decent and fair-minded – seemed unable to see that we needed to change how we thought and how we behaved in football. I didn't like the injustice, the hypocrisy, the unwillingness to even consider the possibility that there might be a different way – a better way – to do things. And, of course, the more aware I became, the more I understood. Some people were reassuring me that we didn't have a serious problem. Others would say the right things, say they wanted to move forward, but would then do nothing. If most people in football weren't even aware we had a problem, how could anything change? It was a game in denial.

15

The controversy around the Rooney Rule made me realise just how long a struggle lay ahead. We met so much resistance. Even when people came along to meetings and seemed to nod their heads in agreement, they'd go away and do nothing other than recycle the fallacy that the Rooney Rule was about handing jobs to ethnic minority coaches at the expense of their white peers. I had to start judging people on their actions rather than on their words, while trying to appeal to their sense of shared humanity: Put yourself in that black coach's shoes. *Be honest, come on. How would you see the situation now from their point of view?*

It seemed more important than ever to me that we pushed for coaches from minority backgrounds to get qualified, to make sure there was one less excuse, at least, for denying these hard-working professionals the opportunities they deserved. I resolved to do the best job I could in supporting other black coaches who were struggling. Convincing players to take their first steps in coaching was vital if we were going to challenge the myth. I knew – and the PFA, as an organisation, knew – that change had to happen. And that change would only happen if people were prepared to make it happen.

It took courage for those players and coaches I worked with while I was at the PFA; going into coaching was demanding and difficult enough, but most black coaches knew there'd be extra challenges they'd have to face, however much hard work they put in to gaining their qualifications. We'd pushed to increase the numbers but, even though we were now seeing more minority coaches getting qualified, there were still very few getting opportunities in the senior game. It was painful to witness: after *He's not qualified*, the next excuse people put forward was *He's not got the experience*.

My work with the PFA around diversity became a driving energy for me. It's still something I feel extremely passionate about. For the first few years of my time at the PFA, I enjoyed delivering the Level 2 coaching programme into the half dozen clubs I was responsible for. The content of the courses we delivered – and the commitment we got from the clubs – improved a lot as time went on, and the coach education department expanded. I believed in the people around me. The department was led by Jim Hicks, who I had huge respect for and who I recognised as someone who improved me in the work I was doing. Jim had a genuine understanding of the diversity issues I felt so strongly about, too.

Eventually, we had three black and one female coach educators in place and helped hundreds – if not thousands – of players through their coaching qualifications. Numbers attending our courses grew year-on-year. On one London course, 80 per cent of the candidates were from minority ethnic backgrounds, which was amazing to see and be a part of. Early on, there still weren't many women on our courses: women's football was marginalised and had very little infrastructure in place. That said, I remember a few women – Rachel Yankey and Kelly Smith, for example – who joined what had historically been all-male courses. That was a big step in the right direction, and they turned out to be outstanding candidates, maybe with their own points to prove.

The numbers attending our courses proved how wrong the idea was that black players weren't interested in coaching or management. After completing their Level 2, a few went into coaching roles at professional academies. Others progressed to doing the 'A' licence and a handful became candidates on the Pro licence. Still, though, very few were getting opportunities at the senior end of the professional game. There were outliers: Paul Ince was one, Chris Hughton another. But generally, it was very frustrating to see guys I'd worked with – and who I knew had what was needed to excel – being overlooked. I saw candidates with real ability drift out of the game. I knew that I'd had to learn to find my own way to survive.

I think I got better in my role as a coach educator, delivering courses to the next generation of players. I hope I did. I did everything I could to keep learning, to keep moving forward professionally. As well as completing my Pro licence, I'd attend FA training days at Lilleshall, at Bisham Abbey and then at St George's Park. I took every chance I was offered to further my own learning, all with the support of the PFA. I'd re-educated myself – re-invented myself, really – and got accredited to deliver our highest coaching qualification, the Pro licence, supporting coaches from all over the world on the courses.

There was good collaboration between the Professional Footballers' Association and the Football Association over working with players who wanted to go on from Level 2. It was rewarding being on those journeys with coaches going all the way through to their 'A' licences, and even to Pro. I was supporting candidates from all backgrounds and – not before time – all genders, each of whom had his or her own strengths and weaknesses, each with his or her own very distinct personality as a coach. My job often involved supporting candidates through the most difficult transition many will ever face in their professional lives: from playing the game to doing whatever comes next.

15

I tried never to be too overbearing: I tried to be available and supportive, but I needed to see that inner drive come from them. It was their learning, and they had to be prepared to lead on it. What helped, I think, is that I understood from my own experiences a lot of the challenges they had to face. I understood how nerve-wracking it could be, presenting to a room full of your peers. As a player, you might have been comfortable performing live in front of 50,000 fans – with perhaps millions more watching on TV – but that won't necessarily stop you freezing when you stand up in front of other candidates and present or put on a session. I remember how scary that was for me. For me, it was always about offering support, not about showing anyone how much I knew.

I took so much from 13 years at the PFA but, eventually, I found myself needing to move on: I'd always seen myself at the senior end of the game. What had always held me back was probably my mistrust of the football industry at that level. Day-to-day, though, I'd begun to feel I knew my job inside out. The PFA's coach education department was moving forward, but I wasn't sure I was personally. I'd turned 50 and needed a new challenge. In 2016, the Football Association advertised a post for a national coach educator. My main role at the PFA had always been working with academy scholars. This was an opportunity to work with more experienced players, coaches and managers on their advanced qualifications, up to Pro licence. Like a manager wanting to work with the first team at a club, this seemed an opportunity for me, as a coach educator, to work with candidates who already had lots of experience.

I took a deep breath and applied and got called for an interview at St George's Park. I just tried to be myself. I believe, by and large, I've been able to remain true to who I am. I'm able to sleep at night: that's a true indicator for me. Older now, I've also been able to reflect on my experience and my values. As a player and as a coach, I've never felt comfortable trying to work out how other people might want me to be. Better to do what feels right, to be honest about who you are. Maybe it's held me back, I don't know, but I've not been willing to bend on my integrity and my principles. The interview with the FA must have gone well. A few days later, I was offered the job.

I was now going to work for the national governing body as one of more than 900 members of staff. Based at home, I'd travel to St George's Park for meetings and to support individual coaches and deliver the courses. When I started, it felt like change was in the air at the FA: quite a few senior administrators and coaching staff were moving on. The England DNA philosophy was just starting to be implemented. Ambitions were high. *To produce a World Cup-winning team and, in doing so, to inspire the nation.* I was to be part of a plan to develop a world-class education department. We already had learners from all over the world wanting to get on to our courses. I was going to get the chance to work with some outstanding people.

My move to the FA was overdue, but it was still difficult leaving the PFA after such a long time. I appreciated that the organisation had given me the opportunity of a career beyond playing the game. An opportunity few others had seemed ready to offer me. They'd helped me develop, trained and supported me, just when I'd been coming to terms with the brutal reality which can face a player after he retires and is looking to take his next steps in the game. The PFA had offered me some stability in my life when I needed it most. But now, joining the FA, I felt like I was starting on something that was going to ask very different questions of me. I didn't know what lay ahead, but I knew it wasn't my time yet to stand still.

16

Mum had been ill for a while and passed away in 2016, August 11th. My sister, Sandra, was there for her. She was at the hospital when Mum got her diagnosis of myeloid leukaemia in 2015, but Sandra remembers she wasn't struggling too badly for the next six months or so. Mum was too independent to move in with Sandra, who was living in West Norwood, not far from Mum in Stockwell. So, it was a case of keeping an eye on her. In 2016, she had to go to Guy's Hospital every Monday for a blood transfusion. Sandra took on most of the responsibility. I did what I could. I remember feeling a little helpless. Mum was getting weaker month by month, but she had a lot of pride. She was a fighter.

Mum was admitted to hospital a couple of times and, the last time she came home, Sandra understood it was only going to be a matter of weeks. Sandra used to stay with her overnight. Natalie, Anthony and Paul, my niece and nephews, all helped, too. I'd visit Mum at the weekends. Everybody did their bit, and we just tried best we could to look after Mum as a family until she passed away. We had the funeral at Christ Church, Clapham, which had been Mum's church for 20 years and was just along Wandsworth Road from the Lansdowne Green estate. Church had become more and more important in her life, ever since Sandra and her eldest son, Anthony, were confirmed. Sandra still goes to church every week in Coventry, where she lives now.

Mum was buried at Streatham Park Cemetery, down in Streatham Vale, which is a couple of hours' drive away from where we are in North London. My partner, Angela, and I go to visit the grave probably three or four times a year. A few months ago, we headed down together, just before Mum's birthday. We'd been at the cemetery no more than five minutes when my sister, Sandra, arrived. She'd driven from Coventry. Neither of us had any idea the other was going to be there, at that time, on that day. Quite spooky, but in a good way. I'm not a particularly spiritual person in the way Sandra and Mum have been. But when things like that happen? I do stop and wonder.

There are two years between Sandra and I. She was born in '63, in Wandsworth. Neither of us know who our fathers were. We don't even know if our fathers were the same man. There were never any pictures around, no bits of paper with a name or a date. Not even a father's name on a birth certificate. Mum always kept that side of our story to herself, made it clear she didn't want to talk about it if I ever plucked up enough courage to ask. So, Sandra and I were both Davis, and happy with that. Mum brought up two kids on her own – at a time when society still frowned on a single mother – until my stepdad, Rupert, came into our lives when I was around 12. A lot must have gone on in Mum's life – here and in Jamaica – that she never told us about. There's plenty I'll never know.

I always had a focus: I was determined to become a professional footballer. The flip side of that, though, was that, once I started at Arsenal as a schoolboy, I lost touch with what was going on in my sister's life. I knew there was tension between her and Mum sometimes; I knew Sandra had her first child, Natalie, when she was 17, and there were arguments and challenges which came with that. But it's only been by thinking back over my own life, that I've started to wonder about Sandra's, too. Talking to her, she's filled in some gaps for me about Mum and our family back in Jamaica. But, also, I've learned more about Sandra's own experience: how different her circumstances have been to mine.

Especially, I'd say, since Mum took ill in 2015, I've started to appreciate the challenges Sandra's had to face. That difficult experience brought us a little closer, Sandra taking the lead as we dealt with the challenges that come when your mum needs help. Sandra had children of her own she was raising. She had her work and other things to deal with that I know were out there and that she had to face up to the best she could. She and I fought a lot growing up but, as we've both grown older, I've come to better understand and respect the life Sandra's been able to create for herself and her family.

After she had Natalie, Sandra went back to college to take 'A' Levels. She made that decision about her future, not wanting to rely on other people to make things happen for her. Mum was the same: independent, never wanting to ask for handouts. Sandra started out working in social care for a charity in New Cross, helping young mothers. After the funding ran out, she found her way into a job at the Passport Office at Victoria, filling in passport details by hand. And she's been a civil servant ever since, moving between departments, taking on more and more responsibility. She's worked on monitoring programmes aimed at social cohesion in minority communities; represented the Home Office in court over asylum appeals; and investigated immigration cases for the department. She's still in the civil service, with the Home Office, working in a senior HR role now.

Sandra's managed to create and manage a professional life, with some stability and structure. We've had interesting conversations about work that have made me think about what people are trying to do, around football and in the wider world. Working in HR, Sandra knows all about diversity programmes and training. She's particularly motivated around neurodiversity and recognising the strengths that people with conditions like autism and ADHD can bring to the workplace. Like me, Sandra sees that people are talking the talk now, maybe even walking the walk a little more. But, in the civil service, she thinks the problem is that good people come in with good ideas but then, because they're high-flyers, they move on. The processes they put in place get parked, and the energy goes out of all the good intentions. The next person comes in with their own ideas, and the whole cycle starts up again, without plans ever getting properly followed through.

Maybe that's true in football, too. Maybe it's one of the reasons it always seems to take the game so long to do the right things. I find myself wondering what will happen at the FA when Gareth Southgate moves on. Will we bring in someone else with the same human values and professional skills to replace him? It'd be foolish not to. If we really want to achieve positive lasting change, enlightened and capable leadership is – and will be – the only way forward.

Sandra has three grown-up children: Natalie, Anthony and Paul. And her children have had children. She's even got one great-grandchild. Mum helped her with childcare early on and Sandra's had a couple of long-term relationships since. She spent 15 years with Anthony's father, Tony, who she's still good friends with. And she's been married to Pat now for 21 years. So, she wasn't a single mum like our mum but still, to steer children through growing up in our part of South London wasn't easy: distractions, kids falling in with the wrong crowd, gang violence and postcode wars. Sandra had worries about schools, about employment, just about the kids being out at night, that I didn't ever have for my sons. That's real life, and she's seen them through it: they're good kids – good people – working, settled, in good relationships. Close with their mum, too. I like that.

When Mum passed, she had her whole close family round her, and she knew she was loved by us all. She was proud of what I had achieved in football. Even if, at the beginning, she hadn't really understood my interest in it. Was it ever going to be a real profession? Mum had imagined me going into banking or insurance, and perhaps I'd have ended up doing something like that if it hadn't worked out at the Arsenal. She worked so hard to give me a good upbringing – in what I know now weren't easy times for her – and just wanted a more secure life for me. But she never discouraged me from following my passion. And she understood in the end. Mum became a huge Arsenal fan. She loved watching the 'Invincibles' team of the early and mid-2000s and was delighted she had the chance to meet Arsène Wenger more than once. She liked Arsène a lot!

I understand much more now about the relationship between Mum and Sandra when we were growing up. Mum loved her grandchildren and was there for them whenever she could be. The bond between her and Sandra deepened over the years. Mum had so much respect for her daughter: her independent spirit, her values, her professional achievements. She was full of admiration for how Sandra grew up to become such a caring, brave, and capable mother. Mum was proud of my sister, for sure. I am, too.

17

The new role at the FA didn't quite go to plan at first. The job description had been to work with senior coaches on the 'A' and Pro licence courses but, straight away, I got asked if I would help academy coaches with their Advanced Youth Award qualification instead, looking after a couple of clubs: Barnet, who were in League Two then, and Brentford, who were in the Championship and ended up disbanding their academy altogether. It wasn't the job I'd applied for, but I understood that the FA had lost quite a few coach educators who'd gone into clubs as heads of coaching in academies, a position that had only existed in football for a couple of years. So, I found myself filling in because we were short-staffed. That went on longer than it should have, and it was a couple of years before I was able to focus on what I'd joined the FA to do.

I had another surprise, too. The FA were very keen for all their coach developers to study for a post-graduate diploma. I heard that word – 'diploma' – and straight away thought of classrooms and essays, and I wasn't keen. *I'm in my 50s now. Surely, I'm done with the academic stuff. I just want to get on with putting theory into practice.* The course was called the Post-Graduate Diploma in

17

Coach Development. Long title. Long course, too. It ran over three years, part-time, and had been designed by the FA in collaboration with Leeds Beckett University. I wasn't the only candidate who was unsure about taking it on. And quite a few dropped out while we were doing it. But my nature is to stick things out. And I did. It even says 'With Merit' on my diploma.

There were quite a few modules to work through. There were group workshops. Essays to write, lectures to attend and a long thesis to produce at the end. Theory, history, coming up with ideas to improve coach development. We'd go up to Leeds for a day or two at a time and then do stuff at home in the evenings and at weekends. Towards the end, it got even more complicated because of Covid, although that at least left me a little extra time to work from home on it. Some of the literature we were given was super-academic, written in a language I could barely understand. The lecturers worked hard to connect all that study to the practical work we were doing day-to-day as coach developers. I just kept going, kept going, and asked for help when I needed it.

The big thing was the thesis: we all had to produce 10,000 words on an issue in football that we felt strongly about. A big piece of work. There were lots of ideas which interested me and which I'd have been happy to work on. A lot of my colleagues looked at developments in football in terms of tactics and the technical side. How the game has changed as a game. But I thought: *Well, everybody's doing that, so I'm going to try something different.* I decided to research an issue that I'm passionate about, an issue we have to tackle to propel the game onto a new level in future. I decided my dissertation was going to explore how we could increase the number of black coaches and managers working in senior professional football.

It wasn't as if this was a completely new subject for me, although doing a university thesis on it definitely was. The academic side of it was hard. But I was studying around a topic I felt strongly about, and which had affected me and many of my peers. While I was working for the PFA, I'd spoken to hundreds of players at every level, to players like Paul Ince and Leroy Rosenior, who'd been managers, and to younger guys who were wondering what to do once they retired from playing. I'd asked them about their experiences and about how they saw coaching as a potential future pathway. Almost all of them shared the same frustrations, a sense of not being able to trust a game in which so few people of colour were getting opportunities as coaches or managers.

I'm not sure, even now, that football understands the dissatisfaction and deep misgivings so many of us continue to feel. Some people will point to the outliers, but if you look at the overall situation in any objective way, you have to ask serious questions. *Why?* So, the thesis for my diploma was a chance to revisit the subject and to be a bit more analytical, and as clear-eyed and objective as I could. I did a series of interviews, trying to make sure I got a good spread of ages, backgrounds and geographical locations. I gathered fresh first-person experience of how things had been in the past and what the landscape looked like now. I studied the data, trying to make sense of my own and other people's numbers. And what was clear was that those numbers had barely moved over the past 30 years. The experiences I was being told about now were the same as those I'd been hearing about since the '80s and '90s. There was an overwhelming sense that nothing, fundamentally, had changed.

Although the thesis was focused on coaching and management, working on it brought me back to thinking about the player's perspective, too. What's it like for Marcus Rashford, Raheem Sterling and Bukayo Saka now? Is it any different to how it was for me, Bob Hazel, Brendon Batson, Garth Crooks and Paul Canoville? The abuse we got inside stadiums in our day was much worse, much more obvious. The heightened profile of football nowadays explains that, in part: the fact that broadcast cameras and CCTV are everywhere inside grounds. If you racially abuse a player in a stadium, you're likely to be caught on camera or you might get reported by a steward or another fan. Racist abuse is now illegal whereas when I grew up and started playing, it was a normal part of everyday life.

But racism hasn't gone away. It's a cancer in the system and has migrated online, onto anonymous social media accounts. The personal impact of the abuse today's players get must be the same as it was for my generation. I'm sure they feel what we felt inside stadiums and in front of packed terraces. In a strange way, I feel as if I can handle someone who's up front and obvious when it comes to their feelings about the colour of my skin. At least I know where we stand. I wonder if it's even worse now, when people don't voice their feelings but, instead, go through life secretly or unconsciously discriminating against people of colour. So much of the abuse is 'invisible' now: the people attacking today's black players are hidden away, faceless. You can't see them. You can't count them. You can't confront them.

I was at the final of the Euros. I could tell the whole story about what went on beforehand: walking over beer cans and broken glass down Wembley Way three hours before kick-off; the drunkenness and the poor behaviour; the ticketless fans rushing into the section where I was sitting; the people in the seats behind me swearing and abusing players from start to finish. But what about afterwards? Bukayo Saka said that as soon as he missed his penalty, he knew he'd be racially abused online. Watching the penalty shoot-out at Wembley, the same thought had crossed my mind. *Him, Rashford and Sancho. It will be the three black lads getting it on social media, that's for sure.* It's bad that it happens, even worse that you know it's going to happen. The only positive thing was how many people were aware enough to openly condemn the abuse those young England players received. That, at least, has been a major shift since my playing days, when we'd just have been left to get on with it on our own.

The Euros were remarkable in one way: from the moment some fans at Middlesbrough booed the England players for taking the knee before a warm-up friendly, race and racism was being talked about through the entire summer. Usually, the racial abuse of players is a story for a couple of days before it disappears and is replaced by the next headline. Gareth Southgate and the players, though, made their feelings clear, even in the face of hostility from some of our own supporters and some of our leaders in government. I had real respect for the way they stuck by their values, held their nerve, knowing it was the right thing to do, and continued taking the knee before every game. They asked people – including the Prime Minister and the Home Secretary – to show more understanding. And this wasn't club football; it was the national team. Nobody could miss the message.

I felt this England team, perhaps more than any other in my life in football, represented me. I know many other people in the black community felt the same. I was proud of how the England players, as a group and as individuals, conducted themselves in 2021. Proud they were brave and courageous enough to insist that enough was enough, brave enough to say: *These are our values. This is what we stand for. This is what we want all of you to think again about. We won't just follow the media's interpretation of events.* It's important to recognise that there's a lot of complacency around racism in football in this country. England play in eastern Europe and are regularly subjected to the sort of discrimination in stadiums that used to happen here in the '70s and '80s. You'll hear people – and the media – getting outraged about it. *Those supporters are a disgrace! Kick their countries out of football!* Are they saying we don't have our own issues, right here?

It's a difficult conversation for most of us, black and white. In a way, I've always felt protected from the abuse in many ways. Because I was a professional footballer, people perhaps treated me with a little more respect. I've been able to travel and see how others live: those experiences have opened my mind. But I've been aware for a long time now how our society continues to struggle with racial division. I have a personal perspective that comes from my family, my community, and my own lived experience. I'm fortunate to have the opportunity to see things from more than one point of view, though. And I try to understand why others might hold different points of view. What I'm sure of is that we need to have more action if we're serious about crossing the divides that still exist between us, inside and outside football, in 2022.

18

My involvement with England under-17s was just an informal arrangement to begin with. In 2018, I'd been at the FA for a couple of years, working within the coach education department. There wasn't really a connection between the work we were doing and the national teams: we weren't linking up with those coaches. The age groups were doing well: it felt like English football and the academy system were developing some exceptional players. Our under-17s, with Steve Cooper as head coach, had just won the World Cup with a very good team: Phil Foden, Jadon Sancho, Callum Hudson-Odoi, Emile Smith-Rowe and Conor Gallagher were all part of that group. Now, Steve was getting a team together for the Euros, which were being played in England: we had Bukayo Saka, Harvey Elliott, Curtis Jones and Mason Greenwood coming through.

I didn't really know Steve. We'd bumped into each other a few times around St George's Park, but we'd never worked together, other than him doing a couple of presentations on our 'A' licence courses. One of those times we crossed in the corridor, though, he asked me if I'd be interested in joining up with him and his coaches for one of the under-17 camps. My reaction straight away was: *Yes, great.* It wasn't the kind of arrangement that existed in the organisation at that point, so we needed to let our respective line managers know what we wanted to do. We met up again, so Steve could explain how he thought it might work. He wanted someone older – thanks, Coops! – who could be a fresh set of eyes on what he and his staff were doing; someone to bounce ideas off, a different perspective.

I appreciated Steve's invitation. I was excited about working with him, the staff and, of course, some of the country's best young players. It was a chance to see how it all worked, to be involved in a training camp for the duration, something I'd never done before, and to see the standard for myself. In my day-to-day, I was in regular contact with coaches, but not with players. I knew it would be good experience for me, an opportunity to get to know our brightest young talents and find ways to support them. It gave me a boost, too, knowing that a coach who'd just won a World Cup thought I could offer something when it came to preparing his next group of players.

The first camp with Steve was a week in Portugal: a couple of friendly games, and a chance to meet everybody. I was able to see first-hand how the players dealt with being away from their clubs, in an England environment, with team-mates they didn't know. The boys had GCSEs they were preparing for, too. I watched how Steve and his staff worked, individually and collectively. They'd been together for a couple of years, had been away to India and won a World Cup, and so they were a very close-knit coaching team. He took that same group to Swansea with him when he left the FA in 2019. And, in 2021, some of them moved with him to Nottingham Forest.

I was extremely impressed with Steve's methods: he had an excellent relationship with his players. He got his messages across clearly and put on sessions the boys obviously enjoyed and learned from. Steve knew how to deal with people and make everyone in the group feel comfortable, even when decisions on team selection might involve disappointing individual players. He struck the right balance between winning games and developing and getting the best from the talent he was looking after. With the under-17s, Steve was dealing with youngsters. But I had no doubt that, given an opportunity in senior football, he'd succeed. When the call came from Swansea, my only surprise was why it had taken so long to recognise what he had to offer.

It was the first time I'd been away for any length of time with an England team, and the one thing that really stood out to me about the players – apart from their obvious talent – was the make-up of the group. It's natural for people of colour to be aware of being represented: here was a pool of English talent who were maybe 80 per cent black or mixed-race. At the same time, though, across 15 or 16 members of staff, I was the only black person. This didn't come as a complete surprise to me – I'd been tracking which coaches were getting which opportunities for many years, after all – but it was a stark reminder.

During the first few days of that first camp with the under-17s, I could sense all the players trying to work out who I was. Steve did introduce me but, even so, it takes time for trust and understanding to develop. The boys knew Coops was their head coach and that he was the one they needed to impress. They knew the regular staff, too. But people like me who they didn't know? A few probably went on the internet to look me up. It didn't take long for some to start asking me questions about my Arsenal career. At first, the players came to me to talk about football, and about me as a player. I had the chance, at the same time, to find out a bit more about them.

Once trust was established, the conversations became even more interesting. Some boys wanted to know whether I'd experienced racism when I played, about how I'd reacted and how I'd dealt with it. A couple were obviously thinking about this stuff a lot, trying to work out how to handle it themselves. They needed to talk, needed to consider ideas, and I was someone they felt they could approach. Maybe they felt a connection with me: this wasn't anything sinister, just young black men trying their best to get support and advice to help them. It was an extremely powerful experience for me. It showed me that we must be aware of our young players as young people, and to understand where they're coming from and what they need. I wanted to know more about how they were dealing with the issues we discussed, but they were the ones who first asked the questions.

Steve and I sat down after we got back from Portugal and tried to work out how to move forward. The whole arrangement was being driven by him. It wasn't exactly 'official', so I could only be with the group when I was able to fit that around my full-time role as a coach developer. It was a little frustrating: I missed the next two or three camps and couldn't join up with under-17s again until the European Championships in the summer of 2018, when we were based at St George's Park. The tournament was staged at Football League grounds, and we ended up getting knocked out on penalties in the semi-finals by the Netherlands. Mason Greenwood was away for pre-season training with Manchester United's first team and we probably missed his goals. He missed a tournament that players like Bukayo Saka really benefited from. Those Euros were a great experience for those under-17s. And for me.

Even at the younger age groups, a tournament is a massive logistical operation. It was interesting to see how it was all managed. There's a lot of information that has to go backwards and forwards between us and the players' clubs, sharing data on fitness, playing times and training loads. The relationship between the FA and the clubs has steadily improved over the years. Gone are the days when clubs refused to allow their youngsters to go on international duty, something that happened on a regular basis when I played. We realise the academies are doing a good job and that we have some exceptional international players to choose from across the age groups. I think the clubs trust the FA now to look after their players and to offer them valuable football and life experiences.

I used to hear talk about our young players lacking dedication and drive, suggesting they only cared about money and prestige. I don't hear that too much now. The boys are playing for England, and the ones I've worked with have shown respect and a willingness to learn. They appreciate the opportunity they've been given and are humble and proud to represent their country. It's a pleasure to be involved on their journey and to support them in any way I can. Everybody's seen how the seniors under Gareth Southgate have functioned as a team: players come from all over, they're happy to be there, and are committed to England just as much as their clubs. Our aim is to replicate that 'club' feel at every age group now.

The academies are nurturing these young players, often from as young as eight or nine years old. At under-17 level, Steve faced the challenge of bringing his squad together for a few days and trying to get everybody on the same page in terms of team shape and tactics. The players are from different clubs, with different cultures and playing styles. They are at varying stages of their physical development, too. But there seem to be good things happening everywhere: every player we see is comfortable on the ball. They're all athletic, agile, sharp. Their football understanding and psychology are improving all the time.

I've been impressed by how quickly this generation of young players can take on information and apply it. They'll only be out on the grass for an hour or so during an average day, and they have their education commitments to keep up with, too, which are extremely important. We're also very mindful of them needing rest and recovery. A lot of the coaching is done in the classroom: video analysis, team-building, getting the boys working together in small groups, and making time for one-on-one conversations. All that's happening as part of the planning to win games. The players need down-time, too, and to see their families and friends whenever that's possible.

It's a massive honour to play for your country at any level. Not every boy – very few, in fact – will go on to become a full international, but the idea is they learn, develop and have a great experience while they're with the under-17s. The players want to play for England and their clubs are happy to release them because they see the benefits: players get exposed to different challenges in international competition, get asked questions that they wouldn't usually be asked playing in academy football. With us, they'll play against the best, against different types of players, against teams playing completely different styles. And they'll have to deal with the pressures of tournament football, the travel and everything else that comes with playing abroad. Those are experiences of real value to any young player.

It's been a long time since I was their age but, being around these boys, I have a strong sense that I know how they feel. In many, I see a reflection of myself: quietness, uncertainty, a desire to fit in. I understand what's happening to them. A lot of the experience of growing up and becoming a footballer – and a lot of the emotions that come with that – are still the same. I recognise when they're nervous or anxious. They're quiet because they're around new people and a new environment, finding their way in a competitive sport. Wondering about their places in the scheme of things, maybe. This generation is serious about their work. You don't ever think there's going to be a boy misbehaving or getting sent back to his club. Mobile phones and social media, though, are a big part of life for this generation. Making sure we have face-to-face conversations with every player is really important. So is stuff we do together as a group: karaoke sessions, quiz nights, or whatever. We can keep those human connections in place.

The England experience is different in many ways now, though. The under-17 age-group team didn't exist when I played. There was an England Schoolboy team – under-15s – but then it skipped straight to under-21s and England B. I was never involved with the Schoolboys, so my first time with England was at under-21. We didn't have camps. You'd get a letter saying you'd been selected. You'd turn up at the hotel three or four days before a game, have a few sessions together, and then play. I didn't come into the set-up until I was older. I got called up as an over-age player. I won 11 caps and I don't think I got my first one until I was already 22: each team could have two over-age players, to help the younger ones. For me, even in my early 20s, there was always so much to learn, especially in terms of being flexible and able to get on with team-mates and staff.

It's important that young players find ways to work with different coaches, to respond positively to different personalities and styles of leadership. When I started with the under-21s, Dave Sexton was the manager: quiet, gentle, and very considered in every-thing he did. I liked him. Everything Dave did was thought-out, thorough. He knew exactly what he wanted from every moment of every training session. He was a one-off, a bit like Arsène Wenger, maybe. Then, Terry Venables took over. In terms of personality, he and Dave couldn't have been more different. Terry was gregarious, funny, enjoyed telling stories. He was almost one of the boys, but had the air of authority he needed, too. And, like Dave, he was a brilliant coach: two different personalities, but both very effective when it came to working with players. I always felt that we were well-organised in terms of kit, training, hotels and team meetings. It always felt like something special for a player to be involved in.

One difference I'm very aware of now is the attention paid to young players' educations. On camps and at tournaments, teachers are with us as members of staff, and time for schoolwork is part of the daily schedule. It's the same for the boys when they're at their clubs. A player's education is taken extremely seriously now. When I was 16, after I signed on as an apprentice at Arsenal, that was it as far as school was concerned, although every Wednesday we were supposed to study something we were interested in. I remember the club fixed us up at North London College, on Holloway Road. You had to turn up, but some lads took it more seriously than others. I chose to do what they used to call Home Economics. I wanted to learn about diet and nutrition, and to learn how to cook properly.

The whole idea of continuing your education at the same time as playing the game was only starting back in the '70s. There wasn't anybody else from Arsenal doing Home Economics. I didn't do things on purpose just to be different but, somehow, a lot of the things I ended up doing did turn out that way. Because she used to work late shifts when we were kids, Mum would leave food ready for Sandra and me to warm up. *Don't leave the cooker on and burn down the flat!* When it came to college as an apprentice, I remember us making cakes: cakes all the time. I've come back to the kitchen recently, though. I did a lot during lockdown: steaks, pastas, all sorts of stuff. I've always been interested. Maybe it's why I started reading books about diet, thinking about what I was putting into my body, when I was still in my teens, before clubs were starting to take an interest in the subject of nutrition at all.

Steve Cooper moved on from the FA to become manager at Swansea in 2019. He joined Nottingham Forest last year. The arrangement I had with him and the under-17s finished when he left. But, in 2020, John McDermott, who I've known for a long time, left the Spurs academy and joined the FA as Technical Director. It was just before Covid hit and we all had to go into lockdown: a difficult time for anyone to start a new job. It wasn't easy to judge where we were going during the pandemic: those were very strange and different times. I did get a message to John to wish him luck and to say I was looking forward to working with him. It was only once the restrictions eased off that he was able to get into his work and put in the changes that he wanted. One of the first things was to get people from our department – coach development – working with all the national teams. Thanks to my experiences with Steve and the under-17s, I'd already made a start as far as that was concerned.

19

Without me realising, there had been other things I'd done during my career which helped get me ready to take on that Leeds Beckett post-graduate course: from writing reports on young players at Arsenal through to the theoretical parts of taking the Pro licence. While I was with the PFA, I'd studied for a Certificate in Applied Management at Warwick University, too. That had included lots of financial and management modules. I still remember a conversation with the careers officer at Beaufoy where we talked about banking and insurance being options if I didn't make it in football. The Leeds Beckett qualification was a big step up for me, though. It probably hasn't made a huge difference to how I do my job. But I'm proud that I stuck it out. It wasn't something I'd have imagined doing when I left school with just average grades in a handful of CSEs. Completing the diploma gave me a different sense of what I was capable of. Even at 58 years of age.

I've been lucky: I've found opportunities, first with the PFA and now with the Football Association. I've re-invented myself in many ways to stay in the game. And I've kept learning, too. I'm watching matches all the time, talking to people working at every level. I'm taking in all the presentations and workshops we put on for the learners on our courses. Picking up new ideas, seeing what the best people are doing and how the game is evolving: I love that part of the job. On the teaching side, I've had to work hard at getting the most out of a computer; had to develop the skills to do research and to put a report or a piece of statistical analysis together; had to push myself to be able to stand up and speak confidently to a room full of people.

When you're a professional footballer, most of your time is managed and accounted for by others. You get told where you need to be and when you need to be there. There's a lot of routine: training, games, recovery. The club looks after your schedule. I'm sitting here looking at my diary now, and it's another world. I have to keep a diary, for a start! Make appointments, keep appointments, and organise my own schedule. The FA aren't going to plan things out for me. That's my responsibility. And every day's different. I am now a Senior Professional Game Coach Developer. There are six of us. The job title covers quite a bit of ground. And covers every single page of the diary on my desk.

I'm trying to help coaches develop, working mostly at the senior end of football, in the professional game. They'll either be doing their Pro licence, the most senior coaching qualification in football in Europe, or their 'A' licence, the next one down. I'm also involved in our Alumni Programme. Every Pro licence holder – ever, and there's about 600 of them! – is on that programme. We organise events, conferences and workshops, to help those coaches on their continued professional development and to foster a community network which, hopefully, keeps them connected to each other. Around a third of my time is now allocated to working with our National Teams department and specifically with the under-17s.

My core role, though, is supporting coaches progressing through the FA's senior courses. It's interesting to see how much it's all changed. When I took my 'A' licence in 1998, it was all about the coach educator. He talked. We listened. He led every session. I got taught by people like Dick Bate, John Peacock and Steve Rutter, the very best of their time. But it was all about them showing you exactly what to do. It was laid down: *This is how to coach.* Now, it feels like the challenge is to recognise what each individual coach has to offer, and then guide them towards finding their own way of doing the job. A coach developer today is there to support rather than to instruct, although there are key principles and core values which you need to help every candidate to understand.

There are quite a few players who come out of the game, want to coach, and assume they know how to just because they played. It's different in different countries: some, like Holland and Spain, parachute senior and international players in at an advanced level. Here, though, we've always wanted players to go through the whole process and that's been frustrating for some. If you've played 50 times for England, do you really need to go back to the technical basics all over again? But the FA's thinking is that being able to do something doesn't mean you'll straight away be able to teach it to others.

We need to do everything possible to make sure outstanding players stay in the game. If you won trophies at club level or played international football for your country, you're going to have something unique to bring to coaching and management. I've had some input with our International Player to Coach Programme, which started two years ago and invites applications from a handful of ex-players each year. An individually designed programme is created for each of them, with ongoing support to aid their development and help keep their talent in the game. The first four were Wayne Rooney, Ashley Cole, Michael Dawson and Carlton Cole. It's right that we should be helping in any way we can to make sure players with that level of experience progress as coaches if they want to.

To get on an 'A' licence course, you already need to be serious about what you want to do as a coach. Ideally, a candidate will have a group of between 14 and 22 players to work with on a regular basis in order to get the best practical benefit from the course. That will usually mean they're already in a club job. The 'A' can't ever just be about getting your qualification, rushing through it as quickly as you can. I do see players who retire and expect to go straight into a job coaching a first team. But if you come in with that attitude – just getting the piece of paper as soon as you can – you won't get the most from the course. Coaching needs a new set of skills. There's a lot to learn, however talented you might have been as a player.

I can think of players coming to the end of their playing careers who've come on our courses and not really connected with the learning. I've seen players getting jobs before they've got any qualifications or experience, and that seldom ends well. I can understand, if you're offered an opportunity, the temptation is always to grab it, not knowing if it'll ever come round again. But I want the coaches I work with to enjoy the process of learning. I want them to be appreciated for what they achieved as players, but also to embrace the learning of important new skills. It's almost impossible today to step straight off the pitch into coaching as people did in the past. The courses should be about pushing themselves to be the best they can in a new career. I want to help that happen. It's not for me to drive the process, though.

Coaching qualifications do count. When I started out, people got jobs simply because they knew someone, or on the strength of their reputation as a player, or the media pushing their name. It was about who your friends were. You didn't have to have any qualifications. Now, you usually need an 'A' licence to coach in professional football and a Pro licence to manage in the Premier League or the Championship. Similar guidelines are in place across all the major European leagues. The 'A' & Pro licence courses are standardised and monitored by UEFA, but there's flexibility given to each national association on how their courses are run. I'm proud to be a part of how we've grown in this area. The FA has set the standard in coach development.

Managers and coaches in my time were expected to be tough, autocratic and dogmatic. Clubs had almost total control and players had very little power. But the relationship between player and manager has changed, and the influence of more experts – data analysts, sports scientists, psychologists, media officers – has grown. Some clubs now have more support staff around the first team than they have players. There may have been a feeling that all these new specialist disciplines were taking over football but, to be a manager these days, you need an understanding of all those elements. You have to know how to listen and be ready to take advice from others who might have more expertise than you in a particular area. A successful manager knows how to let go of his ego! Effective leadership is about taking people along with you, by creating a culture, by involving the staff around you. It can't just be telling people what you want them to do.

I took my 'A' when I was in my mid-30s and there was a very set way of coaching. The 'A' wasn't just about what you coached; it was about learning exactly *how* to coach. If you weren't prepared to shout at your players most of the time, the feeling was you weren't doing your job and weren't going to get very far. For someone like myself, who felt more comfortable with a quieter leadership style, that was always a challenge. It wasn't just the FA: it was football generally. Don Howe was a great example: I played for him, and he was head coach in the Arsenal academy when I went back to work with the under-12s. Don was fantastic: knowledge, enthusiasm, passion. But often at full volume and often with quite a bit of aggression in his manner. I didn't feel that was what would get the best out of me as a player, but I had to find a way to deal with that style.

I understand that Don was just trying to get me to do what he needed me to do, and that he was passionate about that. I wouldn't question Don when I was playing for him: I had too much respect for him as a coach. But I often found myself thinking that what he wanted couldn't always be done the way he wanted. Once they've been given direction, I believe players should be trusted to get the job done, to adapt to situations they find themselves in during a game. The best teacher is game repetition and competition. Don always wanted us to close down opponents quickly, but sometimes, that wasn't possible. As players, we needed to know how to judge for ourselves how to adapt to any circumstances we found ourselves in.

I never thought the ruling by fear approach got the best out of me as a player. And it wasn't how I felt comfortable being a coach. I always thought there had to be other ways to get what you needed from your team. The FA have evolved their approach and helped encourage coaches to develop their own individual styles. There aren't that many 'screamers-and-shouters' coming out of our courses. Today's players don't respond well to that approach and will down tools if they feel they're being unfairly treated. Today's coaches need to find other ways to manage individuals and groups.

Gareth Southgate is a great example of that new approach to coaching, leadership and management. When I was still playing, in the '80s and '90s, would Gareth have been able to get work as a coach or a manager? When he was appointed as the national head coach in 2016, there were still plenty of people who weren't sure. *He's too softly spoken. He's not tough enough. He hasn't got the authority to coach international players.* But Gareth's intelligence and his commitment both to footballing principles and to human values have proved the doubters wrong.

I've nothing but respect for how Gareth – and the players – have got the nation enjoying our national sport again. I admire the way he's been able to guide the England team through some challenging political situations at the same time as reaching semi-finals and finals in major competitions. I can think of other England managers who've always stuck to their moral principles, whose styles of leadership I think I'd have responded well to: Sir Alf Ramsey, Dave Sexton, Sir Bobby Robson and Graham Taylor, for example. As far as my own coaching career was concerned, I'd have stayed at Arsenal if that had been possible. But it wasn't, and I'm glad I was able to find a different way to stay in football after finishing as a player.

So, coaching's changed. The 'A' licence used to be like a driving test. There was a right way and a wrong way. Two assessors would come, watch you coach, and then you'd either pass or fail. They told you right there whether they thought you were competent or not. I'm sure I wasn't the only candidate who found the experience terrifying! But the FA's course now is adapted more to the individual learner's circumstances. The candidate will be supported in their own working environment, visited regularly by a dedicated tutor. It works. The core principles of the game are the same as when I started out. Coaching styles and vocabulary may have changed, but football's still football, and the FA's coaching licences still carry the same weight they always have.

A big part of coaching is being able to communicate to different groups of people and to get others to understand and believe in your methods and messages. Those skills don't necessarily come naturally to players. As a top-level footballer, you do a lot of things instinctively, and for yourself. You don't usually have time to think twice in the middle of a game. When it came to coaching, I found it took me a while before I was able to put thoughts and ideas down on paper about the game I'd played for so many years. I had to break things down, work out how I did what I'd always done without thinking, in order now to help people learn and improve.

I see some ex-players on our courses and recognise they're doubting themselves like I used to: you know football, you know how the game feels, but it doesn't come naturally to talk about it using specialist language. You can end up questioning the value of your own experiences. I try to counter that. *You've played the game professionally at the highest level. Don't take that experience for granted. You've achieved something only a very small percentage of people are ever able to.* Sometimes, players need encouragement to acknowledge what they've done. You have to listen and learn from people who may have something positive to offer. But it's important not to let data, science and analysis over-complicate what's always been a simple game.

Every new group starting on an 'A' licence course will come to St George's Park for a week: meeting the other coaches; having lectures, presentations, workshops, some sessions out on the pitches; getting an overview of the whole course. I'll be allocated six or seven coaches to work with during the rest of the year, watching them coach, filming their sessions, and then discussing them afterwards; helping them prepare written work; or just having a coffee to catch up on how things are going. You work through each module with each candidate. The idea is for me to be questioning them all the time. *Why are you coaching defending in that way? What do you want your players to get out of your session? Might there be a different way of getting them engaged?*

Most coaches who go on to make a success of the job are asking themselves questions all the time, anyway. It makes them flexible, open-minded, able to respond to situations. When we're looking at candidates for the FA's courses, we'll always ask about a coach's philosophy. *How do you see the game? How do you want the game to be played? Are you clear on what you want from a team?* Each candidate has their own way of saying it but, right now, almost everyone, when you break it down, wants to play either like Guardiola or Klopp. You can understand why! But the best coaches can adapt to the players they've got, and find different ways to win football matches. The course is designed to give them the tools to do that.

The 'A' licence is a process: you need to take on the knowledge and then be able to plan your sessions, to communicate with your players and, finally, to reflect on what you've done. As a coach developer, I understand that different people go about things in different ways. Coaches have their own styles. But it still comes down to attitude. When I did my qualifications, I looked at the courses as a chance to learn. That's what I hope to see in the men and women I'm working with now: you want them to be self-driven, trying to improve all the time. Chasing people up for their course work isn't really what I ought to be doing!

I find it incredibly satisfying, when I'm watching a game, to look at the benches and recognise managers and staff I've worked with. It's one of the best parts about my job: watching people continue to learn and develop and achieve some success, knowing that you've had a part to play in that process. You watch their teams play, and you know that doing their qualifications has helped them be better. There's a knock-on effect, too, that I see in academy football: coaches we've developed who are working in that setting are helping to produce a new generation of homegrown players. I believe that, within the next ten years, English coaches will have broken through and be managing top clubs. And that the national team will be winning major tournaments. There are excellent coaches and players in the system right now.

When you're a player, it's all about you. That's your job: to be the best you can be. Although football's a team game, you're always competing for a place in that team. So, players are, in the main, selfish people. To be a footballer, you need that single-minded attitude, the drive to get the very best from yourself and from your career. But to be a successful manager or coach, you need a personality and an ambition focussed on getting a winning performance out of others. To get to the top, it can't just be about you. It has to be about everybody else. You have to know how to read people, how to develop empathy. The job becomes about helping and inspiring your players and staff to get to where you want your team to be. *Empathy*: we talk about it a lot in coaching now, but it's probably not a word – or an idea – any of us had much use for when we played.

Once you've done the 'A', the next step up is the Pro licence course, which runs for 18 months. The plan wouldn't usually be to go straight to that next level. Ideally, you'd want a coach to spend time putting what they've learnt on the 'A' into practice: experimenting, trying different systems, working with different players, finding out about their own strengths and weaknesses. That's obviously more practical if you can work at a club, either as backroom staff or in an academy, maybe even spending time at more than one club. If you straight away find yourself in a manager's job where all the pressure is on winning, having room to make mistakes and develop as a coach isn't going to be easy. Two games a week for the best part of ten months doesn't leave much time for learning, although that's not to say you can't develop that way.

The Pro licence concentrates on management and leadership. One of the pre-requisites is that you're already working at the senior end of the professional game. From the hundreds of applicants each year, only 24 make it onto the course. People come from all over the world: our Pro licence has a very good reputation. Again, it starts at St George's Park, and you get a real mix of backgrounds and experiences. Very different personalities, too. But all the candidates are encouraged to work together, and do presentations and study together. We'll bring in people from other sports and from other industries, to get different perspectives on how to get the best out of a team. Gareth Southgate usually comes in on the first day, delivering a presentation to kick off the course.

Over the next 18 months, candidates come back to St George's Park for three days at a time to work through the nine modules. So, for example, a module might be Talent Identification. We'll bring in experts from that field to pass on their very specific knowledge and experience. Then we'll split into small groups to watch games, analyse data, pick out talent, and discuss what we're looking for in players. I'll work closely with four or five coaches over the time they're on the course: supporting them through each module: going into their clubs to see them, or talking on the phone, or setting up small group workshops. It got a bit complicated during the Covid-19 lockdowns, but it forced all of us to become experts at working online.

What's amazing is how many of the coaches I'm helping now are people I played with or against, Steve Bould being the perfect example. There are others I've had the chance to get to know since retiring. It's rewarding to see how those relationships keep coming round. Maybe I've got the best of both worlds now: I'm involved, in touch with people and with the game, watching football, thinking about football, and talking about it with the coaches and coach developers. But I don't have to endure the pressures that come with making a living as a coach or a manager. Instead, I'm supporting others on their journeys.

I believe the FA is in a good place, both in terms of our national teams and the governance of the game. There is still room for improvement, though. I'd like to see us lead even more positively on diversity issues, for example. But there are some outstanding and very talented people working for the organisation. People I'm privileged to work with and learn from. If the right opportunity to go into a club environment were to come along? That'd be great. But I'm not actively chasing it. After so many years spent carving out a career outside of club football, I have to say I'm happy with where I am.

21

Working with the under-17s, watching them out on the pitches during camps, reminds me of all the physical stuff I was once able to do with such ease. I'm at home today. It's June and at least it's warm. I've been out running. It's easier on grass, so I go on the Common rather than on the road. The aches and pains of old injuries don't go away, though. It's rare I'll meet an ex-player who hasn't got something going on: if it's not hips, it'll be knees or ankles or back. Our bodies get worn and, because we were professional athletes, we're even more aware of that. Fortunately, the culture around injuries in the professional game is very different now. Things changed in the '90s. With the Premier League starting, there was more money to spend on facilities and medical staff. Players had more control over decisions which were being made about injuries and rehab, too. I only had one bad injury – the torn thigh muscle – during my career, but that was enough to keep me out for well over a year and, afterwards, to make me change the way I played.

I was lucky to be at Arsenal: Gary Lewin was fully qualified and had been tutored by the great Fred Street, the England and former

Arsenal physiotherapist. We had access to the best resources and were ahead of most other clubs. But the level of medical care everywhere now has gone to another level. There's more awareness of what injuries and training methods might mean for footballers' bodies further down the line, too. However, one area the game has struggled with is the link between heading the ball and dementia. The position I played, heading wasn't something I was doing repetitively, but I got my share of bangs to the head, and went up for my share of aerial challenges. Recently, I signed up to be part of a major study looking at the link with dementia in former players. My results came through all clear, but the overall findings haven't been published yet.

The FA has brought in guidelines: no more than ten full-force headers during any week in training. Maybe it'll go further when the full study data comes in. Jeff Astle's daughters have had to campaign hard for years on raising awareness: they lost their dad to dementia, and it's been proved that heading the old leather footballs was the reason Jeff suffered like he did. I believe there are many former players suffering in silence with their families, guys from the generations before mine. At the top level, the game's been changing anyway. It may be coincidence, or it may be because people are more conscious of the dangers now: I see far fewer headers in training sessions, and fewer in games. Playing the ball on the ground has become the way the game's played at most clubs in the Premier League, and that's filtered down through the divisions and into grassroots football.

I can see football having to bring in even more restrictions around heading as the scale of the problem becomes clearer. Look at how many of the England 1966 World Cup-winning team have had to battle dementia. And then include all the players of that time that we don't know about. Football with fewer headers sounds extreme and might compromise an English football tradition, but we know now what we didn't know then. Most ex-players carry injuries. That's part of the deal, right? But it's one thing struggling with a knee or a hip: you can go into hospital and get a new one. If it's proven that heading the ball does long-term damage to players, though, we'll need to change, won't we? Dementia isn't just pain and inconvenience. It's a disease which kills people, and we've no cure for it yet.

Covid was a bad time for everyone. It was difficult for academy football, too. Players and their clubs were very restricted in terms of training and games. The boys missed out on the best part of 18 months of football at an important stage in their development. Last summer, though, we gathered 48 players for two four-day camps at Loughborough University. I didn't know any of the players, but they'd been identified as the country's best under-17s. There's more to it than when I first worked with Steve Cooper but, fundamentally, my role is similar. I'm assisting the head coach, offering what John McDermott describes as 'a little grey-haired thinking' to the set-up.

Originally, the coach leading the camp was going to be Kevin Betsy, who'd replaced Justin Cochrane after Justin was appointed Head of Player Development and Coaching at Manchester United's academy. But just before the Loughborough camps, Kevin was appointed under-23s coach at Arsenal. I know Justin and Kevin well. Both have great futures in the game at senior level. Tom Curtis, an experienced FA coach/coach educator, stepped into the under-17s role. Tom had previously worked as Justin's assistant with the under-16s, so already knew this group and understood the role. He knows the boys and, in some cases, their families, and understands their individual characters as well as anyone. He knows the coaches at their clubs, too. There are two of us supporting him. Omer Riza is the other assistant coach, someone else I took through his coaching qualifications and who I've known since he was a young player at Arsenal. Omer worked hard to have a career in the game, and he's brought that same attitude to his coaching: enthusiasm, commitment, always wanting to learn. He works in the academy at Watford full-time.

I'm very aware that, with so many staff members around them and so many voices to listen to, there can be a danger of overloading the players with too much information. That's something we work hard not to do. All through my career as a player, what I needed was a structure, but then I wanted space to be myself and to show my individuality. It's what I think players still want today. Over the course of those camps at Loughborough, the players had a lot of ideas and details to absorb in quite a short time. Our job as a group of coaches was to put a squad together for our first friendly tournament and then a set of Euro qualifying games in Belarus.

All these players were born in 2005: they were 16, going on 17. At that age, they're still developing physically. They've still got a lot to learn technically, and we can only help a little in the short time they're with us. What we can give attention to, though, is their social and psychological experiences while they're away with England. We take these young players out of club environments where they feel comfortable, and that can be a challenge. Some are outgoing, others are shy and quiet. Most have a phone with them a lot of the time. We do our best to work with them as individuals, helping them find a way to become part of the group very quickly. Not just on the pitch, but off it, too, even if they're surrounded by players and staff they don't know. We want them to feel confident enough to be themselves while they're with us.

Come September 2021, I travelled to Poland with England under-17s for a UEFA tournament, the Syrenka Cup, to play friendlies against good teams like Romania, Portugal, and the Netherlands. Even without the circumstances of the pandemic, travelling with an age-group team is a complicated business: as well as 22 players and four coaches, we had a team operational manager, a doctor, a physical performance coach, a physiotherapist, a video analyst, an education and welfare officer, a kit manager, a security officer and a psychologist on the trip. Probably one or two others I've not mentioned, too! The job is to make sure all those specialists work together to give the players the best experience possible.

The vision, at every age group, is to develop international footballers good enough to play for our senior team in a few years' time. Playing in tournaments abroad on a regular basis has made a big difference across the age groups. We've always sent teams to World Cups and Euros, but it was Dan Ashworth who pushed ahead with a programme to get our younger teams playing competitive football overseas in between tournaments, too. Being away with an England team for perhaps six weeks – if you go all the way to a final – is a developed skill. Getting on with others, being away from family and friends, dealing with unfamiliar surroundings, creating a good team environment: all those elements need to be in place before you even start on team shape, the opponents' style, the weather, the pitches and so on. It's important our young players have those experiences.

Away at a tournament, the games are often every three days. We'll rest those players who've played, and train those who haven't. All of them have two or three hours of schoolwork to do every day. We choose the right time for analysing the opposition and for preparing our own game plan, ensuring the players understand and feel part of that process. Each boy has a well-being check every morning. Every training session is filmed and reviewed by the coaching staff. Preparation for matches is usually in small groups: defenders, attackers, midfielders. We discuss what we're trying to do together as a team. There'll be workshops on refereeing and on the possibility of racial abuse, and what to do if it happens. The boys still have quite a bit of down time, and we set up a games room, with music in the background to help create a relaxed atmosphere. I'd guess it can all feel a little claustrophobic for them at times, but tournament football can be like that: we're preparing these lads for life as international footballers.

Most of the young players will have been in the academy system from the age of eight or nine. They'll be used to structure and may know each other from their club games or, of course, from social media. I need to get to know them myself as quickly as I can. I was allocated half a dozen boys to work with one-to-one in Poland, to talk about football generally, and about their lives and their ambitions. These lads have no idea of my playing history. Why would they? I didn't dare tell them when I played. *Before you were born. Let's leave it at that!* We still have plenty in common, though, because of our journeys into football.

The lads knowing I played helps establish an understanding, I think, but then it's about building trust. A couple of them asked me about my Arsenal debut, as a 17-year-old, at White Hart Lane. I was thrown in when I was about the same age as these boys. It crossed my mind that I hadn't seen a single boy in the group who I'd thought looked ready – physically or psychologically – for that level of football just yet. That's not to say these weren't good players. Quite the opposite, and I'm sure a lot of them will go on to have great careers. But young players like Jude Bellingham, for example, or Bukayo Saka, are exceptions: ready at 17, or even younger. The average age at which a player makes his first-team debut in the Premier League is between 22 and 23.

Those numbers tell you things have changed. These days, we understand more about the stages of development youngsters go through. Clubs are more patient, to ensure boys aren't pushed too early. Coaches and sports scientists and psychologists understand that too much too soon can cost a player down the line, can mess him up physically or undermine him emotionally. The gap, in terms of strength and athleticism, between youth football and first-team football is bigger now than it's ever been, and the pressure of playing at the top end is greater now: games are shown live all over the world. There are so many eyes on every developing player. In my time, it was just down to individual judgement, a manager's instinct. *Does he look big enough? Does he seem confident enough? Well, we'll just put him in then.* Which is what Terry Neill did when he gave me my Arsenal debut forty-odd years ago.

22

Middle of August, a lovely sunny weekend. First weekend of the football season. But I was watching cricket: Day three of the second Test against India at Lord's. The West Indies team made a huge impression on me when I was young, and I always enjoyed playing cricket. If there was ever a charity match with the Bunburys, or with Arsenal, I'd always put my hand up for it. Like a lot of people, I'll watch the Ashes or Tests against the West Indies on TV. But it's never been a part of my daily life in the way football has. I got a couple of tickets for this particular Saturday, though. Better still, my eldest son, Du'aine, was free to come along. Great. We hadn't spent time together in far too long.

There's that thing about football and families, isn't there? *Dads and Lads*. Fathers and sons going off to the game together. I've had two season tickets, first at Highbury and then at the Emirates, for years for that reason. Both Du'aine and his younger brother, Jordan, are Arsenal fans and one or the other would always come along whenever they could. We had some of our best times together at Arsenal, not least watching Arsène Wenger's 'Invincibles'. But, for spending quality time, perhaps cricket's even better. A whole day,

22

comfortable seats, sunshine on green grass, and something to eat and drink within reach. A game going on in front of you that you can dip in and out of. Test cricket isn't the same heart-in-mouth experience as 90 minutes of football which you can't take your eyes off. Du'aine and I had hours at Lord's that summer's afternoon to chat and catch up.

I catch myself still calling them boys sometimes. Both my sons are young men now. Du'aine was born in 1994, Jordan in 1996. They've had their own very different journeys: Du'aine through Eton and Oxford and into music and finance; Jordan through the academy system in football, a soccer scholarship in the US, and now looking for the right opportunities in sports management. Those are their stories to tell, but my sons are fundamental in my story, too. Their mum, Hope, and I met in Jamaica in 1987 and were married in 2003, but we split up and, eventually, divorced in 2007, while the boys were still quite young. That was a difficult time for us all, particularly for Du'aine and Jordan. When Hope and I went our separate ways, the boys moved in with her.

There's always more than one perspective involved when a marriage breaks down. It's not my place here to say what happened between Hope and I and why things turned out the way they did. I'm very aware, though, that professional football – elite sport, generally, I suspect – puts massive pressure on relationships. The numbers are frightening; something like 75 per cent of players go through divorce or a relationship breakdown once they retire. I can only look at myself and try to understand why I was how I was, while I was playing and afterwards, and how that led to Hope and I divorcing. Hope always supported me through the hard times during my Arsenal career: my nine-game ban, my thigh injury, my bust-up with George, me not getting the under-18s job as a coach. She was there for the good times, too: winning leagues and cups, and for my testimonial season.

Football was the centre of my life, which meant it was the centre of my family's life, too. It had to be for me to get where I was going. I don't know how you'd describe the mindset: selfish, self-centred, being ready to sacrifice almost everything else? But that obsession – that drive to get in the team, to stay in the team, to earn that next playing contract – can do things to you that you're not even aware of. It can put a huge strain on a marriage and on family life. And then, the excitement, the attention, and the regular income all stop. You retire. That bright, burning thing at the middle of your life isn't there. What happens then? Twenty-five years focussing intently on football, your days measured out in training sessions and games, doing whatever you need to do to stay at the top. Suddenly, that's gone. And the transition isn't ever as straightforward as you hoped.

It was difficult for Hope and me. That made it difficult for our children, too. Once we split up, my sons and I weren't under the same roof. I wasn't a daily part of their lives. That was the most painful thing I've ever experienced. It didn't stop me wanting to be there for them, though. I tried to find a balance. I wanted to be available. I wanted Du'aine and Jordan to know how I felt about them, that I hadn't abandoned them and that none of what had happened was their doing. But I didn't want to make their lives any more complicated and challenging than they already were. At times we were close, for periods it was like I hardly existed. I tried to figure out where they were with their lives, and then do whatever seemed the right thing for them as regards our relationship. Sometimes that meant stepping back, letting things go. But I was always ready to step forward, too.

When I was growing up, there wasn't a man around our house until I was about 12, when Rupert moved in. I know Sandra and I have very different memories of what our stepdad was like. At first, it was uncomfortable for both of us: Mum and two children had worked out how to get along okay and now, suddenly, there was someone else around. But I was already out of the house a lot, with my paper round and school and playing football. I was out another night every week, too: playing Subbuteo with a couple of friends, Greg Morbin and Peter Watson. We had our own league table and hours of fun playing that game. So, I wasn't at home as much as Sandra, and never had as clear a picture as she did of what Rupert was like. I don't think the two of them ever got on. The opposite, in fact. Sandra saw a lot more of our stepdad than I did. She'd have been much more aware of how he treated our mum.

Rupert was in the building trade, a bricklayer, and in and out of work. A Jamaican guy. His big passion was cricket, so we'd talk about that, and I remember us watching matches on TV in the front room at Stafford Court together. The West Indies were the best in the world. Rupert loved it and would go off to the Oval with his friends to watch whenever they played in London. Cricket was at the heart of every West Indian household back then: everywhere, it was cricket and dominoes. He liked football, too, but he just let me get on with what I was doing: he didn't ever get involved or interfere. Rupert was just there. For me, it was just as if he'd suddenly turned up and become part of Mum's life. Mine and Sandra's lives, too.

Mum and Rupert seemed happy to me, going out to parties and to see friends in and around Brixton. They got married when I was 14, going on 15, in 1976. It was low-key: just a few of us in Stockwell at the Registry Office. Rupert had been married before and had children from that marriage. Mum became Mrs Jones. But, to me, he was always Uncle Rupert. I've got one photo from their wedding day that still makes me smile. It's in bleached-out '70s colour and Ruby's looking lovely, getting into a blue Volvo with white ribbons on it, outside the Registry Office. Rupert's in his suit, and wearing a pair of white gloves, looking very proud of himself. He and Mum were together until Rupert passed away, at the flat after a battle with cancer, in 2000.

When I was a young boy, I'd go round to my friends, to Rob's house or Dean's, usually after a Sunday morning game, and I'd think: *This feels good. Normal. Dad's here.* It was a social thing as much as anything: having two parents around was seen as how a family should be. Otherwise, there was a stigma. But I never dwelt on that for too long. Maybe I threw myself into football so hard because it was something I found all on my own. For me, it wasn't ever to do with anyone else, with a father pushing me on or me trying to please him. There were people in football who encouraged me. Pushed and challenged me, too. I'm thankful to them. But playing, really, was about me and what I wanted to do with my time and my life. I think that gave me some resilience, having to make it happen all on my own.

With my two sons, when it came to them playing football, the situation was different. I'd always try to be around when they were still young, especially for training and games. I was very conscious of giving them the support that I didn't have when I was their age. At the same time, though, I didn't want to get in the way. At games, watching your sons play, there's an instinct to shout out advice or instructions. But I know from my own experience that you don't learn by always being told. That can take away the fun, too. There'd be other parents on the touchline, screaming their heads off, telling me: *Paul! Why don't you say something to the kids? You know what to say to them. You're a footballer, aren't you?* I always tried to bite my lip. Encouragement is all children need. *Just let them get on with it. Let them find out for themselves.*

Du'aine and Jordan played for our local club in Hadley Wood when they were young. Both of them enjoyed the game and being with their friends. They were both good players, too. Du'aine picked up quite a bad knee injury, though, just when things were starting to get competitive, at 11 or 12 years old. It was a big disappointment and he started to think differently about the game after that. Du'aine was always strong academically and willing to put the effort into his schoolwork, so he followed that path. A pretty amazing path, really. He loved reading: read more books in a month than I'd read in my life! He was especially keen on the Charlie Higson stories about the young James Bond. I don't think Du'aine ever planned on becoming a spy. But he decided the school where young Bond went was the school where he wanted to go: Eton College.

I thought about it then, and I still think about it now. Du'aine was second generation, his grandmother had come from Jamaica in the 1950s with next to nothing, bringing up her son in one room and working as a cleaner and as a seamstress to get by. From that to Eton was a very big jump, any way you looked at it. I'll be honest: it concerned me. I didn't know what Eton was like, of course, but I knew what it represented, and I thought I knew the kind of people who were supposed to go there. Which wasn't people like us. But Du'aine pushed on. He passed all the entrance exams and started when he was 13. There was a certain distance between us by then and him going to Eton made that distance seem wider still. Eton's a boarding school. It isn't just a day-to-day thing. It's a boy's life. Du'aine being there took us even further away from each other, physically. Emotionally, too.

Talking to Du'aine about Eton now, I know he appreciates the fantastic education he received. He went on to university at Oxford. At the same time, though, he's aware the boys at the school didn't learn a lot of the skills you need to live: cooking food, looking after your clothes; looking after yourself! Eton drove students hard academically, but all the other stuff got taken care of for them. Football was a big deal for him during his time there. I didn't even realise they played it at Eton. From the very start, Du'aine decided that football was a way to carve out a place in the hierarchy and create an identity for himself. He was captain of the school team all the way through. I know he fought for that. He even got me along to coach a few sessions.

I wish I could have been more involved. But I was conscious Du'aine wanted room. It was difficult for me, but I didn't want to make things any more difficult for him. I trusted that he'd know I was there to connect with whenever he was ready. Eton was his thing, and he was strong enough to navigate it on his own terms. He was always ready to stand up for himself. I remember a time when he was wearing his hair a particular way, with twists, and that became an issue at school. And at home, too. But Du'aine insisted. It was part of who he was, and that was for other people to deal with, not him.

Du'aine told me once that there were maybe ten black students at the whole school when he started at Eton. The situation was probably a little like when I first stepped into the first-team dressing room at Arsenal. There wasn't ever racism directed at me; I just had to come to terms with being part of a culture I couldn't ever feel fully accepted in. I hope Du'aine will share more about that experience with me in future because I'm conscious of how little I know about Eton and his time there. I didn't have the whole picture and I probably had my own preconceptions, which need challenging. He actually found people's attitudes when he went up to Balliol College more difficult to come to terms with than anything at Eton.

Du'aine completed his degree at Oxford, but his plan to do an MA at Carnegie Mellon in Pittsburgh didn't work out. Instead, he took some time to decide where it was he wanted to go with his life. That was a tricky time for him, I'm sure. Tricky for me, too. It's natural to worry about your son if you think he's struggling. And we didn't have the kind of relationship then which made it feel natural for him to turn to me for emotional support or to talk things through. He tried to get a social enterprise idea off the ground, connecting university students up with grants and research funding opportunities. He got into writing and playing music, and I probably felt like my mum did at first about me playing football. *That's fine. It's not really a job, though, is it?* He went off to California for a while. I really didn't have any idea what he was doing over there.

I contacted David Dein at one point, just after Du'aine left Oxford. He was helpful and arranged a placement at a private wealth management company in Mayfair. It only took Du'aine a few weeks to realise that world wasn't for him. He had the skills, but wasn't comfortable in the environment. Now, he's following his own path in finance. He can read a company balance sheet, understands stocks and shares and how markets behave. Du'aine's up at about five every morning, studying prices and movements and deciding on investments. He's got interested in Sound Therapy, too. It feels like he's finding his feet and is beginning to have a clear idea of where he's headed.

I've got so much I want to ask Du'aine. Eton, Oxford and what he's doing now: all of it's so different to my life. I want to understand how he sees the world. Sitting in the sunshine at Lord's that afternoon, watching the cricket, he was asking me about my career as a footballer, at Arsenal and after. There's plenty about my story he doesn't know. During those times when he and I lost touch, he lost touch with my mum and my side of the family as well. Even though Mum's passed away, he wants to understand how life was for her, about the culture she was raised in, and how it brought her here half a century ago.

Du'aine took the day to travel up with me when I had my graduation ceremony at Leeds Beckett University, too, which meant a lot to me. He's his own man now, and I'm proud of what he's achieved. I think Du'aine's in a good place. And I believe there's a lot more to come from him. There have been times when I wondered where he was going. Early 20s, he probably wasn't even sure himself. We'd have conversations back then and I couldn't get a feel for the world he was in. There was so much I didn't understand. It was almost as if we were talking past each other. I missed a lot while he was at Eton and at Oxford and then away in America. I hope we can make up for lost time now.

Du'aine was strong on the academic side. His brother, Jordan, was much more committed to his football than he was to his studies. But he went to good schools so, even though he found it difficult, he worked as hard as he could to pass his exams. Jordan had a competitive streak that football was a great outlet for, and he was playing regularly from under-7s onwards. He was still young and Du'aine was playing at the same club, so I used to go to most of the games, watching him with the other mums and dads. At home, I think Jordan's older brother shielded him from a lot of the upset so, when I moved out of the family home in 2006, the transition wasn't as hard for him as it was for Du'aine. I still used to take him to training and games, and we went to watch Arsenal together sometimes, too.

Jordan had ability and wanted to look at the possibility of academy football. I tried to make sure he never felt I was pushing him towards that, or towards one club or another. He had a trial at Arsenal. I left him to it because I didn't want to add any extra pressure with my own history with the club. They didn't pick him up anyway. Spurs did, though, and he started training with them a couple of nights a week. John McDermott was running the academy, and he and I got on well, which made Jordan feel comfortable. Made me feel comfortable, too. They had games at weekends and went on a tour to Italy, playing against teams like Barcelona and Inter Milan. Harry Winks was in his age group and has gone on to play first team at Spurs.

When the time came to go back pre-season at Tottenham, though, Jordan told me he didn't want to do it anymore. He said he wasn't enjoying it. I think the club were looking for their school-boys to do day-release, where they'd miss one day of school and go into the club instead for extra training. Jordan wasn't keen. He didn't want to miss classes, and I think the fun he'd had when he was playing Sunday football wasn't there any longer. I advised Jordan to take his time with his decision because this opportu-nity might not come round again. I didn't want him to leave. But Jordan was sure. I remember having to phone John and explain the situation. John handled it really well. *Let him take a break and, if Jordan wants to come back, he'll be welcome.* He never did.

For a year or so, apart from at school, Jordan didn't play much football. I think some of the enjoyment had gone for him. But then he said he wanted to get back into an academy, so I got him a trial at Watford. Jordan would have been about 14, and really wanted to give it a go. He started going to sessions but had some health issues: an irregular heartbeat. He had to take six months off and was on medication, having tests to diagnose the problem. He even-tually went back to training. Watford used a school locally for their sessions and, one evening, I went to pick him up. We were going to go to Arsenal together to watch them play AC Milan in the Champions League. But, coming round the M25, Jordan suddenly went faint. *I'm really struggling here, Dad.* He was going in and out of consciousness. I drove as fast as I could to the nearest hospital, Chase Farm, where Jordan had been born. I was panicking.

Jordan came round that evening, but had to rest and have tests over the next few months. Football wasn't important while that was going on. It was a scary time, especially because nobody was able to tell us what was wrong with him at first. Eventually, they discov-ered he had a little heart murmur, and the better news was that it was a condition they could fix. He had to go in for minor surgery, and that set Jordan right. He's not been troubled by it since. He missed quite a bit of football, though. He went back to Watford but, when it came to the end of the season, the club felt they hadn't seen enough of him to offer him a scholarship. Jordan was disappointed. I was, too. I wasn't a dad pushing his boy into professional football. I just didn't want him to be left with any regrets.

Jordan decided he was going to go to college in the US on a soccer scholarship. It came a bit out of nowhere. I had no idea he was even thinking about it. It was just, suddenly: *This is what I'm going to do.* Our situation as a family meant there were often those moments of disconnection with both my sons, times when I felt I wasn't really in touch with their lives. Having that ambition to go to the US was motivation for Jordan as a footballer, and motivation for him when it came to getting the right grades in his 'A' levels. He had to sit other exams as well: they're called SATs and they determine what college you can get into in the US. He went to a place just outside New York called Cazenovia because he didn't get good enough SATs results to get onto a top-tier soccer programme.

Cazenovia College was good academically, though, so Jordan did his SATs again and was able to transfer to a different university, which was higher-ranked for football. Valparaiso was in Indiana, about an hour's drive from Chicago. The idea was to aim for MLS as a player, but he was never happy about the football at Valparaiso. I went out to visit and, straight away, understood why. It was a beautiful place, and the facilities were pretty good. The pitch they played on wasn't, though. Nor was the coaching. And, because there were so many students enrolled on the programme, they didn't ever play enough games. From a football perspective, it was maybe time wasted. But he met a lot of interesting people, from all over the world, his classmates and team-mates. The experience of living in the States was great for him. When Jordan talks about it now, though, he says he should have stayed at Cazenovia, which was a better all-round college.

Football was always something that kept Jordan and I in touch and, once he got back to England, we went to watch some games, met up for pizza and talked about the Arsenal, while he looked around for what to do next. Like Du'aine, Jordan enjoys music and was planning for a while to manage a band he'd got to know. Then he did some work experience with a football agency. I was there to support him but, by now, Jordan was driving everything for himself. He connected with a company called ASM, who help young athletes to get onto sports scholarships in the US, with the idea of representing them after they graduate. They wanted Jordan to identify talent, and then use his own experience to help students through the whole process. Before I even knew, he'd signed up and was off to Florida: apartment, office, life in West Palm Beach. It turned out not to be the opportunity he'd hoped it might be. Jordan's back in London now, planning his next steps into the world of sports management.

My relationship with my sons has always been driven by my love for them and has been grounded in my own experience. I wouldn't think to tell anybody else what to do. But not knowing my dad, not even knowing who he was, made me want to make sure my sons didn't grow up like that. Sometimes it was difficult. It always will be, I guess, when a family breaks up. But walking away was never ever an option. Whenever – and for whatever reason – they didn't want to be in touch, I tried to just hang in there. I knew pushing things wouldn't help, but I always wanted them to know I was around and that I cared. There have probably been times for Du'aine and Jordan when a relationship with Dad wasn't something they felt they wanted or needed. I hope we've gone past that. They're young men, living their own lives, and I hope they know I'm still here for them and always will be, no matter what.

My environment growing up was very different to theirs, and they're both aware of that. I get the sense they understand, as well, that where I've come from is an important part of who they are, too. They want to know what I've done and why. And how I did it. How being a black man has impacted my life. They've had their own experiences with racism and will find their own ways of dealing with it. But I'm here to help. It's interesting for me to get their generation's perspective. Du'aine, especially, wants to know my thoughts about a lot of other things besides. We were watching England v India at Lord's and found our way into a long conversation about how culture can shift over a single generation. Du'aine knows how to ask a good question: that's one thing Eton definitely taught him!

23

I feel I can make a difference to the game: working in coach education, in coach development and, all the while, pushing for more diversity, encouraging black players, in particular, to take their qualifications. I looked at the coaching landscape 25 years ago and made the judgement that football management wasn't where I was going to get opportunities to succeed. My background and my personality didn't fit that environment.

Like a whole generation of black players, I didn't feel comfortable with the game's denial of what was happening to us. On the path I've taken instead, though, I've been able to make some impact. With the PFA and now at the FA, I've been able to push for change from within those organisations.

I've got my own personal perspective on diversity, and my own experience: so often, and in so many situations, I've been the one black person in the room. I have my history, and I can reflect on a lifetime of conversations I've had with other black players and coaches, too. I see what's gone on – what's still going on – in the professional game, especially when it comes to making senior appointments. I see highly qualified coaches, people who've put an incredible amount of work and energy into being the best they can be, just not getting the opportunities they deserve. It's tough for those coaches, but it's the game that misses out. Real ability gets lost to the game because so many people who should be getting a chance never do. We need to take on other points of view and push for change together: we're all affected by the environment we've created. The alternative is to be like the person who's ill but puts off going to the doctor until it's too late: that's how football's been for too many years.

The FA itself has made mistakes, but there are good people working in the organisation, trying to do the right things. On the Pro licence, for example, we make sure that black coaches are able to access the course: Asian coaches and female coaches, too. The intakes are the most diverse since the Pro licence's inception in 2003. And the course is the best it's ever been. But there's still so much to do. Both the FA and the PFA have recognised that the problem exists and have looked for ways to re-think, to adapt and to change. Leaders like John McDermott and Jamie Robertson at the Association, and Gordon Taylor and Jim Hicks at the union, are people I've worked alongside. I've seen them try to back up words with action, watched them push against the football industry's norms. You look around the game and at society in general: it can be a bit overwhelming. Recognising that things aren't right is a start. But it's only a start. It's important that the FA leads the game by example now, in the hope that other stakeholders will follow.

One area I'm not directly involved in but follow with interest is the FA's Technical Director course. If we're talking seriously about the coaches who study with us getting opportunities, it seems to me that we need to align them with the people we're training on that Level 5 course, which is equivalent to the Pro licence. It's already an important role at several clubs, and it's going to continue to develop. When he was at the FA, Dan Ashworth pushed to create the Technical Director qualification. He's a perfect example himself of what the job involves, and what you need to do it successfully. He had a big influence on our England teams while he was at the FA. Dan's gone on to club football at Premier League level, too, first with Brighton and now with Newcastle United.

The role of Technical Director varies from club to club. Director of Football or Sporting Director are other titles for what's basically the same thing. Everywhere, though, it's usually a much more stable position. Long-term planning is written into the job description, and the responsibilities of the role cover everything across the running of a football club. The FA course reflects that. Football, in terms of setting up for a game on a Saturday afternoon, is only a small part of it. I think we're going to move towards it being the model at most clubs, like it is around the rest of Europe. Technical Directors will be the people hiring coaches and managers, so we need to make sure they know all about the coaches who are studying for their 'A' and Pro licences with us. If nothing else, the FA should be looking at how to put clubs and our candidates together in the same room. And ways of making sure our Technical Director courses are diverse and attract the very best people.

The other way the FA is trying to help with those final steps into the professional game is to give opportunities to younger coaches – and coaches from different backgrounds – to lead the national teams. Steve Cooper, a World Cup winner with the under-17s, is a great example of how it can work. He came to the FA from a background in academy football. The FA identified him as a talented coach and, for a number of years, Steve proved it by developing players and creating successful teams. That led to him getting the opportunity to go back into the professional game, but as a head coach at senior level in the Championship, first with Swansea and then at Nottingham Forest. The FA played an important role in developing Steve as a coach by giving him his chance with the under-17s. That looks to me like exactly the kind of pathway we should be helping make possible.

Now, I want to see those same doors open for the younger black coaches who've been learning and developing inside the FA's structure. After Steve Cooper left, Justin Cochrane was appointed to head up the under-17s, but soon got head-hunted by Manchester United. Then, Kevin Betsy was promoted to replace him but, almost straight away, got a good offer from Arsenal to manage their under-23s. Now, he's been appointed manager of Stevenage in League Two. The FA can be proud of them both. I worked with Justin and Kevin from very early on in their coaching careers, and I know how much they've both got to offer. I believe they're both capable of the kind of success in club football which Steve Cooper's enjoying now, promoted to the Premier League with Nottingham Forest. I hope they move on to working with senior players like he has. Justin and Kevin can be role models for a whole generation coming up behind.

I believe in what the FA are trying to do with our national teams at every level now. Obviously, the main objective is for the senior men's and women's teams to have success at international tournaments. Our disability teams, too. We've got 28 England teams, all based at a world-class training centre at St George's Park. There's been a concerted effort to get the whole organisation functioning and feeling more like a club. Both Gareth Southgate and Sarina Wiegman are doing great jobs with the senior teams: a World Cup semi-final, a European Championship final, and qualification for the World Cup in Qatar for the men. And the Lionesses are going from strength to strength, too.

The idea now is that the age-group teams, like the under-17s I'm involved with, work almost like a club academy, pushing talent through as soon as players are ready to follow in the footsteps of young talents such as Bukayo Saka, Phil Foden and Jude Belling-ham.

I watched a lot of football during the Euros summer of 2021. Tournaments are a chance to learn, to see what other countries are doing, to look out for new ideas and to see the best play against the best. I took in as many games as I could, specifically from a coach development viewpoint: making notes, sketching team shapes and patterns of play, trying to assess the impact of coaches on the performances of the players. Come the semi-finals and the final, though, I let myself get caught up in the excitement a little, to just be an England supporter. A bit like watching Arsenal at Anfield back in 1989. I watched from a coaching perspective, of course, trying to be as observant and as analytical as possible, but those experiences were also about the atmosphere and the passion and, in the end, the disappointment.

It was great being at Wembley, cheering this England team on. There's so much to admire about them as a group of players. When I was a kid, I'd never seen a black man playing for my country. I look at this England team now, though, and I recognise myself in it. It's a team that looks and feels like the country I want to live in. It was exciting being in the stands, but it was pure emotion all around me and not the best view in the world, either. To be fair, watching both semi-finals behind the goal, down near the front, some things had a real impact seen up close: the speed of the game, the changes of pace and direction, and the physicality of the players. To do my work and analyse the games properly, though, I had to go straight home afterwards and watch them over again on TV.

The England players who got so close at the Euros – and who we hope can take the next step in Qatar – are the obvious success story, but the FA deserves credit for how things have moved forward at every level. It's such a big organisation, with so many responsibilities, but a lot of hard work has gone into connecting it all together.

Communication has improved, people are much clearer about their roles and responsibilities, me included. Naturally, everybody looks at the senior England teams. That's the focus for the glitz and the glamour and the media profile. But the FA has made a real effort to make sure that what Gareth and Sarina and the players are doing is part of a plan that reaches right across football: women's football, the England age groups and through into the grassroots game. There's an army of people working in the background: it's now around about 750 at the last count, spread between Wembley and St George's Park.

I know the organisation has taken a lot of criticism, and some of it's been deserved. But there have been some bold and forward-looking decisions made more recently. There's been a lot of good work done which hasn't been highlighted enough. Success for the senior teams down the line will depend on the right things being put in place at grassroots level, with the next generation of players and coaches. That's where everything starts from. I hope we're headed in the right direction with respect to coach development, too. Certainly, we're getting more and more people coming from abroad to look at what we're doing and to learn from it. They've recognised there's something good going on here.

Learning can be a two-way process, too. I try to watch football from other European leagues, to pick up on what people are doing elsewhere. During lockdown, we arranged a couple of online sessions with the Dutch, German and Belgian FAs and their Pro licence learners, with maybe 100 people on the call. The Belgian FA arranged for Roberto Martinez, Thomas Vermaelen and Kevin De Bruyne to join us and speak. What they had to say was valuable from a coaching point of view. After the presentations, each senior coach developer took a group of eight learners – some doing their Pro licences elsewhere in Europe, others doing theirs with us here – into smaller sessions to discuss what we'd heard. A few months later, there was another event – this one with Jürgen Klopp – which the German FA organised. Lockdown had its benefits: I'm not sure those events could have happened with those numbers in person.

I'm intent on seeing real change as regards diversity at the top of the game. It won't be easy, but we have to push on. In the Premier League, there's a log jam: it's hard for English coaches to get jobs because so many managerial positions go to guys from overseas, who then bring in their own staff. That adds up to another half dozen jobs at each club which don't go to English candidates: maybe 60 or 70 senior coaching positions across the Premier League. I'm not sure how clubs go about choosing their managers. It still seems to be about having the right profile: sometimes as if it's done on an agent's say-so, or on the strength of the last conversation an owner or CEO has had with someone at a game. And with both European and British coaches, it seems the same names go round again and again. Names people know. Perhaps that's just now starting to change.

The FA can't really do anything beyond putting good candidates through their qualifications and then recommending the best of them, hoping they'll be interviewed before decisions are made. Looking across the whole of the professional game, I'm more aware than ever of the need to shift people's attention towards black and ethnic minority coaches. It's been interesting to watch this huge organisation, the Football Association, trying to work out what needs to be done and how best to do it. A good start's been made; the FA recognises that there's been a problem. It's still there in front of us, though, not least because so many people in football haven't woken up to it yet or aren't willing to disturb the status quo, or don't want to see their own positions come under threat.

We're creatures of habit, especially under pressure. Those habits are what we must challenge. If we're going to make change happen, we probably can't just look at things in isolation, within the FA or around football. There's a weight of history, of bias, of perspective that needs shifting first, not just in our game but everywhere you look in our country. Even for many people who mean well, who understand the message and talk the talk, the issue of diversity is just something that comes up now and again. For every person of colour, in every walk of life, though, racism is something we have to deal with all the time. It's not just a subject on an agenda. It's part of our lived experience, 24/7, and always has been. Understanding our experience has to be the starting point if we're all going to move forward together.

I hope people recognise now that building a new landscape in terms of diversity isn't just for the benefit of black coaches, Asian coaches, female coaches. It's for the benefit of all of us. In the FA's case, it's for the benefit of the whole of football. Over the course of my career as a player, as a coach, and as a coach developer, I've watched so many people who had something to give being discarded or ignored or denied opportunities. And let's be honest. Let's not pretend otherwise: the colour of their skin was always the key to it. The biggest obstacle laid across their path. Those people have been defined, judged and dismissed because of that, before they've had the chance to prove what they can do.

It seems crucial to me, for the good of football, that coaching, management and administration become as diverse as dressing rooms became over the course of my career as a player. Stopping the next generation of coaching talent drifting out of football is in all our interests if excellence is what we want in our game at every level, from grassroots through to the England national team. That's true, too, in relation to every kind of position of responsibility: in ownership, in administration, and in the media, as well as around the training ground. We have to open up pathways, take risks and challenge misconceptions. We need to do the right thing by black and ethnic minority candidates and create a genuinely level playing field.

I'm coming up on nearly 50 years in professional football. I keep trying to have the conversation, whether people want to take it on or not. I get tired of the trying sometimes. Of the having to try. Maybe people get tired of me, too. But I won't be letting it go. I want to have the integrity, the courage and the determination to keep fighting, to keep pushing back. That commitment was hard-wired into my character a long while ago. Do you know the feeling? It's tough to keep going. But, when it matters this much, I'm not going to quit. Especially when I know for sure, in the core of me, that if we can work this out together, we won't all just be better off. We'll be unstoppable.

ACKNOWLEDGEMENTS

Over the years, quite a few fans have asked me why haven't I written a book. I must be honest: the idea didn't appeal to me. However, as the years went on, I started to feel that If I did write one, I'd want it to be an in-depth, open and honest book. My story, and more than just football. Perhaps it would be something best done once I'd had time to truly reflect and when most of my life was behind me. That time is now.

My partner, Angela, is the one person who's come back to me on the subject time and time again. Not pushing me; but gently nudging me: *You've got a great story to tell. People need to hear it. I'd read it.* Angela loves to write herself and reads a lot. She persuaded me of the importance to others of sharing my story. So, it was Angela who kept the idea of writing down my story in my mind. And then there were my sons, Du'aine and Jordan, who would ask me how I had achieved what I'd achieved, why I'd made the choices or decisions I had. That got me thinking about an autobiography seriously for the first time.

I first met Angela in town while socialising with friends, and it turned out we lived not far from each other in North London. Angela had worked in the travel industry in management positions with companies such as Thomson Holidays, British Airways and Intercontinental Hotels. She then took a job travelling the world visiting the finest 5+ star hotels, resorts and spas as a secret hotel inspector, checking they were keeping up with

ACKNOWLEDGEMENTS

and meeting hundreds of globally recognised and benchmarked luxury standards.

It was important that Angela was not identified by the hotel staff as an inspector during her stay and I would sometimes travel with her because a couple blends into the environment far better than a woman on her own. All hard work for Angela – observing, recording, writing up reports, liaising with hotel management and presenting her findings at the end – but free holidays for me! I'd just be there as her cover. I remember being recognised by hotel staff – Arsenal fans – on occasions which really took the attention away from Angela and what she was doing.

Our relationship began after my marriage was over and, as it developed, we decided to move in together. I know Angela wouldn't thank me for going over the details of her life here, but I must put down on paper just what an important part of my life she's been. Angela has given me support and stability as I continued to find my way after playing football and after Arsenal.

But that's only part of what she's brought to my life. I'm not sure where I'd have been without someone I could talk to about anything and everything: Angela has always been the person I could turn to for support, whether it's about where I was at personally in life or about making the next big decision in my professional career.

Angela is very caring and giving, and she brought into my life a gentleness that I needed. Our backgrounds are very different. Angela was born in Sunderland and grew up in Bristol. The family moved South when she was three years old, after her dad was offered a great career opportunity and promotion. Her dad, Jack, was an engineer, a life-long football fan and a keen amateur player. Mum Jean, who received the MBE for her services to charity through her work with the Keep Fit Association, was also an enthusiastic fan of the game.

Both Mum and Dad were Sunderland supporters, of course.

Angela has an older brother, Grahame, who is a massive Sunderland fan, too. But Grahame supported Arsenal throughout his school years and remembers fondly their dad treating him to a visit to Highbury for one of his birthdays. Angela also remembers Mum, Dad and Grahame driving off to Wembley in 1973 in Dad's white Ford Cortina – red sticking tape across it to make it look striped – to watch Sunderland beat Leeds United in the FA Cup Final.

Coming from such a football-loving family, it's little wonder Angela, a football fan herself, has ended up sharing her life with me. Angela is intelligent, articulate, witty, naturally confident, comfortable around people and well-travelled. I'm a South London boy who left school at 16 and spent 20-odd years at Arsenal, in the bubble of professional football, sheltered from the real world. So naturally the way we see things can be different at times. But I've always valued that difference.

I've learned so much from Angela, and I know this is a two-way thing. Growing to understand each other's thoughts was a process: valuing our very different experiences, attitudes, and interpretations of how we see, experience, handle and enjoy life. We do have different views, but we've managed to turn those differences into strengths in our relationship. Our relationship has helped me to grow and develop into a better person. It's given me the chance to understand better and connect with people from cultures which are different to the one I grew up with. But we share the same core human values which have bound us closer together, and still do.

I'm a glass half-full kind of person, seeing the positive in most situations, but Angela has helped me through some difficult times: the challenges that came with me having come out of a broken marriage and with two young boys. It's not always been easy, but Angela has always been there: loving, caring, open-minded, understanding, and wanting nothing but the best for me and my two sons. She has navigated it all extremely well. Angela developed a close bond with my mum before she passed away. Also with my sister, Sandra, and with my nephews and nieces. It seemed to come very naturally to Angela to become a part of my family, and that's helped me stay closely connected with them, too.

Angela's knowledge of football has gone from an enthusiastic novice to expert, watching games live at the Emirates if I can guarantee a comfortable seat and warm weather! If not, then we'll watch the games on the sofa, and not just Arsenal. As I've progressed with my qualifications as a coach and coach developer, I've had to go back to studying. To researching, analysing and interpreting academic theories, writing dissertations and so on. Angela is an independent thinker and she's always been there to encourage me. I can bounce ideas off her and she can help me consider ways of tackling what I'm doing.

While I've been writing the book, Angela's left me to get on with it. She understands how important it is that these are my experiences, my thoughts expressed in my words. A few times I've checked things with her. *Do you remember that? When did that happen?* I should mention she has an incredible memory! She's asked every now and again, just making sure everything's going okay. But nothing more than that. She's always said she'll be happy to read it when it's finished. Like I say, the core values and respect that we've developed for each other probably explain why we're so settled together.

It's important to me to write these words about Angela, to thank her. I think about what we've experienced, achieved, and shared together. About all the support she's given me. About her prompting me: *You've got a great story to tell. People will want to read it.*

This book is for the fans who have always been great to me. *Arsenal and After* is my story for my sons and for my family, and is dedicated to the memory of my wonderful Mum, Ruby, and the memory of my dear friend Sean Heaney, a life-long Arsenal fan who passed away too young, and for his beautiful daughter Sienna who I am proud to have the honour of being godfather to.

My sons Du'aine and Jordan are the *Why*: I want them to read this book and I want them to know and understand. It's for my sister, Sandra, who really was the *How* when it came to remembering and finding out more about Mum and our wider family.

It's for my generation – and for the following generations – who will, I'm sure, have experienced dreams, joys and disappointments similar to mine. Reading my story will hopefully help them on their journeys. Lastly, it's for anyone and everyone who's interested in trying to understand why we need to help our game to evolve.

My intention was always to be open and honest; not to sensationalise anything, but to give an accurate account of my life, my experiences, my memories, my thoughts and feelings, expressed in my own words.

I want to pay a special tribute to Tom Watt for his hard work, friendship, patience and expertise in helping me to put together this autobiography. It's been fun. Painful and difficult at times, too! Thanks to Mikel Arteta for writing the foreword and to Arsène Wenger, Ian Wright and Amy Lawrence for their support.

Thanks to my literary agent David Luxton for seamlessly and expertly introducing us to our publisher Reach Sport, who have skilfully and calmly helped us to produce a book that I feel you will enjoy reading.

Finally, thanks to you, the reader. We hope *Arsenal and After* has been as rewarding to read as it has been to write.

SPECIAL THANKS...

With my gratitude and special thanks. (Some no longer with us but always in memory):

Family
Rubena Jones
Rupert Jones
Angela Jones
Du'aine Davis
Jordan Davis
Sandra Crawford
Carmen Griffiths
Tasman Bains
Constantine Anderson
Emily Bailey
Claudius Bailey
Cardinal Bailey
Natalie Shirley
Anthony Williams
Raymond Paul Koroma
Terraine Shirley
Taiyon Shirley

Friends
Sean Heaney
Gary MacDonald
Chris Whyte
Tony Phillips
Clive Patterson
Tom Watt
Robert Bray
Dean Tonkin
Robert Armitt
Peter Watson
Greg Morbin
Gary Karsa

School Teachers
Mr Daly
Arthur Barnes
Mr Richards
Graeme Swann
Fred Newton

Sunday Football
Len & June Bray
Alf & Jean Tonkin
Ted Butler

Professional Football
All the Staff at Arsenal Football Club - between 1977-2003
Arsenal FC Fans
All staff at Brentford - Between 1995-1996
Brentford FC Fans
All my team-mates (1977-1996)

SPECIAL THANKS...

All the players I came up against
Ernie Collett
Pat Wiskin
Alf Fields
David Dein
Roger Thompson
Ian Crawford
Terry Neill
Don Howe
George Graham
Theo Foley
Gary Lewin
John Cartwright
Terry Burton

Testimonial (1991-92)
Hope Davis Dias
Harvey Sharpstone
Sharron Sharpstone
Lennard Lazarus
Steve Shaw
Dennis Pinchin
Dave Pierce
Richard Artus
Mark Brown
Pam Cully
Cass Edwards
Sharon McEnhill
Max Clifford
Jean Emblin
Sammy Nelson
Jeff Clancy

Anthony Webb
David Denham
Michael Beare
Malcom Bentley
Stan Jackson
Ambrose Mendy
Zac Harazi
Brian Kerner
Roland Butcher
Jeff Weston
Jerome Anderson
Kevin Connelly
Roger Levitt
Keith Darcy
Liam Brady
Celtic Football Club
Harry Hitchcock
Michael Sanderson
Sue Tully
Jeremy Beadle
Steve Jackson
Michael Watson
Brian Glanville
David Froggett

The Professional Footballer's Association
All at The PFA (between 2003-2016)
PFA Coaching Department
Golden Taylor
Jim Hicks

SPECIAL THANKS...

The Professional Footballers' Association
All staff at The PFA – between 2003-2016
PFA Coaching Department
Gordon Taylor
Jim Hicks

The Football Association (2016-Present)
FA Education Team
FA Senior Professional Game Development Team
FA Youth Coach Development Team
FA National Coaches Team
John McDermott
Jamie Robinson
Phil Church

Charity Organisation:
Show Racism the Red Card
Kick It Out

Inevitably, there will be people whose names should have been included here, and apologies to them.